APOCALYPSE

Louis René Beres

APOCALYPSE

Nuclear Catastrophe in World Politics

With a Foreword by Paul C. Warnke

The University of Chicago Press / Chicago and London

The University of Chicago Press, Chicago 60637
The University of Chicago Press, Ltd., London

© 1980 by The University of Chicago
All rights reserved. Published 1980
Phoenix edition 1982
Printed in the United States of America

89 88 87 86 85 84 83 82   2 3 4 5 6

Library of Congress Cataloging in Publication Data

Beres, Louis René.
  Apocalypse.

  Includes bibliographical references and index.
  1. Atomic weapons and disarmament.   2. Atomic
warfare.   3. International organization.
I. Title
JX1974.7.B457   327.1'74   80–13541
ISBN: 0–226–04360–6 (cloth)
        0–226–04361–4 (paper)

"Bring Back My Smile," by Michiko Sako, is
reprinted with permission from *The New York
Times*, May 22, 1977. © 1977 by The New York
Times Company.

The excerpt from "Nightmare for Future Reference,"
by Stephen Vincent Benét, is reprinted from *The
Selected Works of Stephen Vincent Benét*, copyright
1938 by Stephen Vincent Benét; copyright renewed
© 1966 by Thomas C. Benét, Stephanie B. Mahin,
and Rachel B. Lewis. Reprinted by permission of
Brandt & Brandt, Literary Agents, Inc.

For Valerie

Contents

Abbreviations

ABM	Antiballistic Missile
ACDA	Arms Control and Disarmament Agency
AEC	Atomic Energy Commission
CINCSAC	Commander-in-Chief of the Strategic Air Command
CCD	Conference of the Committee on Disarmament
CTB	Comprehensive Test Ban
DOD	Department of Defense
ECWA	(U.N.) Economic Commission of Western Asia
ERDA	Energy Research and Development Administration
FALN	Forces Armadas de Liberacion Nacional
FLN	National Liberation Front (Algeria)
FLQ	Front de Libération du Québec (Canada)
FPA	Federal Preparedness Agency
IAEA	International Atomic Energy Agency
ICBM	Intercontinental Ballistic Missile
IRA	Irish Republican Army
IRBM	Intermediate Range Ballistic Missile
JCS	Joint Chiefs of Staff
MIRV	Multiple Independently Targeted Reentry Vehicle
MBFR	Mutual and Balanced Force Reductions
MRBM	Medium Range Ballistic Missile
NDER	National Defense Executive Reserve
NORAD	North American Air Defense Command
NPT	Treaty on the Non-Proliferation of Nuclear Weapons

NRC	Nuclear Regulatory Commission
OTA	Office of Technology Assessment
PAS	Primary Accounting System
PLO	Palestine Liberation Organization
PFLP	Popular Front for the Liberation of Palestine
PNE	Peaceful Nuclear Explosion
PNET	Treaty on the Limitation of Underground Nuclear Explosions for Peaceful Purposes
PRP	Personnel Reliability Program
QRA	Quick Action Alert Aircraft
SAC	Strategic Air Command
SALT	Strategic Arms Limitation Talks
SLA	Symbionese Liberation Army
SLBM	Submarine Launched Ballistic Missile
SNM	Special Nuclear Material
SSBN	Ballistic Missile Submarine (Nuclear)
SSOD	Special Session on Disarmament
TTBT	Threshold Test Ban Treaty

Foreword

In accepting the first Albert Einstein Peace Prize this year, Alva Myrdal asked, "How can anyone be worthy of a prize for peace when we are so far from it?" She also commented ruefully, "In the face of stupendous risks, public opinion is asleep."

Mrs. Myrdal of course deserves a prize for peace in recognition of her many years of distinguished service as Sweden's chief delegate at the disarmament talks in Geneva. Professor Beres also deserves acclaim for this powerful effort to awaken public opinion to the stupendous risks of nuclear war.

At this time of increased tensions, just when the danger of nuclear devastation should be perceived to loom largest, nuclear arms control seems steadily to be downgraded on the list of human priorities. There seems, indeed, to be a ground swell of sentiment for all-out military competition with the Soviet Union. Some voices are heard to argue that détente has now become a discredited myth, that strategic arms control is a demonstrated failure, and that those who have supported the SALT process have been proven to be hapless dupes. At the request of President Carter, floor consideration of the SALT II treaty has been indefinitely deferred, while primary legislative attention is given to the situation created by the Soviet invasion of Afghanistan.

Yet as the president said in his State of the Union Address, "especially now in a time of great tensions, observing the mutual constraints imposed by the terms of [such] treaties will be in the best interests of both countries and

will help to preserve world peace." The current proof that
Soviet military power remains a major threat does not mean
that efforts at arms control should be abandoned. In fact,
the likelihood of continued frictions, of continued differences of view as to a desirable world order, confirms the
wisdom of the effort, through strategic arms limitation, to
make it less likely that United States/Soviet confrontations
will lead to the ultimate calamity of nuclear war.

The concept that has come to be known as linkage has,
of course, a considerable emotional appeal. It is tempting to
try to use arms control negotiations as a lure or lever
to obtain better Soviet cooperation across the spectrum of
international problems. The overt espousal of linkage in the
Nixon-Kissinger-Ford years was abandoned in the Carter
administration's insistence that SALT should be considered
on its own merits. The political potency of linkage, however,
has at least temporarily overcome logic.

It is imperative, however, that we get our priorities
straight. Some months ago, Andrei Sakharov made the point
with his usual eloquence:

> I believe that the problem of lessening the danger of
> annihilating humanity in a nuclear war carries an abso-
> lute priority over all other considerations. I believe that
> the principle of practicably separating the question of
> disarmament from other problems, as formulated by
> the United States administration, is completely correct.
> Consequently, the strategic arms limitation talks must
> be considered separately; and considered separately,
> we must ask ourselves whether it will lessen the danger
> and destructive power of a nuclear war.

The successful pursuit of the process of nuclear arms
control requires that the intensity of this pursuit not be
allowed to rise and fall with the fortunes of détente. Indeed,
as détente advances, the urgency of nuclear arms control
recedes. If we could count on the Russians always to behave
as we would like them to do, there would be little need for
strategic arms control. In the absence of any restrictions on
the numbers and kinds of nuclear weapons added to the
arsenals of the two new superpowers, the recurrent crises in
superpower relations take on a dimension of danger that the
world cannot afford.

The coming into effect of the SALT II treaty would mean, for the first time, overall limits on intercontinental-range nuclear weapons and lower ceilings on those weapons most dangerous to strategic stability. Launchers of the intercontinental ballistic missiles with multiple independently targetable reentry vehicles (MIRVs) would be specially limited, as would the number of such reentry vehicles that could be placed on strategic range ballistic missiles. Without these restraints, both the United States and the Soviet Union will continue to acquire a greater ability to attack the other side's strategic nuclear weapons. The forces of each side which are now depended upon for deterrence will continue to become both more deadly and more vulnerable. Adoption of new strategic doctrines under which Soviet and American ICBMs would be "saved" by launching them first when a nuclear attack is feared will become virtually inevitable.

No amount of theorizing and no spinning of mushroom clouds on the head of a pin can obscure the facts. Nuclear war is incompatible with human existence, and only arms control can prevent it from happening. No matter how much money either side invests in doomsday weapons, this can only lessen strategic stability. No increase in the number of U.S. missiles will lessen the destructive power of Soviet missiles.

And certainly no massive increase in the defense budget will block the spread of nuclear weapons. Here again, the only answer lies in arms control under a policy of restraint on the part of the nuclear superpowers that will create a climate in which world opinion will dissuade additional countries from developing, testing, and stockpiling their own nuclear weapons.

Only a change in emphasis from military competition, moreover, will permit proper attention to the other serious threats to international security. Bigger defense budgets won't buy a more stable world in which United States interests can be protected. For that, we need dramatic action to assist the developing countries and to narrow the gap between the rich and the poor nations. The report issued recently by a commission headed by former West German chancellor Willy Brandt describes this gap as responsible for the "immense risks threatening mankind." The report, entitled "North-South: A Program for Survival," recommends a world development fund and increased foreign aid by the wealthy countries. The United States Congress, however, is cutting sharply back on the authorization levels for the Inter-American Development Bank and the Asian Development Bank. Our total foreign aid hardly exceeds one-quarter of one percent of our gross national product.

At this point, when we seem to have lost our bearings along the road to true security, Professor Beres has provided a sound though somber perspective. His perception of the perils of the present policy drift is, I believe, irrefutable. His careful analysis exposes the fallacy of reliance on deterrence in the absence of effective quantitative and qualitative limits on nuclear weapons. The recurrent illusion of a limited nuclear war, in which there would be a winner and a loser, is dealt with and dispelled. Such a war could not remain limited, and everyone in the world would lose.

It may be that the possibility of nuclear war between the United States and the Soviet Union is overdrawn. Perhaps we can count on continuing leadership in both countries that will avoid those conflicts of vital interests that could make it conceivable. But Professor Beres commends to our attention the fact that not even today are the superpowers the only players in nuclear war games. Unless prompt steps are taken to bring Russian and American nuclear arsenals under control, it must be anticipated that tomorrow nuclear weapons will come into the possession of many more nations and, in time, of subnational terrorist groups. These new players could not be counted on to observe the rules tacitly accepted by the current nuclear powers. The message of Professor Beres's book is clear and compelling. I hope there is someone listening.

PAUL C. WARNKE

Preface
The Future in Retrospect

*Listen, are we helpless? Are we doomed to do it again and
again and again? Have we no choice but to play the Phoenix in
an unending sequence of rise and fall? Assyria, Babylon, Egypt,
Greece, Carthage, Rome, the Empires of Charlemagne and the
Turk. Ground to dust and plowed with salt. Spain, France,
Britain, America—burned into the oblivion of the centuries.
And again and again and again.*
*Are we doomed to it, Lord, chained to the pendulum of our own
mad clockwork, helpless to halt its swing?*

> Walter M. Miller, Jr.,
> *A Canticle for Leibowitz*

For as long as the people of Earth were organized into
groups, it is apparent that these groups were in conflict. To
protect themselves, the groups appear to have engaged in the
creation of ever-more terrible implements of destruction. By
continually threatening to use these implements against
other groups, each group seems to have felt that it was pursuing peace.

After the time which earthlings reckoned as their seventeenth century, the largest of these groups—which were
called states or countries—elevated this threat system to the
stature of law. *To preserve the peace, they prepared for war.*
This was the guiding principle of states; the idea which became the cornerstone of their relations with each other. Yet,
despite the fact that this principle was proved false again
and again by successively more destructive wars, the people

of Earth clung stubbornly to their curious logic. By the end
of the time which they called the twentieth century, the
principle of "Peace through Strength" brought Planet Earth
to the point of no return.

What happened? It appears that earthlings might some-
how have unlocked the secrets governing the nucleus of the
atom and used those secrets to obliterate their own habitat.
While much of this may sound incredible, the evidence
through which we have sifted so carefully and systematically
supports no other conclusion. The organisms that once lived
on this desolate planet annihilated themselves by steadfastly
holding to the view that safety springs from terror. We must
conclude, therefore, that these beings were entirely ignorant
of the laws of reason.

This is, of course, a fictitious account. But as a fable for
tomorrow, it describes an event that is all too likely—a thermonuclear holocaust that has burned the world into oblivion. Unless the people of Earth are quick to understand
that a system built upon the threat to use nuclear weapons
can never produce peace, they will surely have nuclear war.
The fable will become fact.

Introduction

This book is about nuclear catastrophe in the context of world politics, the ways in which it may occur, its implications for human life, and strategies that might be employed to avert it. Although, until recently, the focus of popular concern has shifted from nuclear war to more visible economic and environmental hazards, the threat presented by nuclear weapons is still the most devastating.[1] Not only does it dwarf all other threats in terms of the magnitude of its destructive consequences, but it is also far more likely to occur than almost everyone imagines.

The vision of a global nuclear wasteland must not be taken lightly. It is no longer the exclusive vision of men with sandwich boards proclaiming, "The End of the World is at Hand." It is also the prediction of our most eminent scientists, philosophers, and statesmen. We have reached the point where the catastrophic possibilities that lie latent in nuclear weapons are very likely to be exploited, either by design or by accident, by misinformation or miscalculation, by states or by subnational groups, by lapse from rational decision or by unauthorized decision.

To reverse this slide toward a nuclear Armageddon, three basic steps must be taken:

First, the world must come to grips with the enormity of the threat confronting it. The hands on the "Doomsday Clock" advance steadily closer to midnight.[2] We must recognize this movement before we can slow down its progress.

Second, we must devise a far-reaching and feasible agenda for world-order reform. Such an agenda must represent the product of careful, well-reasoned, and creative scholarship. Although we still do not have the kind of World Peace Research Organization proposed by Nobel laureate Linus Pauling in his book, *No More War* (1958), many scholars are currently engaged in seeking a "way out" of the nuclear crisis. It must be *their* primary responsibility to shed light upon the implications of alternative courses of action. In so doing, they can begin to identify various blueprints for survival.

The third step that must be taken requires the implementation of this agenda. Once we have all acknowledged the threat and scholars have drawn up appropriate strategies, national leaders must begin to act. The time for "business as usual" in world politics is at an end. Soon we must begin to construct a reliable ark of renewal. There *is* still reason to hope. Taken together, the three steps toward preventing nuclear catastrophe in the context of world politics point to creative planetary renewal.

This book is offered with a view to inaugurating such a search. Parts I and II reveal the precise character of the nuclear threat in world politics, its myriad forms, and its potential consequences. Part III explores a number of strategies for coping with this nuclear threat and offers several concrete suggestions for reform.

From the standpoint of the three steps toward survival, therefore, this book is oriented toward the first two: increased public awareness of the nuclear threat in world politics and the generation of workable plans for surmounting the problem. The third step—implementation of a workable plan—must be satisfied elsewhere. For as long as the world remains divided into a large number of competing national units, our common fate remains in the unsteady hands of our national leaders. These leaders can ill afford to underestimate the nature of the challenge before them.

The events that signaled the birth of an apocalyptic age, the dropping of atomic bombs on Japan in August 1945, were prefigured by thousands of years of warfare. However, today, with our military megamachines, our capacity for destruction is limitless. We have ironically reached the point where lavishly supported government preparations for "overkill," in the name of "national security" are taken as guarantees of peace, while pleas for dismantling the military megamachines are regarded as invitations to war.

To understand how we reached this point, we must first turn our attention to what has happened since "The Little Boy" was dropped on Hiroshima and "The Fat Man" was dropped at Nagasaki.[3] These products of the now famous Manhattan Project, a genuinely supersecret enterprise whose object was the development of an American atomic bomb, were the beginnings of nuclear weaponry and the nuclear arms race. By August 1949 the Soviet Union had developed its own atomic bomb; and by 1953 both the United States and the Soviet Union—having successfully developed a hydrogen bomb—were thermonuclear powers.

The transition from fission or atomic weapons to fusion or hydrogen weapons has had great significance in destructive terms. By deriving their energy from a process of thermonuclear fusion—the energy source that powers the sun and the stars—thermonuclear weapons release much greater energy than fission weapons. Moreover, in contrast to fission weapons, thermonuclear weapons are effectively unlimited in size and power. We have, in short, achieved a thousand-fold increase in explosive power by shifting from fission energy to thermonuclear energy.

By 1960 the United States and the Soviet Union possessed nuclear stockpiles which together contained somewhere between 30 and 60 million kilotons of TNT, or the energy equivalent of more than 10,000 World War IIs.[4] Since these stockpiles could produce lethal levels of radioactivity over tens of millions of square miles, the truly apocalyptic consequences of a nuclear war became generally understood.

To make the most efficient use of such awesome power, a "marriage" was effected between nuclear warheads and missiles of incredible accuracy with ranges of up to 6,000 miles. Today, American and Soviet strategic forces are diversified in three principal delivery systems: manned aircraft, land-based missiles, and sea-based (submarine) missiles. Moreover, single missiles with many warheads are being deployed in great numbers (MIRV is the acronym for

Multiple Independently Targeted Reentry Vehicles), and anti-ballistic-missile defense (ABM) has become totally impracticable.

Great Britain joined the "nuclear club" in 1951, France in 1960, China in 1964, and India in 1974. Thus, a process of "horizontal" proliferation began to be superimposed upon the "vertical" proliferation of nuclear weapons in the stockpiles of the superpowers. In spite of the Nonproliferation Treaty (NPT) which became effective in 1970, the prospect of having dozens of additional nuclear-weapon countries by the year 2000 is very real. In the words of Thomas Schelling, Lucius Littauer Professor of Political Economy at Harvard: "Although, by temperament, I may be an optimist, a reasoned evaluation of where we may be in 25 years suggests that we will not be able to regulate nuclear weapons around the world in 1999 any better than we can control the Saturday-night special, heroin, or pornography today."[5]

Professor Schelling's portentious prognosis is lent credence by the failure of certain significant parties to join the NPT. Even were the signers of the treaty to honor their commitments, the nonparties would still pose a serious threat. Three nuclear countries—France, The People's Republic of China, and India—have rejected the NPT, and the list of certain nonnuclear absentees is even more worrisome:

Egypt and Israel, while bound by a treaty of peace, have not yet committed themselves to the NPT—Egypt has signed but not yet ratified the treaty; Tanzania and Zambia, uncertain about South Africa's intentions have not signed it; Pakistan, in response to India's rejection of the NPT, also refuses to sign; fearful of each other, Brazil and Argentina, have not signed the treaty, while Columbia has signed but not ratified it; South Korea has ratified the treaty, but North Korea does not appear ready to follow suit; Indonesia has signed but not ratified the treaty; and finally Algeria, Cuba, Turkey, Kuwait, and Saudi Arabia remain non-parties to the treaty.

As the spread of nuclear weapons continues uncontrolled, the superpowers persist with their own nuclear arms race. The Soviet Union, in its efforts to modernize strategic forces, is now focusing on increasing the power, flexibility, accuracy, and survivability of its intercontinental missiles.

They have developed a whole new generation of intercontinental ballistic missiles (ICBMs) and are augmenting these offensive capabilities with an improved air defense capability for early warning of a missile attack as well as with a growing civil defense capability.

Since 1964, more than 1,000 ICBM launchers and more than 900 submarine-launched ballistic missile tubes have been added to the Soviet strategic forces. The Soviet deployment of fourth-generation ICBMs continues at a rate of more than 100 per year, and all of their SS-17, SS-18, and SS-19 missiles can carry multiple independent reentry vehicles. A fifth generation of Soviet ICBMs, consisting of four missiles, will soon be able to hurl warheads at widely separated targets and to enjoy considerable sanctuary from U.S. submarine forces.

The United States, in turn, is forging ahead with strategic weapons programs that go beyond the requirements of "assured destruction" or "minimum deterrence." These include: new mobile missiles known as the MX, which will have the capability to destroy much of the Soviet ICBM force in a first strike; the Minuteman Mark 12A nuclear warhead, which will equip American Minuteman III missiles with ultraprecise and provocative guidance systems; and the Trident I and cruise missiles, which will also increase U.S. ability to destroy Soviet ICBMs and other hardened targets. Finally, in an apparent reaction to Soviet developments in passive defenses, the United States is moving ahead with plans to upgrade significantly its civil defense capability. Taken together, these programs are expected to provide a nuclear-war fighting capability, or—in the parlance of the Pentagon—a "counterforce" capability.

Both the Soviet Union and the United States have, therefore, moved toward the deployment of a counterforce capability. No longer are they satisfied with simple nuclear deterrence, i.e., a strategic weapons capability that can assuredly destroy an aggressor with a retaliatory blow. They are now not only "thinking about the unthinkable," they are also preparing for it. As a result, the fear that the other side will strike first naturally provides an incentive for each to strike first itself.

New technology is also providing new threats. The next major escalation in the superpower arms race is likely to involve laser beam technology. Such technology, based on light amplification by stimulated emission of radiation, could be used both offensively and defensively. Offensively, these beams of light could be used to guide missiles to their planned targets or "blind" an enemy's early-warning system, leaving him vulnerable to missile attack. Defensively, they might be used to accomplish what ABMs cannot accomplish —the destruction of incoming missiles. Since such destruction would take place through "vaporization," the day is not far off when science fiction truly becomes science fact.

Equally fantastic are the prospects for environmental warfare. Techniques already exist for manipulating the very structure of our planet—the solid earth, its flora and fauna, the sea, and the atmosphere—and outer space as well. The consequent changes in weather or climate patterns, ocean currents, or in the ozone layer could permanently alter our environment.

Can the development and availability of all these instruments of destruction really be expected to produce security? Are they worth their drain on the world economy (development of the MX missile alone is expected to cost $30–60 billion, and the U.S. investment in laser weaponry topped $2 billion in 1980)? Can the move and countermove dynamic of the strategic arms race between the superpowers go on indefinitely, without a breakdown? Will neither side ever achieve enough of an upper hand to calculate that a first-strike would be gainful? With the militarization of outer space, isn't the nuclear balance of terror in danger of sudden imbalance?

It is difficult to believe that the superpower arms race can be maintained indefinitely. And, it is difficult to believe the argument that the prevailing balance of terror is a sound basis for peace simply because it has worked for over thirty years. Constantly changing factors throughout the world might at any time serve to upset this delicate balance.

The argument that a nuclear war is simply too terrible ever to be fought seems naïve when viewed in the light of history. Throughout history, the only constraints on human barbarism have been the available implements needed for the task. In fact, the grossest inversion of man's capabilities took place not in the dark and distant recesses of history's memory, but in the twentieth-century death camps of Hitler's Germany. There, the cult of antilife was elevated to levels beyond the wildest imaginings of even the most hardened pessimists. Auschwitz and Hiroshima provide vivid examples of man's ability to perpetrate savagery upon his fellow men. It would be the height of folly to believe that this could not happen again and on an even larger scale.

What makes the situation more frightening today is that warfare may be conducted in a sterile atmosphere of computers, consoles, and dimly lit launch control facilities, far from its intended victims, whose suffering cannot be perceived. Bombs are dropped from great heights, and missiles are launched thousands of miles from their targets.

Whereas the SS guards in Nazi death camps often resorted to permanent intoxication to enable them to carry out their "duty," no such measures are necessary in the thermonuclear context. Imbued with a sense of mission, those who are assigned to the use of nuclear weapons throughout the world have only to complete a series of mechanical tasks and to turn a number of coordinated keys to achieve their objectives. It should not be hard for them to do so.

This is, perhaps, one of the most terrible ironies of the entire system of nuclear "security" which man has created for himself. The perfection of evil, the design and construction of weapons for the obliteration of humanity, has been achieved, for the most part, by good, decent, and well-intentioned people. If it cannot be prevented, the delivery of nuclear weapons, by and large, will be carried out by the same sort of people, individuals free of sadistic motives or of any wish to inflict unprecedented misery. Should we fail to prevent it, the ultimate catastrophe, nuclear apocalypse, will be executed by men who want peace.

Another element that makes our present situation more hazardous than ever before is the ability today of private individuals to make and use nuclear weapons. Recently it was revealed that a twenty-one-year-old undergraduate physics major at Princeton University, John A. Phillips, designed an atomic bomb in four months with information obtained from public documents. Although Phillips did not actually build his bomb, a crude plutonium device weighing 125 pounds and carrying a yield one-third as great as the Hiroshima bomb, experts agree that it would almost surely work.[6] "The point," says Phillips of his thirty-four-page junior independent paper, "was to show that any undergraduate with a physics background can do it, and therefore that it is reasonable to assume that terrorists could do it, too."[7]

Even a nuclear weapon as "small" as Phillips's could generate terrible destruction, by virtue of the radiation it would emit (gamma rays and neutrons) and the blast wave and heat it would generate. Mason Willrich and Theodore Taylor, in *Nuclear Theft: Risks and Safeguards*, give examples of bomb potency.

> A nuclear explosion with a yield of ten tons in the central courtyard of a large office building might expose to lethal radiation as many as 1000 people in the building. A comparable explosion in the center of a football stadium during a major game could lethally irradiate as many as 10,000 spectators. A nuclear explosion with a 100-ton yield in a typical suburban residential area might kill perhaps as many as 2000 people, primarily by exposure to fallout. The same explosion in a parking lot beneath a very large skyscraper might kill as many as 50,000 people and destroy the entire building.[8]

Phillips's weapon design, we remember, is for a bomb with a yield in the range of more than *6,000 tons of TNT*.

The fact is that Phillips's achievement is really not all that remarkable. According to Willrich and Taylor:

> Under conceivable circumstances, a few persons, possibly even one person working alone, who possessed about ten kilograms of plutonium oxide and a substantial amount of chemical high explosive could, within several weeks, design and build a crude fission bomb. By a "crude fission bomb" we mean one that would have an excellent chance of exploding, and would probably explode with the power of at least 100 tons of chemical high explosive. This could be done using materials and equipment that could be purchased at a hardware store

and from commercial suppliers of scientific equipment for student laboratories.[9]

Today, many people throughout the world could design and manufacture a nuclear explosive. Criminals or terrorists who might wish to "go nuclear" have only to turn to the entry about nuclear weapons in the *Encyclopedia Americana* to gain detailed insight into the design principles of fission explosives.[10]

Still easier is the manufacture of a radiation dispersal device designed to disperse radioactive materials. Plutonium, in the form of very small particles suspended in air, is extraordinarily toxic. In terms of the weight of material that represents a lethal dose, plutonium-239 is about 20,000 times more toxic than cobra venom or potassium cyanide. Stolen from some stage of the nuclear energy production cycle, it could be put into the form of an aerosol of finely divided particles for use as a radiological weapon.

The following scenario provided by Willrich and Taylor suggests how such a weapon would work.

> The plutonium aerosol is distributed into the intake of a large downtown office building's air conditioning system by a criminal or terrorist group. Only three and one-half ounces could prove a deadly risk for all of the occupants. Death by lung cancer would probably come to anyone inhaling between ten and one hundred *millionths* of a gram. Death due to fibrosis of the lung would be the probable fate of those who retain a dose of about a dozen *thousandths* of a gram.[11]

Such an explosion would also have grave social, economic and, of course political implications.

Plutonium could be dispersed in other ways. One scenario that has been considered by the Nuclear Regulatory Commission office in Washington, D.C., is described as follows:

> During what appears to be a normal day at the Pacific Coast Stock Exchange, a large beaker filled with boiling liquid is noticed in the window of a nearby hotel. Police investigate, but it is too late. The boiling acid in the beaker has been dissolving and dispersing half a pound of plutonium, enough to expose everyone within several city blocks to a high risk of lung cancer.[12]

Another present-day danger is that criminals or terrorists might steal a finished and sophisticated explosive device from a military stockpile of one of the nuclear powers. Existing evidence (which I shall consider later) suggests that military stockpiles of nuclear weapons in many parts of the world are inadequately protected.

Finally, there is always the possibility that acts of sabotage might be directed against nuclear power plants. Consider the following scenario, another in the collection of the Nuclear Regulatory Commission's Office of Nuclear Material Safety and Safeguards:

Under the cover of night, a dozen men storm the gates of a nuclear power plant, killing the two guards and taking the operating staff hostage. After placing charges of high explosives next to the plant's critical cooling systems, they phone the mayor of a nearby large city. Send $5 million, they demand, or we will blow the plant, sending radioactive particles drifting over the city's neighborhoods.[13]

Although steps have been taken to diminish the vulnerability of nuclear power plants in this country, recent statements by the Albuquerque-based Sandia Corporation and the Nuclear Regulatory Commission suggest that successful sabotage would not be difficult to accomplish. By penetrating the physical barriers between them and the fission material in the reactor and by disabling the cooling systems to the reactor core, saboteurs could cause the reactor to melt through its protective shielding and release deadly radioactivity into the atmosphere. Alternatively, since today's nuclear plants are unable to withstand the impact of large aircraft, a kamikaze-type plane crash into a nuclear plant could create a calamitous reactor core meltdown. Comparatively speaking, however, it would be more difficult for criminals or terrorists to "pulse" a nuclear reactor core to destruction than to make a radiological weapon or crude fission bomb.

The gravity of our situation today is evident. Armed with an understanding of this threat in its various manifestations, we must act to overcome it. This book attempts to make a step in that direction.

Part One

Paths to Apocalypse

Introduction to Part One

There are many potential paths to nuclear catastrophe in the context of world politics. Each of these must be recognized with all of its ramifications in order that it may be obstructed. For the purposes of this text, I have divided these potential paths into three major categories: nuclear war between the superpowers; nuclear war through proliferation; and nuclear terrorism.

The first path to be considered here, and certainly the most obvious, is nuclear war between the superpowers or between the two alliances of states defined by NATO and the Warsaw Pact. A war of this magnitude might be triggered in a number of ways. It might come about inadvertently through competition in risk taking. It might begin through the seizure of nuclear weapons by allied countries. It might be provoked by a smaller power (catalytic war) or by war between smaller powers. It could result from incorrect information processed by field commanders or national leaders. Or, it might take place because of errors committed in calculating the outcomes of various anticipated courses of action. It might even occur as a consequence of a breakdown in the essential requirements of deterrence, such as the use of equipment by unauthorized personnel, or sheer mechanical or electrical malfunction.

The second category involves nuclear war between smaller nuclear powers, or between smaller nuclear powers and one of the superpowers. The deployment of nuclear weapons to allied countries and the proliferation of countries possessing assembled nuclear weapons or the technology from which these weapons can be manufactured make this a likely possibility. Indeed, in the years ahead, the probability of nuclear war involving "secondary" powers is apt to be considerably greater than the probability of nuclear war confined to the current superpowers.

The new nuclear-weapon countries may well differ from the superpowers in several unfortunate respects:

1. They may prove more reckless in nuclear brinksmanship and competitive risk taking.
2. Their governments are more likely to be unstable.
3. They may be less likely to employ reliable safeguards against unauthorized use or accidental firings of nuclear weapons.
4. They may have a greater number of decision makers authorized to use nuclear weapons.
5. They may be more likely to initiate ambiguous command control procedures such as would render the proper source of authority difficult to ascertain.
6. They are less likely to have the secure nuclear retaliatory forces essential to deterrence, thereby inviting a first-strike attack against them.
7. Most terrifying of all, the new nuclear weapon countries are more likely to be led by irrational individuals capable of initiating nuclear warfare in spite of their realization of the consequences. Obviously, this contradicts the "logic" of deterrence lying at the heart of today's precarious security structure, which assumes a rational approach to the common goal of self-preservation.

The third path to nuclear catastrophe could involve the use of nuclear explosives or radioactivity by terrorist groups. A corollary to this would be the use of nuclear technology in a civil war. There are a number of factors that lend credence to this threat:

1. It is becoming increasingly easy for terrorists to gain access to nuclear weapons, nuclear power plants, and nuclear-waste storage facilities.
2. Today's terrorists are unique in the sense that their use of violence may be limited solely by the availability of weapons resources.

3. Terrorists frequently place a higher value on certain political/social objectives than they do on their own lives. This ordering of values renders them insensitive to ordinary threats of retaliation.
4. There exists ample evidence of substantial collaboration between terrorist groups.
5. The prevailing global attitude toward terrorism is remarkably tolerant; indeed, it leans more toward surrender or even active support than to the enactment of effective countermeasures.

These, then, are the three major potential paths to nuclear catastrophe in the context of world politics which must be obstructed. Furthermore, these paths are not mutually exclusive. Activity on one path could "trigger" a reaction from another. For example, nuclear war between the superpowers could engulf smaller nuclear powers and/or terrorist groups, just as war beginning with smaller nuclear powers could involve one or both of the superpowers and/or terrorist groups. Nuclear destruction by terrorists could spark nuclear war between the superpowers, nuclear war between one of the superpowers and smaller nuclear powers, or nuclear war between smaller nuclear powers alone.

A detailed consideration of these possibilities is the subject of the following three chapters.

1 The First Path
Nuclear War between the Superpowers

Much has been written in recent years of the various disasters facing mankind, disasters likely to be brought on by poverty, overpopulation, pollution, and so on. But the greatest single threat to man's survival is, undoubtedly, the nuclear arms race between the United States and the USSR. Whereas other world problems will, in general, take some time to develop to catastrophic proportions, a period which will at least permit the possibility of remedial action, no such breathing space will occur if a general nuclear war breaks out. Civilization as we know it will be destroyed in a flash.

Frank Barnaby and Ronald Huisken

Since the end of World War II, the United States and the Soviet Union combined have spent more than $4 trillion on defense. Yet, today, neither the United States nor the Soviet Union is able to defend itself against the other. Reliable national defense against a determined nuclear assault by either superpower is impossible.

The explanation for this situation can be stated succinctly: offensive nuclear-weapon technologies continue to outdistance defensive nuclear-weapon technologies. Even before the advent of MIRVed nuclear-weapon systems, in which single missiles carry several warheads which can be directed to different targets, anti-ballistic-missile defenses could be easily offset by a simple strategy of saturation. However many antiballistic missiles might be deployed, their effect can always be nullified by additions of offensive land-based or sea-based missiles.

With today's American and Soviet deployment of MIRVed missile forces, the idea of an effective antimissile defense system becomes moot. Since MIRVed missiles have several independently targetable warheads, a separate antiballistic missile is needed to intercept each incoming warhead. Hence, the prospect of overcoming an ABM system by saturation is greatly increased with the presence of missiles with multiple warheads.

A protocol to the 1972 Treaty on the Limitation of Anti-Ballistic Missile Systems restricts the deployment of defensive missile launchers by the United States and the Soviet Union to a single ABM area for each country. This means that the Soviet Union can choose to maintain its existing ABM system now deployed around Moscow (although the Soviet Union is allowed 100 missile launchers by the treaty, only 64 missiles are currently deployed in the Moscow ABM system) or to replace that system with another designed to protect an ICBM complex. For the United States, this means that an ABM system can be deployed at either the Minuteman III missile complex at Grand Forks, North Dakota, or at Washington, D.C. In fact, the $6 billion Safeguard ABM complex at Grand Forks has been phased out, and it is certain that a Washington deployment will never take place.

Not only has the extraordinary expenditure of Soviet and American wealth on military power taken place at a time when a great many human needs are going unfulfilled,[1] but this expenditure has also failed even to produce defense. We have been the victims of a prodigal waste of wealth and intelligence, in a scheme for "survival" that could ultimately result in megadeath or even gigadeath.[2]

The justifying principle for such great expenditures has always been defense through nuclear deterrence, in the belief that maintaining the balance of terror will produce national and international security. However, safety in modern world politics is not, as Churchill once remarked, "the sturdy child of terror." All of the alleged virtues of a nuclear peace are founded upon a set of erroneous assumptions.

The Myth of Nuclear Deterrence

Nuclear deterrence rests on the assumption that the costs of nuclear retaliation are so great that no rational nation would do anything that might invite it, and that neither super-power, therefore, would ever strike first.

There are, however, several things wrong with this kind of reasoning. A credible nuclear deterrence posture—a position that assures any prospective aggressor of an unacceptably damaging nuclear retaliation—requires more than nuclear weapons. It requires the belief, on the part of the nation contemplating aggression, that such a nuclear retaliation will actually take place. Thus it must be believed that the other nation is *willing* to retaliate with nuclear arms.

In the current world situation, it might be difficult to make such an assumption. In the first place, one superpower might believe that once the other is attacked it might decide quite rationally that nothing could be gained by retaliating. Not only could making good on the threat to retaliate create havoc for the civilian population of the attacking super-power, it might even increase the damage already suffered by the attack victim.

Consider the following scenario:

One of the superpowers launches a long-range, high-yield nuclear first strike against the other. This strike is "limited," however, to vulnerable seg-ments of the victim's nuclear retaliatory forces and is accompanied by the assurance of no further damage in exchange for a promise to pass up retali-ation. Under such conditions, it might well be rational for the attacked superpower to accept the "deal" and forego retaliation.

Today, the plausibility of this scenario is underscored by the significant inequality between Soviet and American civil defense capabilities. The United States has only the most marginal of such capabilities while the Soviet Union directs what Paul H. Nitze, former deputy secretary of defense, cor-rectly describes as a "massive and meticulously planned civil defense effort."[3] The destabilizing implications of this inequality warrant special notice, since they point to a con-dition wherein the Soviet Union might believe itself able to hold the American population as a "hostage" to deter retali-ation once a first strike (a "counterforce" attack) against U.S. nuclear forces has been launched.

Another problem that might arise is that one superpower might believe the other to be unwilling to retaliate in response to an attack on one of its allies. Today, the United States maintains about 7,000 nuclear weapons in Europe on the assumption that "deterrence is enhanced by the presence of these weapons in the theater, because WP [Warsaw Pact] conventional or nuclear attack plans must take into account the possibility of early NATO nuclear responses."[4]

But the United States could hardly consider a Warsaw Pact attack on a NATO ally, using conventional or nuclear weapons sufficient grounds to enter into a nuclear war.[5] In this case, American decision makers would realize that the system of mutual deterrence had failed and would probably assume that any attempt to undertake nuclear retaliation would only broaden the arena of conflict and magnify destruction to unacceptable levels.

There are strong reasons to doubt that alliance guarantees of nuclear retaliation would be honored in a postattack situation. After all, can we really expect the United States to honor a commitment when the anticipated costs might involve overwhelmingly destructive nuclear counterretaliation? It is much more likely to decide to place its own survival over its commitment to an ally. In the final analysis, it is the very nature of nuclear weapons that makes it uncertain whether a superpower will make good its threat of nuclear retaliation on behalf of its allies.

This realization has led the United States to consider enhanced-radiation weapons (familiar to us as the neutron bomb). Since it would produce the bulk of its damage by a flood of neutrons rather than through heat or concussive force, the neutron bomb would cause less damage than existing tactical nuclear weapons, to friendly forces, civilians, and buildings. Hence, it has been argued, the neutron bomb—which is essentially a miniature thermonuclear warhead for tactical missiles and artillery shells—would significantly enhance the credibility of the American nuclear commitment to NATO.

However, although the new type of warhead might minimize collateral damage to friendly soldiers, structures, and noncombatants, it would have no special advantages in terms of preventing Soviet escalation to strategic nuclear war. In the words of Arthur S. Collins, Jr., a retired general whose last field assignment was as deputy commander in chief of the U.S. Army in Europe:

> NATO use of neutron weapons developed for limited employment, discrete fire techniques, and pinpoint accuracy in defense of NATO is going to draw a Soviet response with tactical nuclear weapons; there should be no fuzzy thinking on that point. The asymmetry between Soviet nuclear weapons and the neutron bomb would be so great that the larger and less accurate Soviet weapons would be devastating to NATO forces using the small weapons.[6]

Whether the first nuclear weapons used between NATO and the Warsaw Pact were neutron bombs or tactical forces, escalation to unlimited nuclear war would be very possible. Any nuclear exchange could lead each side to press ahead with its entire arsenal, once it became caught up in the momentum of military operations. It was most likely his understanding of this fact that led President Carter, on 7 April 1978, to defer (but not discount) production of enhanced radiation weapons.

Thus, realizing the potential for escalation inherent in the use of even enhanced radiation weapons for the purposes of retaliation, a superpower might hesitate to take the risk. No matter how often or how vehemently the United States, for example, claims that an attack on its NATO allies would be tantamount to an attack on the United States itself, no level of commitment which involves a high probability of nuclear counterretaliation will be seen by the potential attacker as irrevocable. This includes the so-called "trip wire" concept of reinforcing commitments to allies.[7]

The allies, too, are aware of this. The fear that the United States might be unwilling to retaliate against the Soviet Union for an attack against France led the French to develop their own nuclear force. Today, a similar fear—that the United States would balk at steps that might bring it into direct nuclear confrontation with the Soviet Union—has apparently spurred the development of an independent Israeli nuclear force. Both cases support the belief that one of the superpowers—in this case the United States—might be unlikely to retaliate against the other on behalf of an ally.

Now, would the threat to retaliate on behalf of an ally with tactical or "battlefield" nuclear weapons be more credible than a threat to use strategic or large-scale nuclear weapons?[8] An affirmative answer is implicit in a report to the Congress by former secretary of defense Schlesinger on *The Theater Nuclear Force Posture In Europe* which states the following: "Theater [tactical] nuclear forces, because they do not pose a major threat to the Soviet homeland, constitute a retaliatory capability which carries a perceptively lower risk of escalation than the use of strategic nuclear forces." This position, supported by Richard Shearer, NATO's director for nuclear planning, continues to be policy for the United States.[9]

I don't believe, however, that an affirmative answer is warranted here. I believe that nations today regard, both in a concrete and a psychological sense, the distinction between conventional and nuclear weapons as more significant than distinctions among different forms of nuclear weapons. Nuclear weapons *are* different because they are widely *perceived* to be different. There is thus no reason to believe that the threat to use tactical nuclear weapons (even in the form of a neutron bomb) for retaliation would be any less inhibiting for the retaliating nation. That nation would surely perceive that such action could easily trigger a catastrophic chain reaction.

President Kennedy certainly understood this when he stated that "inevitably the use of small nuclear armaments will lead to larger and larger nuclear armaments on both sides, until the worldwide holocaust has begun."[10] This view is supported by a recent issue of *The Defense Monitor*, a publication of the highly regarded Center for Defense Information:

> Once the nuclear threshold has been broken, it is highly likely that the nuclear exchanges would escalate. Radio, radar, and other communications would be disrupted or cut. The pressures to destroy the adversary's nuclear force before they land a killing blow would lead to preemptive attacks. In the confusion, subtle peacetime

distinctions between lower level tactical nuclear war
and higher level tactical nuclear war, and all-out spasm
nuclear war would vanish. Once the threshold is crossed
from conventional warfare to nuclear warfare, the clearest "firebreak" on the path to complete nuclear holocaust will have been crossed.[11]

In spite of this argument, American NATO policy continues to emphasize the special role of theater nuclear forces
as a deterrent to conventional as well as theater nuclear
attacks. What is most peculiar about this emphasis is that it
is coupled with the understanding that "Operational Soviet
military doctrine apparently does not subscribe to a strategy
of graduated nuclear response," and that the limited use of
nuclear weapons is "fraught with the danger of escalation."[12]
With such an understanding, it is difficult to believe that the
United States would actually be willing to make good on its
theater nuclear commitments to NATO allies.

Another aspect of this problem concerns the effects that
theater nuclear forces would have on the countries being
protected. A recent study by the Center for Defense Information reveals that the use of only 10 percent of the roughly
7,000 tactical nuclear weapons which the United States maintains in Europe would destroy the entire area where these
exchanges took place. Indeed, the study points out that in
the course of a recent NATO war game called (interestingly
enough) Carte Blanche that was played on German territory,
"a very conservative estimate placed Germans killed at between 1.5 and 1.7 million plus an additional 3.5 million
wounded."[13] Since 3 million Germans were killed and 7 million wounded during the six years of World War II, this
means that a "very limited" tactical nuclear war could produce more than half that number of German casualties in
only two days. What we have, then, is a policy to destroy
Europe in order to save it.[14] This situation would not be
altered by deployment of the neutron bomb, since—as we
have already noted—the expected Warsaw Pact counterretaliation would be devastating and unlimited.

All in all, the American nuclear NATO doctrine is implausible. Even if we were able to accept the reasonableness of
threatening the use of tactical or enhanced radiation nuclear

weapons, the accompanying role assigned to strategic nuclear weapons to "reinforce theater nuclear forces if needed" and "to deter and defend in general nuclear war" is altogether fanciful. Little wonder, then, that former Deputy Assistant Secretary of Defense Morton Halperin described American nuclear NATO doctrine by saying that "we fight with tactical nuclear weapons until we are losing, and then we will blow up the world."[15]

Recently the foreign and defense ministers of the NATO countries moved to strengthen their deterrence options. On December 12, 1979, they agreed to proceed with plans to deploy 108 Pershing II ballistic missiles and 464 ground-launched cruise missiles in Europe. A reaction to the Soviet deployment of modern MIRVed SS-20s and Backfire bombers in the European theater, NATO's extremely accurate medium range weapons will be operational in 1983.

Regrettably, however, it is unreasonable to suppose that the new weapons will fill a gap in the alliance's spectrum of available nuclear options. As with enhanced radiation weapons and existing theater nuclear forces, the new generation of medium range missiles will be fraught with dangers of uncontrolled escalation. Indeed, these dangers will be especially great since the new weapons will be targeted directly at the Soviet Union. Unlike existing theater nuclear forces, which do not pose a threat to the Soviet homeland, the new missiles will carry a perceptibly high risk of escalation—a risk as great, perhaps, as that of strategic nuclear forces.

There is a third situation in which one superpower might assume the other's unwillingness to retaliate with nuclear weapons, and that is when the retaliation is in response to an attack with conventional weapons against military forces stationed in other countries. Since the consequences of such an attack are likely to be judged much more tolerable than those that would result from nuclear retaliation, the fulfillment of a threat to undertake such retaliation is clearly improbable. The credibility of a threat to retaliate with nuclear force for a nonnuclear attack on military personnel and installations may actually vary inversely with the number and quality of these personnel and installations. This is the case because the presence of a conventional force that appears capable of resisting an attack might signal an un-willingness to resort to promised nuclear retaliation.

We have reviewed three principal reasons why each of the superpowers might doubt the other's willingness to undertake promised nuclear retaliation. Taken together, these reasons point to a fundamental weakness in the strat-egy of peace through nuclear deterrence. If a nation thinking about aggression is inclined to believe that unacceptably damaging nuclear retaliation will not actually take place, the credibility of the nuclear deterrent threat is fatally undermined.

The capability to deliver overwhelming nuclear retaliation is not enough to ensure a credible nuclear deterrence pos-ture. To have such a posture, nations must give the impres-sion that they are willing to use that capability. And then, even the capability ingredient of a credible nuclear deter-rence posture cannot be taken for granted, as the following discussion will show.

The Problem of Secure Nuclear Forces

The mere possession of nuclear retaliatory forces does not imply a nuclear capability. To have such a capability, nations must also be able to assure the security of these forces from a first-strike attack. Secure nuclear retaliatory forces are an essential requirement of a credible nuclear deterrence posture.

Secure nuclear forces, however, cannot be assured indefi-nitely. Their security is subject to technological reversal at any time. Ironically, since each superpower is continually engaged in attempts to poke holes in the "security blanket" of the other superpower, such a reversal is actually the goal of both the United States and the Soviet Union. In addition, there is no assurance that secure nuclear retaliatory forces might not mistakenly be judged insecure by one side or the other, or that the very search for secure retaliatory forces will not produce an accidental, preemptive, or unauthorized nuclear strike.

There is, then, no reason to believe that each superpower will always see itself opposed by secure nuclear deterrent forces. While the current situation is clearly one in which neither side could destroy enough of the other side's nuclear retaliatory forces on a first-strike attack to preclude the possibility of unacceptably damaging nuclear retaliation, the situation is nevertheless an unstable one. Should a technological reversal seriously imperil either superpower's nuclear deterrence forces, the incentive for the other super-power to strike first could be irresistible.[16] As Fred C. Iklé, a former director of the U.S. Arms Control and Dis-armament Agency, said recently:

> Deterrence depends on having military forces that can survive an attack and strike back. The problem is that today's science and weapon technology have such mo-mentum that they are constantly changing the survival conditions for deterrent forces. At one turn, new tech-nology upsets the balance by creating some deadly new weapon that makes deterrent forces more vulnerable— the invention of multiple warheads for intercontinental missiles (MIRVs) for example. At another turn, tech-nology may come up with a way to make deterrent forces more survivable; for example, the missile carry-ing submarine that can hide in the oceans. Deterrence is at the mercy of technology.[17]

And technology is changing all the time. Although the American "triad" of nuclear retaliatory forces—land-based bombers, land-based missiles, and submarine-based missiles —is designed to ensure the infliction of unacceptable second-strike damage on the Soviet Union (and vice versa), the fear is widespread that these forces are becoming increasingly vulnerable. In a report to the Congress, former Secretary of Defense Donald H. Rumsfeld revealed some of the basic reasons behind such fears:

> —aging submarine and bomber forces coupled with Soviet advances in antisubmarine warfare capabilities and defense against bombers;
> —growing asymmetry between American and Soviet strategic offensive forces which favor the Soviet capa-bility; and
> —developments in Soviet strategic programs which may threaten the survivability of the American Minute-man force.[18]

Similar fears have been expressed by the current secretary of defense, Harold Brown:

> Whatever the intentions and motives of the Soviets, we face two related problems as the result of their activities. They are the increasing vulnerability of the U.S. ICBM force and the expanding scope of Soviet active and passive defenses.[19]

Former chairman of the Joint Chiefs of Staff, General George S. Brown, has speculated that:

> The Soviets may become bolder and more aggressive as they perceive their relative military capability improving. The 1981–1982 period appears to be critical in this regard. Many of the most important of their present programs in military research and development, production and deployment will then be complete or nearing completion, while critical U.S. programs such as the MX, B-1 [while the B-1 program has since been canceled, it may still be resurrected], TRIDENT, cruise missiles, and the MK-12A warhead will just be beginning to affect the relative balance.[20]

For the United States to secure its strategic triad of nuclear forces, it must, allegedly, first render its existing silo-based ICBM force (Minuteman and Titan II) less vulnerable to the increasingly accurate Soviet ICBMs (SS-17, SS-18, and SS-19). This would involve further developing the MX missile, which offers a mobile and therefore more survivable basing mode. At the same time, the Department of Defense argues against the complete phasing out of the Minuteman/Titan force on the grounds that such a move would sacrifice a substantial measure of firepower, precision, and flexibility while increasing the vulnerability of the other two triad components.

Second, the United States must modernize its submarine launched ballistic missile (SLBM) forces. This requires moving away from the current force of Polaris and Poseidon submarines in favor of Trident, a quieter boat with longer range missiles to hedge against Soviet advances in anti-submarine-warfare capabilities. It also means looking ahead to replacing the Polaris missile with the Trident missile, which will increase the SSBN operating area by a factor of about ten and thus further complicate Soviet anti-submarine-warfare progress. Plans are presently underway to develop an even more accurate Trident II missile, which would be deployed in the mid to late 1980s.

And third, its land-based bombers must be improved to reflect greater survivability features. With the future of the B-1 bomber uncertain, the United States must turn to a B-52/cruise missile combination. To implement this combination, its B-52 forces will be modernized to continue in a penetrating bomber role, while the development of air-launched, sea-launched, and ground-launched cruise missiles will be undertaken.

Both sea-based missiles and land-launched ICBMs are better suited than bombers to piercing an enemy's strategic defense systems through the use of advanced penetration techniques. The essential advantage of manned bombers, and the basic rationale for their continuance in the strategic triad, lies in their almost instantaneous capability for retargeting and in their relatively great amenability to controlled conflict situations. Also, as in the case of the argument for maintaining the land-based missile force, a phasing out or reduction of the manned bomber component of the triad would almost certainly increase the vulnerability of the other two components.

Soviet strategic nuclear deterrence is also based on a triad of strategic forces, designed to "ride out" a surprise attack with enough deliverable firepower to wreak an unacceptably damaging retaliatory blow. And, as in the case of the United States, these forces comprise land-based ICBMs (which can carry multiple warheads), submarine-based SLBMs (several of which are MIRVed), and manned bombers (with the Backfire bomber capable of reaching targets throughout the United States).

It follows that Soviet leaders, like their American counterparts, are concerned about the effects of new technological developments on the vulnerability of their strategic nuclear triad. Missiles are ever more powerful and accurate, threatening fixed and hardened ICBM installations, just as advances in anti-strategic-submarine warfare threaten SSBN/

SLBM forces. Then, too, the manned bombers have certain inherent problems of survivability and penetrability.

While it is true that both countries are continually improving these components and are developing new, more exotic weapons, they are, at the same time, each pursuing ways to render the other's strategic forces more vulnerable. As a result, each superpower entertains the fear that the other is pursuing a first-strike capability. In the United States, for example, many people believe there is a basic difference in strategic nuclear objectives between the two superpowers. They perceive the American objective as limited to the maintenance of an assuredly destructive second-strike capability,[21] while they perceive the Soviets as bent upon achieving a nuclear-war-winning capability. Irrespective of their accuracy, such perceptions of differences in strategic nuclear objectives render the idea of stable deterrence increasingly implausible. Little wonder, then, that the concept of "mutual assured destruction" is represented by the acronym "MAD."

Another aspect of this problem is that, even if both superpowers are able to maintain strategic retaliatory forces that *are* sufficiently invulnerable, one or the other superpower (or even both) might—through miscalculation or errors in information—*perceive* the other as vulnerable. In such a case, even though both sides have actually been "successful" in protecting their retaliatory forces, a first-strike attack might nonetheless be unleashed. Here, deterrence would fail even though the requirement of secure retaliatory forces had been satisfied.

Finally, even if both superpowers are able to maintain secure retaliatory forces, and each is able to perceive this to be true of the other, the effort to maintain this condition, or balance, provides the basic dynamic of a fearful arms race. Many factors could act to upset this balance, including the accidental or unauthorized use of nuclear weapons by either of the superpowers or by other agents. The search for methods to retain secure nuclear retaliatory forces generates a pattern of fear and uncertainty in both participants which could at any point culminate in a preemptive strike or the accidental breakdown of complex nuclear weapon command/control systems. As George B. Kistiakowsky, the esteemed Harvard chemist, noted recently: "There are no cases in history of absolutely insane arms races ending peacefully by simply laying down arms. Arms races usually end up in wars."[22]

There are then at least three major deficiencies in the strategy of nuclear deterrence from the standpoint of secure retaliatory forces: (1) it is unlikely that survivability can be preserved indefinitely; (2) secure retaliatory forces may mistakenly be judged insecure; and (3) the search for secure retaliatory forces may heighten the probability of accidental, preemptive, or unauthorized nuclear-weapon detonations. Presently, all of these deficiencies must be evaluated against the backdrop of the continuing fear that each superpower is searching for a disarming first-strike capability against the other.

Is the Soviet fear entirely unfounded? Officially, it has always been the policy of the United States not to launch a nuclear strike as an initial offensive move of war. This policy was stated unambiguously by President Kennedy in 1961: "Our arms will never be used to strike the first blow in any attack. . . . We are not creating forces for a first strike against any other nation."[23]

This policy has been reiterated by former Secretary of Defense Schlesinger[24] and by each of his successors. However, it is interesting to note that Schlesinger emphasized the impossibility rather than the undesirability of a disarming American first strike. It is also worth noting that Schlesinger did not declare himself against the *first use of* strategic nuclear weapons, i.e., the first use of these weapons in retaliation for nonnuclear "aggression." Indeed, as Schlesinger said just a few days later on ABC's "Issues and Answers:" "The United States has consistently had a policy of refraining from disavowing first use."[25] This policy is still in effect today. And, as we have already seen in our discussion of NATO nuclear strategy, this policy extends to the first use of tactical nuclear weapons in certain circumstances.[26]

These facts are important to our assessment of the strategy of peace through nuclear deterrence because, in actual state practice, the alleged distinction between the "first use" of nuclear weapons and a nuclear "first strike" may prove meaningless. Once an American adversary has committed an act of aggression, the United States would certainly characterize any intended nuclear response as "first use" rather than "first strike." Since the determination that an act of aggression had actually taken place would necessarily be made by the United States rather than by some specially constituted central arbiter, it follows that certain acts that are judged to be aggressive by the United States might warrant an American nuclear response.

From the standpoint of the Soviet Union, this American policy of "first use" must appear decidedly unsettling, since it allows for rapid escalation to nuclear conflict, and it allows for the possibility of disguising a "first strike" as a "first use" either by deliberately creating conditions which lead to acts of "aggression" or by falsely alleging that such acts have actually taken place. Further, the policy includes a changing targeting doctrine which favors a *counterforce* strategy; a strategy that calls for the targeting of Soviet strategic forces rather than population centers, industries, and resources.

Hence, the American policy of "first use" is extremely destabilizing for the entire strategy of peace through nuclear deterrence. It not only encourages the American use of enormously destructive weapons, but it also offers incentives to the Soviet Union for a preemptive nuclear strike against the United States.[21]

Americans, too, have cause for concern about a Soviet first strike. Like the United States, the Soviet Union has never disavowed the first-use option. Moreover, the Soviets continue to strive for nuclear superiority that is oriented toward a "win the war" capability, and that is augmented by a massive civil defense effort.

More specifically, at the moment American officials are especially concerned about the following: (1) Soviet missile-submarine development is geared to the potential for an effective SLBM attack on American bombers. (2) Soviet land-based ICBMs, through continued improvements in missile accuracy, MIRVing, and increased throw-weights, are being geared to a "hard target counterforce capability" which can effectively threaten America's ICBM force. (3) Soviet ASW forces, through the continuing proliferation of platforms and the steady improvement of sensor technology, are being geared to the capability to destroy America's SLBM force.

To counter these seemingly persistent threats to a survivable second-strike capability, the United States feels itself compelled to take what it regards as appropriate protective measures. The Soviets, in turn, concerned that these and certain other measures on the part of the United States are of a threatening character, will do everything possible to nullify their effectiveness. This will be handled through the production of still more sophisticated and destructive offensive-weapons systems. In turn, the United States will continue to try to render its nuclear retaliatory forces invulnerable to such developments. However, even if the United States should succeed in maintaining secure forces which the Soviets recognize as such, the net effect of this vicious cycle of moves and countermoves is bound to be an increasingly unstable situation for all concerned. At every step in the race, the chances of nuclear catastrophe by preemption, accident, or unauthorized use are increased.

Escalation: A Macabre Dance of Death

Thirteen years ago, during the week of October 22–28, 1962, the two great powers stood near the abyss of nuclear war. It was a fearsome week, one that opened with President John F. Kennedy's declaration on Monday evening, the 22nd, that there were Soviet "offensive" missiles in Cuba, that they must be withdrawn, and that he would establish a quarantine, and that closed with the Soviet promise on Sunday morning to accede to the American demand. It was a time, as Premier Nikita Khrushchev later said, "when the smell of burning hung in the air." During the week, President Kennedy placed the likelihood of disaster at "somewhere between one out of three and even."[28]

The decision to use nuclear forces is not likely to be made in "normal" circumstances. Even the volatile rivalry of the superpowers is not apt to generate a sudden, rational decision to use nuclear weapons. Rather, the necessary and sufficient conditions for such a decision are likely to be met only through various kinds of international crises and through the competition in risk taking that such circumstances bring about. Such competition is called "escalation."

When a "head to head" confrontation does take place, it begins with each side determined to "stand firm" in the hope that the other side will be the first to back down. Such was the case with the Cuban missile crisis. President Kennedy had committed the United States Navy to sink any ship that did not respect the quarantine. A collision course seemed inevitable. While the world waited to see whether the Soviet ships would challenge the blockade, the United States instituted a special SAC (Strategic Air Command) alert, and a Soviet press officer told his American counterpart, "New York will be blown up tomorrow by Soviet nuclear weapons."

In the end, of course, the Soviet ships closest to Cuba altered their course and a potentially apocalyptic escalation was averted. But it very well might have ended differently. The two superpowers, as Dean Rusk was alleged to have said, were "eyeball to eyeball" when "the other fellow [the Soviet Union] blinked." Soviet restraint had prevented a shoot-out at sea that might easily have escalated into full-scale nuclear war.

In this instance, the avoidance of escalation lay essentially with the principal figures, President Kennedy and Chairman Khrushchev. How in the future can we count on superpower leaders choosing humiliation rather than war?

Inevitably, when the superpowers become engaged in the uncertain dynamics of escalation, they find themselves trying to steer a steady course between the sheer rock of Scylla and the whirlpool of Charybdis. Should one side or the other back down out of fear, the retreat would probably be costly in terms of future global influence and power. Should both sides continue to exploit the presumed advantages of a committal strategy, the resulting escalation could well produce nuclear holocaust.

Herman Kahn likens the dynamics of escalation to the game of "chicken" as it is played by two drivers on a road with a white line drawn down the middle. According to Kahn:

Both cars straddle the white line and drive toward each other at top speed. The first driver to lose his nerve and swerve into his own lane is "chicken"—an object of contempt and scorn—and he loses the game. The game is played among teenagers for prestige, for girls, for leadership of a gang, and for safety (i.e., to prevent other challenges and confrontations).[29]

However, since the actual processes of escalation are more complicated than this game, Kahn suggests that "chicken" would present a more accurate analogy if

it were played with two cars starting an unknown distance apart, traveling toward each other at unknown speeds, and on roads with several forks so that the opposing sides are not certain that they are even on the same road. Both drivers should be giving and receiving threats and promises while they approach each other, and tearful mothers and stern fathers should be lining the sides of the roads urging, respectively, caution and manliness.[30]

The second analogy is hardly more reassuring than the first. Whichever way the game is played, the prospect of ultimate collision is unacceptably high.

Accidental Use of Nuclear Weapons

Nuclear war might be begun by accident. No matter how well the United States and the Soviet Union satisfy the requirements of a credible nuclear deterrence posture, their "success" will not reduce the likelihood of accidental nuclear war. Indeed, it may actually *increase* its likelihood.

Also the availability of nuclear weapons allows for the possibility of accidents which, while they may not lead to nuclear war between the superpowers, could still produce a calamitous nuclear explosion. Accidents of this type could be triggered by mechanical and/or human malfunction in the operation of nuclear weapon systems.

As the nuclear arms race continues, the chances of nuclear accidents grow. The number of nuclear weapons in the world system increases continually, and their accompanying command/control systems become more and more complex. At the same time, attempts to maintain a credible deterrence posture strain the safeguards which are designed to prevent accidental nuclear weapon detonations. Yet, our very survival depends upon the presumption that nuclear weapon systems (i.e., the weapons themselves and the personnel who are charged with responsibility over these weapons) can *never* fail, since even a single accident involving nuclear weapons could be overwhelmingly catastrophic.

Nuclear weapon systems—perhaps the most complex systems ever created by man—are required *never* to fail. However, even the commercial aviation industry, which is notable for taking every conceivable precaution to prevent accidents, is unable to ensure perfect safety. Every year there are several major accidents involving commercial carriers. These accidents are a regrettable fact of life, even in this most reliable and safety conscious of industries. An absolutely perfect safety record simply cannot be anticipated.

No mechanical system, however carefully constructed and monitored, can be presumed to be infallible. As a recent publication of the U.S. Arms Control and Disarmament Agency puts it: "We all know that no matter how much we spend in care and resources, mechanical things, from simple tools to sophisticated systems, can malfunction."[31] The same point, of course, can be made about the individual human beings who exercise custody and control over nuclear weapons. They, too, are fallible. What we have, then, is a system of nuclear deterrence in which certain sorts of mechanical, electrical, or human malfunction cannot be tolerated, but where such malfunction is distinctly possible, even probable.

Any nuclear weapon accident may have catastrophic effects. So far, we have been lucky. Consider the American record of accidents involving nuclear weapons, at least as far as that record is known. According to the Department of Defense:

> There has been a total of 33 accidents involving U.S. nuclear weapons throughout the period that the U.S. has had these weapons. Because of the inherent safety features, the control features, the administrative procedures designed into U.S. nuclear weapon systems and the precautions taken during operations with these weapons, there has never been a case where a nuclear

detonation has occurred in a nuclear weapon accident. During the last 10 years, due in part to the Department of Defense's comprehensive program to improve nuclear weapon safety, only five accidents have occurred with the most recent being in 1968.

Nuclear weapons in accident environments are designed to be inherently safe. The probability of an inadvertent nuclear detonation is very unlikely. In addition, there are design features as well as mechanical and administrative controls which prevent deliberate prearming, arming, launching, firing or releasing of nuclear weapons except when directed by competent authority. These features and controls also prevent inadvertent prearming, arming, launching, firing, or releasing of nuclear weapons. After a system is fielded it is subjected to an operational review to reexamine the adequacy and suitability of weapon design features, the safety rules and technical/operational procedures.

Of the five accidents occurring in the last 10 years, two accidents, involving B-25 aircraft, resulted in the dispersal of fissile material. These accidents were at Palomares, Spain in 1966 and in Thule, Greenland, in January 1968. Cleanup operations were undertaken at both locations and the areas were completely decontaminated.[32]

According to the Center for Defense Information, however, there is evidence of many other nuclear weapon accidents that have gone unreported or unconfirmed. In the words of *The Defense Monitor:* "Serious students of the problem estimate that an average of one U.S. nuclear accident has occurred every year since 1945, with some estimating as many as thirty major nuclear accidents and 250 minor nuclear accidents during that time."[33] Some of the specific incidents follow.

"Broken Arrows": Nuclear Accidents Admitted
by the Pentagon

1. *Aircrash over Palomares, Spain.* On 17 January 1966, an American B-52 bomber collided with a KC-135 refueling tanker causing the deaths of five crewmen and the dropping of four hydrogen bombs which were re-

covered after an intensive ground and sea search. Radioactive leakage and conventional explosions occurred in the area.

2. *Bomb accidentally dropped over South Carolina.* On 11 March 1958, a B-47 bomber accidentally dropped a nuclear weapon in the megaton range over Mars Bluff, South Carolina. The conventional explosive "trigger" of the nuclear bomb detonated leaving a crater 75 feet wide and 35 feet deep. One farmhouse was obliterated. Luckily no nuclear radiation leakage was detected, no nuclear explosion occurred, and no one was killed.

3. *Bomarc missiles burned in fire.* On 7 June 1960, a fire at McGuire Air Force Base led to a series of shattering explosions and the destruction of one of 56 nuclear armed Bomarc missiles. Although no nuclear explosion occurred, there was a small amount of radioactive leakage creating a temporary health hazard.

4. *Twenty-four-megaton bomb safety devices sprung.* In 1961 a near catastrophe occurred at Goldsboro, North Carolina when a B-52 bomber had to jettison a 24-megaton bomb. Five of the six interlocking safety devices were set off by the fall. A single switch prevented the bomb from exploding, an explosion which would have been over 1,800 times more powerful than the Hiroshima bomb.

5. *Greenland aircrash scatters plutonium.* On 21 January 1968, a B-52 attempting an emergency landing at Thule Air Force Base, Greenland, crashed and burned on the ice of North Star Bay. The high explosive components of all four nuclear weapons aboard detonated producing a plutonium-contaminated area of at least 300–400 feet wide and 2,200 feet long.[34]

With this record of "broken arrows" (major nuclear weapon accidents) as a background, consider the number and complexity of nuclear weapons held by the superpowers. The United States alone has approximately 30,000 nuclear weapons dispersed across the oceans, in Europe and Asia, and within its own borders. What are the odds that none of these weapons (or those in the huge Soviet arsenal) will ever be accidentally fired? While such odds can, of course, never be calculated with certitude or precision, we surely know enough to realize that they are not so favorable as to warrant the ultimate gamble.

This is not to suggest that each of the superpowers is failing to take certain precautions against the accidental use of nuclear weapons. While very little is known about the Soviet Union in this regard,[35] in the United States the Department of Defense Safety Program comprises four basic standards which are required for all nuclear weapon systems. According to the Department of Defense, these standards are as follows:

1. There shall be positive measures to prevent nuclear weapons involved in accidents or incidents or jettisoned weapons from producing a nuclear yield.
2. There shall be positive measures to prevent *deliberate* prearming, arming, launching, firing, or releasing of nuclear weapons, except upon execution of emergency war orders or when directed by competent authority.
3. There shall be positive measures to prevent *inadvertent* prearming, arming, launching, firing, or releasing of nuclear weapons.
4. There shall be positive measures to ensure adequate security of nuclear weapons, pursuant to the provision of DOD Directive 5210.41.[36]

Pursuant to these standards, specified safety rules govern all nuclear-weapon-systems operations in which the nuclear weapon is vulnerable to being inadvertently launched, prearmed, armed, fired, detonated, released, or lost. The scope of these safety rules is identified in the Department of Defense Directive, *Safety Studies and Reviews of Nuclear Weapons Systems:*

Safety Rules shall include general provisions applicable to all nuclear weapon operations throughout the stockpile-to-target sequence (storage, maintenance, handling, transportation, delivery, etc.) and specific provisions to provide adequate safety for unique nuclear weapon system operations (alerts, operational posturing, maneuvers, exercises, training, etc.).[37]

The principal steps taken to avert accidental use of nuclear weapons by American forces include maintaining strict custodial control of these weapons and implementing a considerable array of redundant safety features.[38] These features are incorporated into the chain of command and into the weapons themselves. Precautions in regard to the chain of command include: a so-called two-man concept whereby no single individual has the ability to fire nuclear weapons; a control system whereby each individual with nuclear weapon responsibility must be formally certified under the Human Reliability Program;[39] and the use of "secure codes." Precautions pertaining to the weapons themselves emphasize "highly secure coded locking devices."[40] Moreover, although the exact release procedures for nuclear weapons are highly classified, it is known that safeguards against accidental nuclear firings do vary somewhat from one weapon system to another.

For example, all tactical nuclear weapons that are deployed overseas include mechanical or electrical devices which prevent their firing in the absence of a specially coded signal issued by higher command. Absence of the coded signal physically precludes firing the weapon. Strategic nuclear weapons under Air Force jurisdiction incorporate somewhat different sorts of command/control devices that nonetheless serve the same purpose as those associated with theater-nuclear forces. Additionally, all nuclear weapons— tactical and strategic—incorporate some sort of "environmental sensing device" that is designed to prevent unwanted detonations. These include switches that respond to acceleration, deceleration, altitude, spin, gravity, and thermal forces.[41]

The submarine-based nuclear weapons, however, are unique in one very important sense: these missiles can presumably be fired without receiving a coded signal from the continental United States.[42] Hence, nuclear missile submarines apparently comprise the only component of the strategic nuclear triad in which firing can be accomplished without activation by remote electronic switch turned on by higher command.[43] The reason for this is simply the problem associated with transmitting electronic signals to submerged submarines. Safeguards against accidental firings on American nuclear missile submarines are thus essentially limited to the use of an electrical firing circuit which requires collaborative action within close time tolerances on the part of several men on board who are certifiably "reliable."

But aren't these sufficient safeguards? After all, the captain cannot fire the missiles by himself. His key closes just one of several switches on the firing circuit. Before the missiles can be launched, several other officers on board must "vote" by turning their respective keys and the weapons officer must pull the trigger.

Before answering, consider the following story of a former Polaris captain: Back at the time of the Gulf of Tonkin incident, in August of 1964, an American nuclear missile submarine cruising somewhere in the Pacific received the order to hold a missile drill. The officer on duty, however, misread the message and announced to all aboard that this was the real thing. The Captain quickly checked the message himself, discovered the error, but decided to preserve the impression of the "real thing" in order to "see how the crew does." The weapons officer and the officer in launch control were told of the deception so that "nothing could happen," and "the whole thing went off perfectly." According to the former captain, the practice of failing to identify a missile drill as a drill is not uncommon.[44]

The outcome would surely have been different if the captain had repeated the mistake of the officer on duty; if the captain detected the mistake but generalized the subsequent deception to include the weapons officer and the officer in launch control; or, if a genuine Emergency Action Message had been mistakenly sent to the submarine in the first place.

On a mechanical level, there is always the possibility that there could be a malfunction in the firing circuit.

Another hazard to be considered concerns collisions involving nuclear submarines. Such collisions are already a matter of record. The House Intelligence Committee's suppressed final report states that United States nuclear submarines have collided with nine "hostile vessels" in Soviet waters during the last ten years. Of these, five collisions are known to have involved Soviet nuclear submarines bearing either nuclear missiles or nuclear torpedoes.[45] According to reports, in one of these incidents, the U.S. nuclear submarine *Gato* collided with a Soviet nuclear missile submarine at the entrance to the White Sea in November 1969. The *"Gato* prepared for action with nuclear torpedoes but the Soviet crew was so confused about what had been encountered that the Americans were able to steal away."[46]

A serious misperception could also arise if, say, an internal accident, such as an explosion, occurred on board a nuclear missile submarine. The explosion might falsely be interpreted as an enemy's first-strike attack, and thereby trigger a chain reaction. At least one such incident has already occurred. In the case of the sinking of the U.S. nuclear attack submarine, *Scorpion,* in May 1968, it took nearly six months to determine that it was not caused by enemy actions.[47]

While such evidence and considerations of potential security problems are disquieting, the implications should be regarded with caution. While they do point to significant problems, there are mitigating factors to consider. In this regard, the following points were put forth by Adm. G. E. Miller, a former high-echelon officer in the U.S. submarine–ballistic-missile program:

> No submarine Commanding Officer (CO) has ever failed to identify a missile drill as anything other than a drill. Written procedures are followed verbatim during missile drills, and are monitored by the Executive Officer (XO), Weapons Officer, and Launcher Officer. These procedures require a positive verbal statement by the Commanding Officer and Executive Officer as to whether the weapons evolution is or is not a drill. This statement is part of a monitored check-off list.
>
> Emergency Action Messages (EAMs) which release nuclear weapons must originate with the President. It is virtually impossible that an EAM would be mistakenly transmitted to a nuclear missile submarine. This opinion is based on the years of experience gained through utilizing built-in test procedures and checks, which are being run continuously.
>
> To preclude a malfunction in the firing circuit, a Nu-

clear Weapon Safety Board composed of military and
ERDA representatives reviews the plans and circuitry
of nuclear missile submarines before they are built.
The nuclear weapon system is approved only after
thorough review indicates that the occurrence of an accident or critical malfunction would be highly unlikely.
In addition, the entire weapons system of a nuclear
missile submarine undergoes periodic, routine prevent-
ative maintenance checks to further guard against the
occurrence of a critical malfunction. Many systems are
designed to fail-safe. Electrical alarms are also built
into the system circuitry to immediately identify an occurrence which might tend to diminish system security
or reliability.

It is essentially impossible that a collision involving
nuclear missile submarines might lead to the firing of
some or all of the American missiles. If a collision could
cause ignition of a missile motor (which is unlikely),
the net result would probably be the loss of the submarine with no effects beyond the immediate vicinity of
the ship itself. A nuclear detonation could not occur
because of the safeguards built into the weapon design.
If an ignition were to occur when a missile hatch is
open (a highly unlikely circumstance since all hatches
are locked shut while the SSBN is underway unless a
missile launch is authorized) the missile would have
no electrical power, the warhead could not arm, and
without guidance the missile would destroy itself in the
first few moments after leaving the missile tube.

There are no circumstances under which any submarine commanding officer has the authority to launch
his nuclear weapon bearing missiles without receiving
presidential authority.

An explosion on board a nuclear missile submarine
that is due to some sort of internal defect rather than
enemy action would not lead to the firing of that submarine's SLBMs. The missiles on board a submarine
are enclosed in missile tubes whose strength and structure essentially duplicate the submarine hull. An explosion internal to the submarine would, therefore, quite
likely cause the loss of the submarine through flooding,
with no effect beyond the immediate vicinity of the ship
itself.

But these points are still not enough to assure us that nuclear war between the superpowers cannot be brought on by accidential firings from submarines. Even the most carefully monitored written procedures during missile drills cannot guard against errors completely. Nothing can ensure against an Emergency Action Message being transmitted by mistake, a malfunction occurring in the firing circuit of a nuclear weapons submarine, or, even a collision involving nuclear weapon submarines that might lead to the firing of missiles.

In addition, how can we know for certain that no predelegation of authority to use nuclear weapons has been given to submarine commanders in situations of extreme duress? How can we ever be sure that our own system of safeguards is matched by that of the Soviet Union? And how much faith can we place in the continuous running of test procedures and checks? In the absence of "the real thing," such procedures and checks can never be regarded as proof positive of reliability. The entire system of safeguards is built upon procedures and equipment that can never be tested completely until the time comes when they are called into action.

There is still another reason to fear nuclear missile submarines from the standpoint of accidental nuclear war between the superpowers. Because in the years ahead, an increasing number of nuclear weapon countries will turn to the sea basing of their strategic forces, it will be exceedingly difficult to identify the country source of a submarine-launched ballistic missile attack. Thus, it would be fairly easy for a "small" nuclear power to provoke nuclear war between the superpowers, creating what is customarily referred to as "catalytic" war.

Members of the "nuclear club" could also inadvertently catalyze war between the superpowers. Such countries, confronted by the prospect of a disarming first strike by other members of the club, might seek security through the deployment of "hair trigger" launch mechanisms (automatic systems of nuclear retaliation based upon the processing of electronic warnings by computers) and through the adoption of "launch-on-warning" strategies with launch authority delegated to field commanders. With such measures the probability of an unintended nuclear attack on one of the superpowers by a third-party state would increase substantially.[48]

Although nuclear missile submarines are especially troublesome from the standpoint of accidental nuclear war between the superpowers, the other components of the American and Soviet strategic triads have important and distinctive problems of their own.

Consider the circumstances surrounding the use of manned bombers. In the United States, SAC bombers—essentially B-52s and FB-111s—are subject to a system of codes and communications procedures to ensure their "positive control." This means that after reaching a particular orbit point on their respective routes, well outside enemy territory, the bombers will be returned to base "unless directed otherwise by the President of the United States."[49] Unless there are positive authenticated voice instructions deriving from presidential authority, to proceed to targets, the SAC bomber force is required not to pass the "positive control point." Without the "go code," the bombers are required to turn back. According to the Strategic Air Command:

> The "go code" would be authenticated at several levels of command and ultimately by at least two members of the bomber crew. It would be transmitted to the airborne force by a variety of means from widely dispersed sites.
>
> Use of dispersed transmitters and different methods of communications insure that the "go code" will be received by the aircraft at the direction of the President.
>
> In case of inoperative aircraft radio receivers, failure to receive the "go code" would, under conditions of actual enemy attack, cause some of our bombers to return to their bases, thus leaving their target uncovered. However, this chance must be taken to prevent inadvertent action.
>
> Thus, positive control guards against the possibility of inadvertent hostile action by the SAC force but guarantees that the bomber force will receive the attack order, if issued by the President.

Positive control procedures are tested repeatedly and have been proved effective.

In addition to the communications procedures of "positive control," the weapons in the aircraft are not armed until the bomber is ordered to attack. Coordinated effort by several crew members under the "go code" authority is required to arm nuclear weapons.[50]

Is "positive control" incapable of failure? Of course it isn't. As in the case of the system of safeguards for submarine-based nuclear weapons, positive control can never really be "proved effective" until SAC bombers are actually called into action. No amount of repeated testing can assure reliability in the event of the real thing. But it certainly comes as close to being a perfectly reliable system as anyone can expect.[51]

On 13 May 1976, I was given a series of briefings by SAC officers at the Command's Offutt AFB Headquarters. Among other points of information, these briefings indicated the following:

1. An extraordinary array of redundant safety systems effectively preclude the possibility that the "go code" could be transmitted by mistake. Before the "go code" can be transmitted to SAC bomber forces, the Commander-in-Chief of the Strategic Air Command (CINCSAC) must receive the weapons expenditure authority from the president of the United States through the Joint Chiefs of Staff via the JCS Alerting Network. Without such authority, CINCSAC also lacks the *capability* to issue the "go code" to bomber crews. Even with such authority, the "go code" must be authenticated at several subsequent levels of command and ultimately by at least two members of the bomber crew. And even after the "go code" is transmitted to SAC aircraft by way of the Primary Alerting System (PAS), coordinated effort by several crew members is required to arm the nuclear payload. In the case of the B-52s, for example, collaboration between the pilot, radar navigator, and electronics warfare officer is required. It follows that the popular movie scenarios of

nuclear attack suggested by *Fail Safe* and *Dr. Strangelove* present highly distorted images of actual command/control procedures.

2. The likelihood of navigational errors by SAC bomber crews which might cause them to mistakenly fly beyond their stipulated "positive control" or orbit points into Soviet airspace is effectively nonexistent. This is because the orbit points are sufficiently far from the Soviet periphery. Moreover, even if such a stray action were to take place, it is unlikely that it would be perceived as the beginning of an American first strike by Soviet command authorities.

Nevertheless, the bombers can still crash; their nuclear payloads can still be accidentally dropped or intentionally jettisoned; the nuclear bombs or missiles which they carry can still be burned in a fire on the ground. Indeed, as indicated above, in the discussion of accidents admitted by the Pentagon, all of these things have already taken place. And, furthermore, so have others. According to Lloyd J. Dumas, one of the leading authorities on the problem of nuclear accidents, a significant number of additional incidents have taken place: [52]

> On the basis of a partial search through public sources (chiefly newspapers), 3 subsequent major accidents, occurring between 1970 and 1973, were discovered. These involved major damage to the weapons carrier, endangering the nuclear weapons aboard. In addition, 20 accidents involving total destruction and 6 more involving serious damage of nuclear capable delivery systems assigned a major nuclear weapons carrier role were found. (Only accidents involving major nuclear weapons carriers, such as the French Mirage-IV or the British Vulcan strategic bombers were included. More than 150 accidents involving total destruction of lesser nuclear capable delivery vehicles were excluded to introduce a conservative bias into the total.) [53]

What all of this suggests is that we do indeed have a problem. While the weapons engineers and the military authorities must be commended for the fact that none of these accidents resulted in a nuclear explosion, there is no reason to expect such good fortune to persist indefinitely.

Furthermore, there is the Soviet Union to consider. What about their system of "positive control" or their system of safeguards? We know very little. For example, how strict and how reliable is their system of codes and communications? What sorts of safety devices are built into the Soviet weapons themselves? What kind of "human reliability program" is operative among Soviet personnel who deal with nuclear weapons? What sort of redundancies are built into Soviet command/control procedures for nuclear weapons expenditure? And, what is the Soviet safety record to date?

The land-based missile component of the strategic triad must also be considered from the standpoint of accidental nuclear war between the superpowers. Unlike the manned bomber, these missiles cannot be recalled once launched.[54] This suggests, of course, that every conceivable measure must be taken to prevent inadvertent launches in the first place. Presently, before a Minuteman missile can be launched, "at least two missile combat crew commanders and their deputies must authenticate launch orders and activate necessary controls." Moreover, "all launch crew personnel must work separately and individually, but within very close time tolerances to carry out their tasks."[55]

What can go wrong?[56] There is always the possibility that the missiles will be launched because of a mistaken belief that a disabling first-strike attack is on the way. In the United States, there have already been at least five major incidents involving false warnings that have been publicly reported:

> BMEWS. On October 5, 1960, the central defense room of the North American Air Defense Command (NORAD) received a top priority warning from the Thule, Greenland, Ballistic Missile Early Warning System station indicating that a missile attack had been launched against the United States. The Canadian Air Marshal in command undertook verification, which after some 15 to 20 minutes showed the warning to be false. The radars, apparently, had echoed off the moon.
> NEWC. On February 20, 1971, the National Emer-

gency Warning Center at NORAD headquarters transmitted an emergency message, authorized by the proper
code for that date, directing all U.S. radio and TV stations to cease normal broadcasting immediately by
order of the President. The message, designed for use
only in grave national emergencies such as enemy attack, was not cancelled until 40 minutes after its nation-
wide transmission. The same NORAD headquarters
complex is the point of transmission for messages to
trigger nuclear retaliation in the event of enemy attack.
    SECT.   On at least 2 occasions during 1971, Subma-
rine Emergency Communications Transmitter Buoys,
accidentally released from U.S. Polaris nuclear missile
submarines, signalled that the submarines involved had
been sunk by enemy action.[57]

On November 9, 1979, a mechanical error sent "war game"
information into the sensing system that provides early
warning of nuclear attack. The "war game" tape, which was
loaded into the North American Air Defense Command
(NORAD) computer in Colorado Springs, Colorado, simu-
lated a missile attack on North America. Read as a "live
launch," the error initiated a sequence of events to determine whether the United States was actually under attack.
It took six minutes, during which the country was in a low-
level state of "nuclear war alert," to discover the error. A
spokesman for NORAD stated that he could not recall another incident in which an alert had actually gone out from
the NORAD complex to the command centers of the vast
American defense chain. On the day following the incident,
Tass, the official Soviet press agency, criticized the error
and warned that another error "could have irreparable consequences for the whole world."

    In view of (1) the steadily increasing accuracy and power
of ICBMs, and (2) the fact that missiles cannot be launched
on warning to ensure their survival, the amount of time
available to decision makers who must decide whether or
not to retaliate is extremely limited. Coupled with the understanding that missiles cannot be recalled, these developments point to a very serious hazard in the area of accidental
nuclear attack. This hazard is aggravated during periods of
peak tension and alert, when the need for quick reaction is

most apt to impair the safeguards of redundant verifications and authorizations.

As a potentially vulnerable component of the strategic triad, land-based missiles leave decision makers with the least amount of time to decide what to do. Hence, the relative vulnerability of these missiles heightens the probability of their accidental use, either by American or Soviet forces. Faced with the understanding that a first-strike attack might succeed in obliterating its land-based nuclear missiles, each superpower is placed under intense pressure to launch these missiles when an attack is threatened or believed to be impending. The more survivable triad systems, therefore, are substantially less subject to the harmful effects of reduced decision time than are land-based ICBMs.

The pressure of false alarms can bring about accidental nuclear war between the superpowers even where it does not lead to an immediate launch of vulnerable missiles. Consider the following scenario:

> American radar warning systems mistakenly sound the alarm (the problem might be something as "ridiculous" as the rising of the moon, the fall of meteors, a flock of geese or a mechanical error). In response, all triad forces are placed on alert. The Soviets, of course, witness these preparations and respond in kind. A chain reaction of preparations and counterpreparations ensues that ultimately fulfills the original mistaken "prophecy"—nuclear war between the superpowers.

This idea is not new. Nor is it confined to the conditions of nuclear world politics. The idea that a false alarm can set off a catastrophic chain reaction between adversaries in a tense and hostile situation is as old as the story of King Arthur's last battle:

> It seems that King Arthur's son, Mordred, revolted against his father. After some fighting the two contenders met, with all their troops, on the field of Camlan to negotiate. Both sides were fully armed and desperately suspicious that the other side was going to try some ruse or strategem. The negotiations were going along

smoothly until one of the knights was stung by an asp and drew his sword to kill the reptile. The others saw the sword being drawn and immediately fell upon each other. A tremendous slaughter ensued.[58]

The false-warning scenario could take a different, more bizarre, form. Consider the following:

In response to false warnings, the United States begins to launch its nuclear missiles against Soviet targets. Almost immediately after the launching process begins, American officials confront the terrible truth that a grievous mistake has been made. Aware, however, that a Soviet retaliation is certain, the American National Command Authority decides that the only "sane" course is to press forward with a full-scale, no-holds-barred, nuclear assault. To do otherwise, i.e., to immediately announce the error to the Soviets while ceasing all further hostilities, would simply be too risky. The logic of "damage minimization" compels the initiation of unrestrained nuclear attack. An irreversible nuclear holocaust begins.

This scenario, of course, need not be limited to situations involving false warnings. It could be played out wherever nuclear missiles—whether land based or sea based—are launched by accident.

Land-based nuclear missiles are also subject to the same hazards of proliferation as sea-based nuclear missiles. With the anticipated increase in nuclear weapon countries in the years ahead, it would be extremely difficult to identify positively the country source of an ICBM attack. Under these conditions, a secondary nuclear power could actually "catalyze" a nuclear war between the superpowers, whether by deliberate choice, by unauthorized use of weaponry, or by inadvertent action occasioned by the deployment of "hair-trigger" launch systems and the adoption of risky "launch-on-warning" strategies.

Finally, there is the risk of accidents involving tactical nuclear weapons. The United States has maintained an arsenal of approximately 7,000 tactical nuclear weapons in western Europe since the 1950s. Most of these, about 5,000, are in West Germany while the rest are in all NATO European countries with the exception of Norway, Denmark, Luxembourg, and France. The United States also has tactical nuclear weapons in Asia (approximately 1,700 in South Korea, the Philippines, Guam, and Midway), on board U.S. Navy combat ships (approximately 2,500), and in the custody of selected Army, Navy, and Air Force units in this country (approximately 10,800).

Despite the seemingly innocuous sound of the word "tactical," these weapons range from "small" systems with blast effects that are equivalent to only 100 tons of TNT to one megaton systems that are 80 times as powerful as the Hiroshima bomb. Indeed, the principal difference between tactical and strategic weapons concerns range rather than yield. In certain instances, tactical weapons are actually more powerful than strategic ones.

The wide dispersion of this type of weapon (not to mention the coming deployment of 572 Pershing II and ground-launched cruise missiles) suggests a substantial risk of catastropic accidents. Tactical nuclear weapons could be involved in air crashes; they could accidentally be dropped from aircraft or jettisoned; they could be burned in fires at weapons storage sites; or they could be damaged in explosions on board carrier ships or at artillery, surface-to-surface, or surface-to-air installations.

In view of the continuing American policy of "first use" (as distinguished from "first strike"), tactical nuclear weapons also heighten the prospects of escalation to strategic nuclear war and greatly increase the incentive of Soviet-Warsaw Pact forces to strike first.

In the event of false warnings, the presence of tactical nuclear weapons might make the consequences of "retaliation" extremely costly. This problem (which is already exacerbated by the use of Quick Action Alert Aircraft, QRA) would be especially great during times of crisis.

And the hazards inherent in the proliferation of tactical nuclear weapons are the same as those for land-based and sea-based strategic missiles. The greater the proliferation, the more difficult it becomes to identify an attacking country. Hence, another tactical nuclear power could "catalyze" a nuclear exchange between the superpowers, again, by design, by inadvertent action, or by unauthorized use of weapons.[59]

What more can be done about the problem of accidental use of nuclear weapons by the United States? The answer is as simple as it is disappointing: little, if anything, beyond what is already being done. The "fault" lies neither with the existing system of American safeguards (they are surely as sound and well maintained as is humanly possible) nor with the military people who oversee these safeguards (they are certainly dedicated and capable), but rather with the underlying strategy of peace through nuclear deterrence. The implementation of even more stringent measures to prevent the accidental use of nuclear weapons would in most cases certainly impair the credibility of this country's nuclear deterrence posture. As long as we continue to base our hopes for peace and security on the ability to deliver overwhelming nuclear destruction to a Soviet aggressor, the risk of accidental nuclear war and of other nuclear weapon accidents will simply have to be endured.

Unauthorized Use of Nuclear Weapons

For anyone who remembers the movie, *Dr. Strangelove* (or *How I Learned to Stop Worrying and Love the Bomb*), the idea of a nuclear war begun without proper authorization evokes images of maddened Air Force generals, incompetent national leaders, and war-loving scientists. While such images tend to be caricatures which lend an air of unreality to the idea of unauthorized use of nuclear weapons, there is nothing unreal about the problem itself. Indeed, *Dr. Strangelove* does for the problem of unauthorized use what *Fail-Safe* does for accidental nuclear war. However much these films play "fast and loose" with particular facts, they *do* point to real and important problems.

Like the accidental triggering of a nuclear war, the possibility of a nuclear war provoked by the unauthorized use of nuclear weapons cannot be prevented by our present systems of nuclear deterrence. In fact, the requirements of a sound deterrence policy might even promote such a possibility.

While presumably only the president of the United States has the authority to order the use of American nuclear weapons, many people may be capable of operating them. Individuals with nuclear weapon responsibilities, who clearly lack the authority to use these weapons on their own accord, may still, in certain instances and in certain patterns of cooperation, have the capability to use these weapons. In short, the area of capability extends far beyond the area of authority.

This is not to suggest, however, that both superpowers are failing to take proper steps to guard against the unauthorized use of nuclear weapons. While not very much is known about the specific features of the Soviet safeguards, it is generally understood that they are roughly the same as our own. And in the United States, the Department of Defense Safety Program comprises basic safety standards which pertain to the problem of unauthorized use as well as to the problem of accidents. As we have already seen, these standards include positive measures to prevent nuclear weapons involved in "incidents" from producing a nuclear yield; positive measures to prevent the deliberate use of nuclear weapons except when properly authorized; and positive measures to ensure the security of nuclear weapons.

By and large, these measures are the same as those implemented to prevent accidental nuclear war. They include strict custodial control and redundant safeguards built into the command and control of nuclear weapons and into the weapons systems themselves (the "two-man" concept, secure codes, reliability screening of nuclear weapon personnel, and coded locking devices). In addition, they include the ability to communicate with adversaries via a so-called "hot line."

These measures *are* impressive. Without doubt, they are well founded, intelligently conceived, and carefully implemented. And the record of success in preventing even a single instance of unauthorized use of nuclear weapons appears to suggest a persuasive case for optimism about the future.

Nevertheless, there are areas of potential difficulty. In the first place, although no American nuclear weapon can be properly employed without authorization from the president of the United States, it has now been publicly reported that this authority may already have been delegated—under strictly defined conditions—to at least one other person. According to Vice Adm. (Ret.) Gerald E. Miller's recent testimony before a House International Relations subcommittee,[60] the North American Air Defense Commander (NORAD) *has* been given the authority to fire nuclear weapons without the specific approval of the president. Such unusual delegation of authority allegedly goes back twenty years to a time when American air warning networks were not very good and there was some concern that a NORAD commander might not be able to respond quickly enough to a surprise bomber attack if presidential authorization were required.

As far as anyone can tell, no other military commander is presently authorized to use nuclear weapons without the express approval of the president. Moreover, NORAD's weapons are relatively low-yield defensive missiles that are to be fired only when the situation is *in extremis*. And according to Admiral Miller, it is highly doubtful that the NORAD Commander still retains such delegated authority.

Testifying before the House Subcommittee on International Security and Scientific Affairs on 16 March 1976, Congressman Richard Ottinger made it clear that even members of Congress are very much in the dark about the question of authority to use American nuclear weapons. Inquired Ottinger: "Who has the authority to launch a strategic nuclear attack today? Is it just the President in this country, as the American people have been led to believe? Or has the authority been delegated, and, if so, to how many commanders?"

Under existing law, the president of the United States, by the authority vested in his constitutional role as commander in chief, may delegate the right to use nuclear weapons to subordinate officers in the chain of command as he sees fit. Thus, even if no such delegation of authority exists today (and we can never know this for certain since such delegations would be highly classified), the prospect and the implications of such delegations being made in the future must be taken seriously.

It might be argued, of course, that there is really no alternative to some sort of presidential delegation of the authority to use nuclear weapons since it is essential to the credibility of our nuclear deterrence posture. After all, if it were true that only a presidential order could lead to a nuclear weapon release, then a would-be aggressor could effectively preclude the possibility of American nuclear retaliation by incapacitating the president. It follows that unless the ordinary provisions for presidential succession are deemed adequate, the requirements of our existing strategy of peace through nuclear deterrence necessarily include certain contingency plans whereby command and control of nuclear weapons would pass to some person or persons other than the president of the United States.

What this suggests, of course, is that our prevailing system of ensuring peace may have built into it an unavoidable risk of the unauthorized use of nuclear weapons. As long as our security hopes are based upon the ability to assuredly destroy an aggressor, we cannot operate without some stipulated plan for alternative authorities to the president of the United States. As Congressman Stephen J. Solarz of New York put it, during hearings before the House Subcommittee on International Security and Scientific Affairs:

> While on the one hand we obviously have an imperative and overriding national interest in preventing and precluding the unauthorized use of nuclear weapons, it seems to me that we have a comparable interest in preventing the other side from operating under the belief that they could effectively preclude us from retaliating through a surgical strike at those who are in command of the apparatus.[61]

The prospect of the unauthorized use of American nuclear weapons, therefore, is an integral feature of our overall strategy of nuclear deterrence. To deny this fact is to admit that our nuclear deterrence posture is not a credible one.

Beyond the question of the delegation of authority to use nuclear weapons, there is the problem of the growing number of individuals with access to U.S. nuclear weapons. For example, under certain conditions American field commanders may be capable of firing the nuclear weapons in their commands without presidential authorization. According to Edward L. King, a former staff officer with the Joint Chiefs of Staff:

> Once armed nuclear warheads have been released to the control of forward-positioned troop commanders (some warheads are currently stored near forward units), control over firing in effect passes to these field military personnel. To cite an analogy, it was impossible for the National Guard commanders on the scene at Kent State to prevent their troops, armed with pre-loaded rifles, from firing indiscriminately on students who individual guardsmen later claimed presented a danger to their lives. Similarly, it would be impossible for the President and senior military officials in the United States to prevent SACEUR (Supreme Allied Commander Europe) or a forward-based artillery commander in the field in Europe from firing his allocated nuclear shells to protect his unit from being overrun and destroyed.[62]

Whether or not King is correct in his assumption that field commanders might actually have this kind of capability is impossible to determine. The release procedures for American nuclear weapons are highly classified. All that we can tell from available public information on this matter is that all U.S. nuclear weapons are under strict custodial control and subject to a variety of safeguards to preclude improper firing. These safeguards include physical barriers such as permissive action links, which are systems included in, or attached to, a nuclear weapon to preclude arming and/or launching until the insertion of a prescribed, discrete code or combination by authorized personnel. However, we simply do not know whether these measures are sufficient to prevent the unauthorized use of nuclear weapons by all field commanders.

We must also consider the reliability of our "positive measures." In the case of the Personnel Reliability Program implemented by the Department of Defense—a program "designed to help assure the highest possible standards of individual reliability in personnel performing duties directly associated with war reserve weapons"—there is evidence of significant unreliability. According to Congressional testimony, 3,647 persons with access to nuclear weapons were removed from their jobs during a single year because of mental illness, alcoholism, drug abuse, or discipline problems. During 1972 and 1973, 20 percent of the discharges were due to drug abuse.[63]

In the course of my own briefings on the Department of the Air Force's Human Reliability Program, I was told that 1,500 to 2,000 individuals are disqualified annually by the Strategic Air Command for nuclear weapon assignments. Approximately one-third of these disqualifications occur during the initial screening process and two-thirds during the first two years of service. After the first two years, there is very little disqualification.

When, in 1969, a Cuban defector brought a MIG plane through radar defenses and landed in Florida, the subsequent investigation led to the arrest of thirty-five men assigned to the Nike-Hercules missile crews. The men were charged with using, among other things, LSD. According to Adm. W. P. Mack, in charge of the Pentagon's drug abuse program, "only ten had responsible positions—and there was only one per battery. In other words, no battery had more than one case in it."[64]

Perhaps we should be even more concerned about those individuals who are not disqualified and who are certified to be "reliable," since a basic reliability standard is "positive attitude toward nuclear weapon duty." As the matter was put recently by a seaman on the U.S. nuclear submarine, *John Marshall:* "Maybe crazy guys do better on this duty. If you're normal, you couldn't stand it."[65]

Another possibility that bears on the unauthorized use of nuclear weapons is the seizure of nuclear weapons by allies. More than half of all U.S. nuclear weapons are stationed abroad or on the high seas. No matter how much care is put into ensuring proper custodial control over these weapons, the sheer number of weapons and weapon sites involved bodes an intolerably high risk of unauthorized use.

This risk is underscored by the understanding that if an allied country to which U.S. nuclear weapons have been deployed ever becomes hostile to the United States, the

United States might find itself in the position of having to fight its way into "allied" territory in order to recover its own nuclear weapons. This problem is discussed in *The Defense Monitor:*

> In countries plagued by civil wars and coups, U.S. tactical nuclear bases may not be safe from our "allies." During internal political disruptions in allied countries, U.S. bases might find themselves caught in the middle of a firefight. One side or the other might find it advantageous, or even necessary, to seize U.S. tactical nuclear weapons to gain the upper hand in the local struggle. Nor can we discount the possibility that allies such as the Republic of Korea might seize U.S. weapons in order to defend themselves from—or possibly to attack—their antagonists.[66]

How well protected are American nuclear weapons abroad? According to the Department of Defense, they are well protected indeed. Judging by the content of Department of Defense directives which deal with nuclear weapons custody and accountability procedures and nuclear weapons physical and storage security, every conceivable step is being taken to ensure proper custodial control of nuclear weapons abroad.[67] These steps are summarized in the Department of Defense publication, *Nuclear Weapons Safeguards:*

Nuclear Weapons Custody and Accountability Procedures

Detailed procedures have been promulgated by the Department of Defense which require continuous property accountability of nuclear weapons and nuclear components throughout their stockpile life. The primary objective of the nuclear weapons custody and accountability procedure, together with appropriate security safeguards, are to insure that none of our nuclear weapons, components, or information fall into the hands of unauthorized individuals.

Nuclear Weapons Physical and Storage Security

Nuclear weapons are secured in alarmed storage structures, in secure areas aboard ship, or given compensating sentry and/or physical facilities protection when outside of these secure facilities. The area immediately surrounding the weapon is designated as an Exclusion Area and these areas are usually located within a larger area known as a Limited Area. Limited Areas are usually delineated by fences or other physical barriers. The smaller Exclusion Areas are sometimes defined by the cement or steel walls of secure facilities. These areas are specifically established to control entry to the area and access to the weapons. The physical barriers and alarm systems on secure facilities provide a means of controlling authorized access and impeding or warning of unauthorized entry. Reaction forces, trained, armed, and drilled, respond immediately to any detection of alarm or irregular condition.

The Center for Defense Information, however, is less than sanguine about the actual effectiveness of these steps and feels it is essential that we, "substantially increase the security precautions around U.S. nuclear weapons compounds and more intensively screen U.S. personnel who handle tactical nuclear weapons." One of the Center's principal concerns is that the military security police who are charged with enforcing nuclear weapon security are often unqualified:

> Many of the military security police are less qualified than their civilian counterparts in law enforcement, and run into many of the same problems of morale and recruitment. Military training of security police is less extensive than that given civilian policemen. Lack of adequate screening hampers recruitment of high-confidence security forces. Military police have a record of higher-than-average crime and drug abuse rates and record more failures under the human reliability program than is found in the rest of the U.S. armed forces as a whole.[68]

The fear that American nuclear weapons abroad are inadequately protected was also voiced by former Sen. Stuart Symington:

> The United States has some 7,000 "tactical" nuclear weapons stockpiled in European countries and thousands more in other countries around the world and

aboard U.S. ships. Reports during the past year have indicated that some of these weapons may not be well protected against potential nuclear thieves—especially those who may have the armed capability and intelligence information necessary to overcome security systems protecting these weapons. The mere presense of such large numbers of nuclear weapons around the globe provides an ever-present risk of seizure—not only by criminal groups, but host governments themselves. A change in government, or government policy, in a country where U.S. nuclear weapons are stored could lead to a takeover of these weapons. It is no secret that during the Cyprus crisis, which persists to this day, the United States has been concerned with the security of its nuclear arsenals in Greece and Turkey.[69]

Symington learned about the problem of nuclear weapons security firsthand. Not long ago, the following letter was sent to him by a concerned U.S. soldier abroad: "No more than four to six U.S. soldiers guard the bunkers which store the nukes. Most of the troops (about 40 per detachment) are housed about a quarter of a mile from the bunkers and could easily be isolated from the warheads."[70]

Indeed, the problem of securing American nuclear weapons abroad came to the attention of certain members of the Congress as early as November 1972. At that time, as chairman of the Joint Committee on Atomic Energy, Sen. John O. Pastore directed the deputy director of the committee staff, Mr. George Murphy, to go to Europe and review security conditions for nuclear weapons at certain NATO installations. According to a statement by Senator Pastore, made on 25 September 1974:

> His [Murphy's] report to the committee on this matter pointed out weaknesses in the security arrangements to protect nuclear weapons in peacetime as well as raised questions on the vulnerability and usefulness of these weapons in the event of a surprise attack. To verify these disturbing findings, Senator Baker and I visited a significant sampling of nuclear installations during the week beginning March 19, 1973. We not only verified the findings of the November report but we were even more disturbed by the situation.[71]

Senator Baker, who accompanied Senator Pastore, cor-
roborates these findings:

> There are literally thousands of these [nuclear weap-
> ons] now, and they are no longer protected with the pre-
> cautions at the height of World War II. As the Senator
> from Rhode Island pointed out, they are presently in
> many parts of the world in numerous enclaves protected
> with various degrees of efficiency. They are vulnerable.
> . . . We have to be exquisitely careful in our storage of
> nuclear weapons, and I do not believe we are now.[72]

Perhaps the most serious problem of all with respect to
unauthorized use concerns safeguards for the really big
weapons. Previously we considered the possibility of accidental nuclear war involving the components of the strategic
triad—land-based ICBMs, manned bombers, and SLBMs.
Now we must consider the possibility of a nuclear war
resulting from the unauthorized use of these weapons. In
other words, how vulnerable are they to the hazards of
unauthorized use?

Our submarine-based nuclear weapons (SLBMs) are an
appropriate place to begin. By and large, the SSBN weapon
system is well designed to prevent unauthorized launch. It
would be very difficult and complicated to open the hatch
covertly, apply power to guidance systems, and man switch-
boards and launcher stations in the presence of two-man
watch stations.

The firing circuit with its four switches is not the only
safeguard against an unauthorized firing of the submarine's
nuclear missiles; a number of other procedural/system
engineering requirements exist to replace external controls.
Indeed, more often than not, the high-ranking naval officers
who are concerned with SSBN operations are more fearful
that the constraints involved in the launching process are so
excessive and redundant that firing might become too difficult in the face of "the real thing." As the matter was put to
me by Adm. G. E. Miller, "Our combat history is loaded with
cases of weapons that would not fire because the safety
'checks' were too many and too complex." Again, we see the
conflict between the requirements for a credible nuclear

deterrence posture and those for preventing unauthorized use of the weapons.

Further security against unauthorized launch on board submarines bearing nuclear weapons is also provided by the two-man rule and the Personnel Reliability Program (PRP). During any operation which may afford access to a nuclear weapon, a minimum of two authorized personnel, each capable of detecting incorrect or unauthorized procedures and familiar with applicable safety and security requirements, must be present. And all personnel on board are formally evaluated and under continuous observation. From the moment that a man's participation in activities involving nuclear weapons is finally approved by the commanding officer, his records are marked: "This member is in a position requiring extraordinary reliability. Report any medical or behavioral changes that may affect his reliability and/or may require further evaluation to his Commanding Officer." Inspection teams, from Navy and DOD commands independent of the ship, conduct periodic inspections to ensure that PRP is being followed and that it is effective.

In addition, the Navy is particularly cautious in selecting men for duty in nuclear submarines, and it is this Personnel Selection Process, according to Admiral Miller that is "the more effective security measure." As the process has been described to me by Admiral Miller:

> Special screening procedures are involved to first, select men for entry into ratings eligible for submarine duty; second, select men for entry into submarine school (which is followed by close observation during the school); third, select those for entry into the missile and fire control programs; fourth, select those to receive a special "qualification" in submarines after suitable time on board ships; and fifth, select those to be commanders and executive officers, etc., of submarines.

Although it is doubtlessly true that the Navy has taken extraordinary care in safeguarding its SSBN weapon systems from unauthorized use, and although such care is almost certain to reduce the probability of unauthorized use to a very low level, the fact remains that the possibility cannot be eliminated altogether. This is because the nuclear missile submarine has, within its own walls, all of the capability for firing. While the actual details of command and control on nuclear missile submarines are highly classified (the "silent service" is truly silent on these sorts of questions), it is virtually a certainty that SLBMs can be fired without activation by coded signals from outside the ship.

The following hypothetical scenarios show what might go wrong. They are, in priciple at least, plausible.

A submarine commander conspires with the executive officer, weapons officer, and launcher officer to deceive the crew into believing that an Emergency Action Message has been received. As a result, the submarine fires its nuclear missile complement.

A submarine bearing nuclear missiles collides with a Soviet submarine. As a consequence of the collision or of any follow-up torpedo action, the submarine begins to flood rapidly. There is no chance to escape. Survival is impossible. The captain, fearing that his boat has been mortally wounded as part of a Soviet first strike, resolves to make use of his assigned nuclear missiles. His officers and crew obey.

Since the present U.S. force of nuclear weapon submarines can deliver more than 20,000 times the explosive force of the bomb dropped on Hiroshima, and since any one of these submarines can destroy any country on earth (the Trident submarine can "overkill" any nation), it is surely reasonable to question whether the existing safeguards are really good enough.

Before considering this, however, we must realize that these nuclear weapon systems were created in the first place for the purpose of nuclear deterrence. Thus, the addition of external safeguards against unauthorized use of nuclear weapons on board missile-bearing submarines (i.e., permissive action links) would be contrary to the requirements of effective retaliation. After all, it is hardly in the interests of a nation bent upon assuring possible aggressors of devastating retaliation to impede the processes by which that retaliation must take place.

The dilemma therefore is that either way we stand to lose. On the one hand, should the Navy ever decide to supplement its existing safeguards against unauthorized use of nuclear weapons with permissive action links, the American ability to retaliate with its SLBM force might suffer. Once recognized by a potential aggressor, this inhibited retaliatory capability might diminish the credibility of our nuclear deterrence posture. On the other hand, if the Navy continues to rely on its existing network of safeguards, there will always be the possibility, however remote, that a covert collaboration among critical individuals on board a nuclear missile submarine could result in a nuclear Armageddon.

The real problem is not with existing safeguards, the Navy, or the Department of Defense. Rather, the problem results from the idea that spawned the SSBN weapon systems in the first place, that peace can be attained by threatening to obliterate any aggressor.

The other two components of the strategic triad—manned bombers and land-based ICBMs are also subject to unauthorized use. Both systems are under the command and control of the United States Air Force Strategic Air Command (SAC). And both are safeguarded by the measures prescribed by the Department of Defense for nuclear weapons—strict custodial control, use of the two-man rule in all nuclear-weapons operations, and reliability screening for all personnel performing nuclear weapon duty. Additionally, both are safeguarded by coded switch devices.

It appears, then, that just as in the case of the SSBN weapon systems, the American force of manned bombers and ICBMs is well designed to prevent unauthorized firings. In the case of the SAC bomber force, a system of "positive control," including the external safeguard of a "go code" that bestows capability as well as authority, supplements the requirement that three persons (pilot, radar navigator, electronics warfare officer) must cooperate for firing purposes. In the case of the ICBM force, a similar system of positive control is in effect, although, of course, missiles cannot be launched on warning since they cannot be recalled.

What can go wrong? Under what conditions can an unauthorized firing take place? Presently, the most significant danger seems to lie in the possibility that MX-ICBMs might be deployed without coded switch safeguards. As in the case of SSBN weapons systems, this would make the MX system effectively independent of external control. Although such deployment would appear to be counter to Minuteman/Titan controls, which *are* allegedly safeguarded by coded switch instrumentation, the growing fears of a Soviet first strike might make it attractive.

Since all components of the strategic triad were designed for the purpose of nuclear deterrence, the prospective benefits of any safeguard against the unauthorized use of nuclear weapons must be compared to the prospective costs to our nuclear deterrence posture.

Like the Navy, the Air Force appears to have done almost everything humanly possible to prevent nuclear weapons from being used without authorization. Both services, led by capable and dedicated officers, are continually seeking to balance the requirements for safety with the requirements for strategic deterrence. In the final analysis, however, it is bound to be a futile, albeit valiant, effort.

Premeditated False Warnings

The unauthorized use of nuclear weapons can also originate with personnel charged with issuing warnings of an impending strike. These personnel man the early warning satellite and radar systems which are essential to the survival of American strategic forces.[73] Should any of them deliberately slant or falsify information about hostile action, the result might be an American nuclear "retaliation." The likelihood of this is greater today than ever before because of the reduced checking time available. Because of the speed of today's nuclear missiles, the decision to "retaliate" would have to be made in a matter of minutes. This ability to react to false warnings applies to all three components of our strategic nuclear forces, irrespective of the extent to which the missiles and bombers are protected by other safeguards.

Soviet Safeguards against Unauthorized Use

The foregoing discussion has been concerned with American safeguards against unauthorized use. Needless to say, these safeguards are meaningless in the absence of an equally stringent and reliable Soviet system of safeguards. While the redundancy of Soviet command and control systems is something that has been mentioned many times in the open press and can surely be taken for granted, little else is publicly known. As Adm. Gerald E. Miller (Ret.) indicated in his recent testimony before the House Subcommittee on International Security and Scientific Affairs, "We really don't know as much about their system as they know about ours, I am sure."[74]

Presently, Western experts on Soviet military affairs believe that the authority to initiate the use of nuclear weapons rests in the Communist Politburo, specifically with the Communist party's general secretary, Leonid Brezhnev. But there is no available information about contingency arrangements whereby this authority may be delegated to subordinate officials or field commanders. However in view of the requirements of a credible nuclear deterrence posture and a nuclear win-the-war capability (Soviet strategy calls not only for nuclear deterrence, but also for a capability to wage and win a nuclear war), we may assume the existence of such arrangements.

Safeguards against Unauthorized Use among Other Nuclear Powers

The greatest danger by far of unauthorized use of nuclear weapons rests in the command and control systems of nuclear powers other than the United States and the Soviet Union. This includes those already in existence (especially China and India) and those bound to join the nuclear club very shortly. Unlike the superpowers, these new nuclear powers are unlikely to have the expensive and sophisticated equipment and methods required to protect their nuclear forces from preemptive attack. Thus they will almost certainly turn to the deployment of more risky nuclear weapons systems provided with hair-trigger launch mechanisms and toward the adoption of launch-on-warning strategies with the authority to launch predelegated.

The United States and the Soviet Union have been able to provide at least temporary security for their triad forces. Missiles are located in hard silos or in submarines hiding in murky seas, while manned bombers can take off on warning under "positive control" conditions. It follows that, *at least for the time being*, neither superpower must stand in fear of a disarming first strike by the other. This relative security from preemptive attack allows each side the opportunity to operate with carefully safeguarded command and control systems—systems that are designed to avert precipitous and unauthorized retaliation.

The absence, however, of such secure systems among the newer nuclear powers thus presents a precarious state of affairs. Their probable dependence on hair-trigger launch mechanisms and launch-on-warning strategies, which require the delegation of authority, increases the likelihood of unauthorized use and is a threat to everyone.

The hair-trigger system is best described by Dr. Herbert K. York, professor of physics at the University of California who worked on the Manhattan Project during World War II. In testimony before the House Subcommittee on International Security and Scientific Affairs Dr. York stated:

> I mean that it [the "hair-trigger" system] is a combination of technology, and organization, and procedures which makes it possible to react extremely quickly to either an attack, or the warning of an attack. An extreme case of that, . . . as far as I know never adopted by the United States, . . . is a system in which, upon receipt of electronic warning and the processing of that warning by the computers, the system would launch the offensive system before the attack actually arrives. This is a kind of launch-on-warning system that has been discussed many times.[75]

But the full implications of nuclear proliferation will be dealt with in a later section of this book. For the moment, we are concerned with the possible implications of misconceived command and control systems for nuclear war between the superpowers. In other words, how might the spread of hair-trigger, launch-on-warning strategies affect the likelihood of nuclear war between the United States and the Soviet Union?

Two ways come immediately to mind:

First, the generally greater likelihood of nuclear war associated with relaxed command and control over nuclear weapons implies a general increase in the number of conflicts which might ultimately involve superpower participation. This is especially the case if the initial nuclear conflict were to involve an ally of one or both of the superpowers, a situation fraught with "trip wire" dangers.

Second, with the steady increase in the number of nuclear powers, it is conceivable that a new nuclear power could launch its nuclear weapons against one or the other superpower without the victim knowing for certain where the attack originated. Were the victim to conclude that the attack came from the other superpower, a full-scale nuclear war between the United States and the Soviet Union might ensue. In such a case, the new nuclear power—as a result of its own inadequate system of command and control—could "catalyze" nuclear war between the superpowers.

Irrational Use of Nuclear Weapons

Everyone has now heard the story of the "final days," during which former President Nixon, sobbing, praying, and beating his fists upon the floor of the Lincoln Room, is comforted by Henry Kissinger.

Some people have heard the story in which the former president, only hours before stepping down, muses to some of his congressional friends that he still holds the authority to unleash worldwide nuclear catastrophe.

Fewer people have heard the story about how the then secretary of defense, Mr. Schlesinger, during the last days of the Nixon presidency, established special and extraordinary precautions to ensure against the possibility of an irrational presidential order to use nuclear weapons.[76]

All of these stories, of course, are subject to various interpretations and to differing assessments of validity. However, what is not subject to reasonable doubt is the fact that Richard M. Nixon, at the twilight of his presidency, was in a very unsteady emotional state. When this fact is joined with the understanding that the president of the United States possesses the authority to order the use of nuclear weapons, a terrible possibility is raised. This is the possibility of nuclear war engendered by a president of the United States, or by any other leader of a nuclear-weapons country with a similar authority structure, because of madness, great emotional stress, or physiological impairment.

It is an ironic fact of life that none of the safeguards for nuclear weapons implemented by the Department of Defense applies at the presidential level. There is no two-man rule at this level. There is, of course, no human reliability screening either. And while it is true that the president cannot commit release of nuclear weapons by himself (the idea of the president initiating nuclear war by pushing a single button is irresponsible nonsense), a refusal to comply with a presidential nuclear weapons expenditure order would be unlawful. In other words, although the secretary of defense and the chairman of the Joint Chiefs of Staff would have to cooperate with the president in releasing codes to unlock weapons, their refusal to cooperate would be in violation of the constitutional and statutory provisions of presidential authority.

The absence of the two-man rule can be explained very simply. The president of the United States, by definition, is incapable of the unauthorized use of nuclear weapons. Rather, he is the only source of such authority. Although reason would dictate that American nuclear weapon command and control and release procedures include certain legal provisions to guard against an irrational presidential attack order, this is not the case. In fact, from everything that is known, there appear to be no legal safeguards presently in existence to prevent the irrational use of nuclear weapons by an American president. Rather, security from this particular path to nuclear war between the superpowers must depend, as one expert on command and control problems suggested to me, on "improvisation." According to Gen. Maxwell D. Taylor (Ret.), the best protection against such misuse of power is "not to elect" an irrational president in the first place.[77]

This advice by a former chairman of the Joint Chiefs of Staff lends considerable support to the presumption that no legal mechanisms exist to countermand a presidential order to use nuclear weapons. However, the advice is not easily followed. A candidate's potential for irrational behavior is not always readily apparent to voters. Indeed, even for trained psychologists or psychiatrists, it may be difficult, if not impossible, to predict such a tendency. The experience of reliability screening by the Department of Defense suggests that a substantial number of individuals who are assigned qualifying ratings are later dismissed as unreliable. As the distinguished psychiatrist, Jerome D. Frank, has written:

> A greater risk than the insane are the apparently normal people who delight in destruction or who are extremely hostile and suspicious. Many of these are experts at concealing their feelings and plans, and no brief screening method can detect them.[78]:

Although Dr. Frank's concern is directed toward defects in the Department of Defense's Personnel Reliability Program, it bears even more importantly upon the problem of presidential irrationality.

What we have, then, is a situation in which the president of the United States, unconstrained by legal procedures for thwarting a nuclear weapon release order and unscreened for "human reliability," can on his own initiative, trigger a nuclear catastrophe. This situation is most likely paralleled in the Soviet Union and in other nuclear powers. We live in a world, therefore, in which the security of more than four billion people rests on the continuing rationality of relatively few national leaders, equipped with nuclear weapon responsibility.

This handful is bound to multiply severalfold before the year 2000. While we must now contend with the possibility of no more than a half dozen potentially irrational nuclear leaders, tomorrow we may have to contend with at least fifty. The odds are not very encouraging. As Dr. Frank has pointed out, "At least seventy-five chiefs of state in the last four centuries led their countries while suffering from severe

mental disturbances."[79] Are we really entitled to assume that
such leadership can never take place in a nuclear-weapons
country? The present system of nuclear deterrence *is* explic-
itly based upon precisely this assumption. If it is unreasonable, then we are rapidly approaching the end of the "fuse."

Irrational behavior in a leader may be stimulated by a
variety of means other than what we usually regard as mental illness. Dr. Frank describes, for example, how the "creep-
ing incapacity under the pressure of age" can have the same
effect as flagrant mental illness. According to Frank:

> The characteristic manifestations of hardening of the
> arteries of the brain are general loss of energy and adap-
> tive capacity, impairment of ability to concentrate,
> lapses of memory . . . periods of confusion, emotional
> liability, and irritability. A leader with such disabilities
> is poorly equipped to meet the demands of modern
> leadership, especially when he is apt to be faced with
> prolonged crises in which decisions must be made under
> emotional stress and without sufficient sleep.[80]

In this regard, he points out how in the future, as modern
medicine continues to develop techniques for the control
and replacement of human organs other than the brain, we
may be faced with "an increasing proportion of national
leaders with vigorous bodies and potentially failing
minds."[81]

Another factor which might have an adverse affect on the
ability of a leader to make rational decisions is the *stress*
peculiar to national leadership, especially in dangerous
times.

Physical illness may also affect mental capacity and judgment. Presently Soviet leader Leonid I. Brezhnev appears,
from his symptoms, to suffer from amyotrophic lateral scle-
rosis. The course of this disease may include progressive
atrophy of the muscles of the extremities, difficulty in swal-
lowing, and ultimately paralysis of the involuntary breathing
muscles. During the past several years, Chairman Brezhnev
has often displayed signs of incoherence, absentmindedness,
and general disorientation.

Then, too, some presidents of the United States suffered
physical handicaps capable of impairing their judgment.

Woodrow Wilson suffered a severe stroke during his incumbency. Franklin Roosevelt, during his fourth term, was obviously a very weak man suffering from advanced hardening of the arteries of the brain. And Eisenhower had both a heart attack and a stroke. According to Dr. Frank, Roosevelt was "a dying man at Yalta, unable to brief himself adequately for the conference," while Eisenhower, after his slight stroke in 1957, described his own mental state as "a confusion of mind. I just couldn't pick up a pen. I messed some papers off the desk. I went down to pick them up. I didn't know where to put them."[82]

These are important revelations, not so much for what they tell about the past as for what they suggest about the future when there will be a greater number of national leaders with nuclear weapon capability subject to the affects of madness, stress, or physical illness. From the distant past, we have the examples of Caligula, Nero, and Mad Ludwig of Bavaria, while from more recent times we have Hitler to show us how madness and consummate political skill are easily joined. Although no American president seems to have displayed the obviously delusional traits of James Forrestal, the first American secretary of defense, who feared that the sockets of beach umbrellas recorded everything he was saying and who finally jumped out of a window, the examples of Wilson, Roosevelt, and Eisenhower serve as a warning of how critical judgments might be influenced by factors other than malevolence or madness.

In contrast, the case of Richard Nixon, appears to be one of a president "on the brink" of emotional collapse. If the now-famous Art Buchwald column, in which Mr. Nixon is cast staggering through the White House mumbling, "Where's the button? Gotta push the button," is an obvious flight of satirical fancy, it is also an indication of what was, during those final days, a very real concern in the minds of many thinking people. This concern must not be buried together with the Nixon presidency, despite the fact that remedial action—because it might impair our nuclear deterrence posture—would probably be impossible. Perhaps a wider understanding of just how dangerous the present situation is might generate some incentives to move toward a more durable system of international peace.

Ironically, the Cuban missile crisis should have provided such an understanding. During those thirteen days of October 1962, President Kennedy with full awareness of potential consequences, took steps vis-à-vis the Soviet Union which could easily have culminated in the deaths of approximately 100 million Americans, more than that number of Russians, and millions of Europeans. Indeed, President Kennedy's own estimate of the odds on such a disaster was "between one out of three and even."[83]

With such a calculation of odds at the basis of his decision to impose a naval quarantine of Soviet shipments to Cuba, can the president's action be regarded as "rational"? What if Khrushchev had proved intransigent and refused to back down? What if he had chosen war rather than humiliation? Despite its satisfactory outcome, the Cuban missile crisis points to the precarious nature of presidential judgments in such instances. Given the odds of grave repercussions, we may consider the president's order to have been irrational. Nevertheless, it is that kind of gamble that is built into the present system of peace through nuclear deterrence where risks must be taken from time to time to assure possible antagonists of one's strength and resolve. This suggests, then, that it is the entire system of nuclear deterrence that is irrational.

Our fear of irrational national leaders triggering nuclear war should be no greater than our fear of the very system of security that we expect sane and rational leaders to follow. President Kennedy's decision during the Cuban missile crisis was not the decision of a crazed or enfeebled president. It was the careful, calculated judgment of a man in complete possession of his critical faculties and in complete accord with the prevailing "rules of the game" in international statecraft.

This is the most sobering point of all. Even if national leaders play by the rules, the dangers of nuclear catastrophe are intolerably high. Since the "game" itself is irrational, we must question the possibility of making rational plays. The only sane course is to change the game itself.

2 The Second Path
Nuclear War through Proliferation

If a great number of countries come to have an arsenal of nuclear weapons, then I'm glad I'm not a young man and I'm sorry for my grandchildren.

David E. Lilienthal

Nuclear proliferation is the greatest danger facing the world today.

Sen. Stuart Symington

With the likelihood of uncontrolled, worldwide proliferation[1] of nuclear weapons almost certain, the onset of nuclear catastrophe in world politics is ever more imminent. As so-called "peaceful" nuclear technology spreads throughout the world, so does the capacity for dozens of additional countries to manufacture nuclear weapons. If only as a by-product of developing nuclear energy programs, approximately fifty countries can be expected to achieve a nuclear weapon potential by 1985. By 1995, it is not unreasonable to predict that up to 100 countries will be members of the "nuclear club,"[2] and that plants in the less developed countries alone will be generating enough plutonium to make about 3000 pounds of Hiroshima-scale bombs annually.[3] By the year 2000, the annual worldwide rate of plutonium production will be enough for the manufacture of 100,000 nuclear explosive devices.[4]

A comment attributed to Albert Wohlstetter, the distinguished strategic theorist at the University of Chicago states the problem succinctly: "There are not two atoms, one peaceful and one military. They are the same atom."[5] Nuclear energy has grown increasingly more attractive to all nations in response to oil shortages and high prices. The effects of the decisions of the OPEC oil cartel in 1973 and the Iranian revolution in 1979, combined with a growing appetite for electrical power, have spawned a proliferation of nuclear reactors.

Nuclear reactors that are designed for the production of electrical power produce plutonium, the substance of the Trinity and Nagasaki bombs. When it is chemically separated from other reactor by-products, this man-made element can be fashioned into nuclear weapons. A reprocessing plant for undertaking such separation can presently be constructed for as little as $3 million.[6]

The pell-mell spread of civilian nuclear power systems throughout the world, therefore, would open the door to the countries involved to construct fission nuclear weapons from diverted plutonium. As soon as they had the facilities for separating the plutonium from nuclear reactor fuel, these countries would be well on the way to a nuclear weapon capability. At the moment, much of the world's nuclear industry seems bent on separating plutonium from spent reactor fuel and recycling it into light water reactors and fast plutonium breeders. Commercial reprocessing of spent reactor fuel will soon be possible in many countries, and several have announced plans to construct reprocessing plants.

The situation is ominous. Even where the development of civilian nuclear power is undertaken without an interest in generating a nuclear weapon capability, a problem of "latent proliferation" exists.[7] Countries engaged in civilian nuclear programs could develop a nuclear weapon capability without even seeking it. Once it is generating electrical power by nuclear means and has access to a reprocessing facility to remove the plutonium from reactor fuel elements, a country automatically acquires a nuclear weapon capability. By diverting weapons-grade material from its civilian power program, a country could have nuclear weapons along with its nuclear energy.[8]

Halting Proliferation: Building a Dike to Hold Back the Flood

It was with an understanding of the relation between civilian nuclear programs and nuclear weapons capability in mind that President Carter, in April 1977, acted to prevent the worldwide spread of plutonium. By his proposal that the U.S. government defer commercal reprocessing and recycling of domestically produced plutonium, restructure its breeder reactor program, and begin to emphasize research on nuclear fuel cycles which do not involve direct access to weapons-usable materials, President Carter sought to set an example for other countries. The president also called for an International Nuclear Fuel Cycle Evaluation to investigate alternate and more safeguardable fuel cycles.

Regrettably, there are strong incentives for other countries *not* to follow the lead of the American president. The most important incentive, perhaps, is that plutonium-powered or breeder reactors use uranium so efficiently that it becomes almost limitless as an energy source. Conventional nuclear reactors, on the other hand, threaten the exhaustion of worldwide uranium reserves by the end of the century. Faced with this situation, other countries—whether or not they are expressly interested in nuclear weapons—will find it very difficult to imitate the American act of technological self-denial.

From the point of view of supplying needed energy, the beauty of breeder reactors is apparent. A breeder reactor, while generating power, actually produces more fuel than it consumes. The steadily increasing stockpile of fissile material results, after about ten years, in an amount of fuel equal to twice that put in initially. Thus, as Frank C. Barnaby, Director of the Stockholm International Peace Research Institute, has stated: "enough fuel becomes available not only to keep the reactor operating, but also to fuel a new one of the same size."[9] Clearly, the development of worldwide breeder-energy economies could make large inventories of weapons-grade plutonium available to any country with appropriate reprocessing facilities.

Since exporting plutonium technology is also an important source of revenue for several countries, there is an additional incentive for these countries not to follow the American example. West Germany has gone ahead with its sale of plutonium reprocessing technology to Brazil, and France—while it has cancelled controversial plans to sell nuclear reprocessing plants to South Korea and Pakistan—is still most interested in offering other countries a complete range of nuclear services on a commercial basis. The obvious consequence of such deals is a huge increase in the world-wide supply of plutonium as well as expanded opportunities for governments to acquire nuclear weapons.[10]

Recognizing the inherently dual nature of nuclear energy, we must take great pains to ensure that the worldwide spread of civilian nuclear power is not in the nature of a Faustian bargain. Just as swords can be beaten into plowshares, so might plowshares be fashioned into swords. However pressing the world's energy needs may become, they must not be fulfilled in a manner that encourages the proliferation of nuclear weapons. But the outlook is not promising. Despite the existence of a "non-proliferation regime"[11] —a structure of treaties and agreements designed to halt the spread of nuclear weapons—the atomic secret torn from nature continues to serve the interests of a widening nuclear arms race.

Nuclear Weapons and Credible Deterrence: The Misunderstood Porcupine

Thomas Schelling, a widely known arms strategist, regards proliferation as an "infection."[12] Nevertheless, among the community of international relations scholars, strategic theorists, and atomic scientists, nuclear proliferation has always had its supporters. Today, as in the past, certain members of this community continue to favor the spread of nuclear weapons on the assumption that it can produce security by enlarging the number of countries with credible deterrence postures. This view of nuclear proliferation is often referred to as the "porcupine theory" because it suggests that a nuclear weapon country can "walk like a porcupine through the forests of international affairs; no threat to its neighbors, too prickly for predators to swallow."[13]

Such thinking has been with us for a long time. Winston Churchill surely had a "porcupine" argument in mind when he spoke the following words before Commons on 3 November 1953:

> When I was a schoolboy, I was not good at arithmetic, but I have since heard it said that certain mathematical quantities, when they pass through infinity, change their signs from plus to minus—or the other way round. It may be that this rule may have a novel application and that when the advance of destructive weapons enables everyone to kill everybody else, nobody will want to kill anyone at all.[14]

Throughout the 1960s, Gen. Pierre M. Gallois of the French Air Force wrote widely in advocacy of "porcupine" reasoning in nuclear strategy. The principal lines of his argument suggest that any nuclear weapon country, whatever its size and power, can be secure against aggression as long as it can deliver overwhelmingly destructive retaliation. According to Gallois, "If every nuclear power held weapons truly invulnerable to the blows of the other, the resort to force by the one to the detriment of the other would be impossible." Therefore:

> Because the risks of nuclear war cannot be compared with the benefits that might be obtained from armed conflict, because it is impossible to endure the shock and to continue with an organized military effort (and therefore, impossible to envisage an armed encounter), it is necessary to make nuclear deterrence the foundation of defense policy.[15]

These views of nuclear proliferation are remarkably misconceived. Nuclear weapon countries are not porcupines, and the global political system is not a forest. The tremendous power of destruction that accompanies a nuclear weapon capability does not necessarily bestow safety from attack. For reasons which shall now be made clear, policy makers throughout the world should look upon proliferation with the same measure of fear and caution that was exhibited by early explorers in uncharted waters.

Willingness to Make Good on Nuclear Retaliatory Threats as an Aspect of Deterrence

The acquisition of nuclear weapons does not automatically signal a credible deterrence posture. Unless a nuclear weapon state is believed willing to use its weapons for retaliation, a would-be aggressor may not be deterred. This is the case even if the would-be deterrer's arsenal of nuclear weapons can deliver very high levels of destruction.

In a world of many nuclear powers, would-be aggressor states might have strong and reasonable doubts about the willingness of certain other nuclear weapon states to retaliate with nuclear arms. If, for example, the intended victim state were to believe that nothing other than vengeance could be accomplished by nuclear retaliation, and that such retaliation might trigger even more destructive nuclear counter retaliation, this state might forego retaliation. Recognizing such lack of resolve, the state considering aggression would possibly not be deterred.

Factors that might make new nuclear weapon states unwilling to make good on nuclear retaliatory threats would be their belief that (1) an attacking power's remaining (i.e., counterretaliatory) nuclear forces are secure from the effects of retaliatory destruction, and (2) an attacking power's civil defense capabilities exceed their own. If, after all, an attacker—through the operation of its active defense, strategic deployment, and early warning systems—were believed able to launch an overwhelmingly destructive nuclear counterretaliation, then provoking such additional damage would surely be pointless. Moreover, if the attacker were to have a genuinely viable civil defense capability, and the victim were not to have such a capability, the former might be able to hold the latter's population "hostage" to prevent retaliation.

Most problematic of all, perhaps, is the possibility of misperception. Even if every nuclear weapon state in the proliferated system were actually willing to make good on its threat to resort to nuclear retaliation, prospective aggressor states might fail to perceive this willingness in certain instances. Here, nuclear deterrence could fail in spite of the fact that every nuclear power had in fact committed itself to nuclear threat fulfillment. Consider the following scenario:

> In response to India's having "gone nuclear" in May 1974, Pakistan—India's longtime rival in the region—embarks upon its own program for nuclear weapon status. Although set back temporarily by the French cancellation of a deal to sell them a nuclear reprocessing plant, Pakistan moves toward membership in the nuclear club by producing its own enriched uranium. (This happened while everyone was worrying that Pakistan might acquire access to plutonium.) It does this by constructing a gas centrifuge plant near the country's capital, Islamabad. Just eight years later in 1982, with outside funding assistance from Libyan dictator el-Qaddafi, Pakistan has assembled a modest number of nuclear bombs that can be delivered from specially equipped fighter planes or from short-range missiles. Recognizing these developments, India, which has fought three wars with Pakistan in the past 30 years, calculates that unless it undertakes a preemptive strike against the developing Pakistani nuclear force, it will face much graver dangers later on. It bases this calculation on the understanding that, although Pakistan has already assembled a number of highly destructive nuclear weapons, Pakistan would prefer to accept the elimination of its nuclear forces rather than face an overwhelmingly destructive nuclear counterretaliation which it could not prevent. With this understanding in mind, India launches a "limited" surgical strike against Pakistani nuclear forces, offering assurances of no further damage in exchange for capitulation. Less than a day later, the Indian foreign minister receives a telephone message: "The Buddha is smiling." Pakistan has acceded to India's demands.

As this speculative narrative suggests, Pakistan's nuclear deterrence fails in spite of its nuclear weapon capability. Of course, if Pakistan's leaders were to fail to fulfill the Indians' expectations of rational response, then Pakistan might still retaliate with whatever forces, conventional as well as nuclear, that it could muster. Such a reaction might be viewed as a distinct possibility if the Indian attack were to generate extremely high levels of Pakistani hatred. As we know from both history and psychiatric research, rational calculations cease altogether when the desire to strike back at an enemy becomes greater than the desire to survive oneself.

This scenario might also turn out differently, although certainly not more favorably, if the effects of alliances and informal alignments were considered. For example, how would Pakistan react to an Indian attack on China, with whom Pakistan maintains close and friendly relations? (Relations between India and China have been estranged since 1962, when a border war erupted after China constructed a highway across part of Kashmir, connecting Sinkiang Province with Tibet.) What would be the reaction to such an attack of the Soviet Union, which has closer relations with India? And what about Afghanistan, whose Soviet installed government continues to support aspirations of Pashtun and Baluchi tribes for independence from Pakistan? Clearly, the possibilities for a much wider nuclear war are all here. Similar questions could be posed in regard to other trouble spots throughout the world; for example Israel and her Arab neighbors, South Africa and its black African neighbors, Brazil and Argentina, North Korea and South Korea, and Iran versus Egypt.

Capability to Make Good on Nuclear Retaliatory Threats as an Aspect of Deterrence

To maintain a credible nuclear deterrence posture, a state must not only give the impression that it is willing to use its capability for nuclear retaliation, it must also first demonstrate that it actually has such a capability. To do this, it must demonstrate more than mere possession of nuclear retaliatory forces. It must demonstrate the security of these forces from a first-strike attack.

Yet, although secure nuclear forces are a sine qua non of a credible nuclear deterrence posture, such forces cannot be assured among new members of the nuclear club. The superpowers have invested many years and vast amounts of money in securing their triad forces. As a result, they "enjoy" a degree of triad force safety which allows for the operation of sophisticated and redundant command/control systems.

New nuclear powers, however, cannot hope to duplicate the level of force security achieved by the superpowers. Few if any such powers can hope to create a diversified and expensive system involving land-based nuclear missiles in hardened silos, manned strategic bombers, submarines bearing ballistic missiles, and multiple, complementary surveillance and early warning capabilities. In response to the resultant vulnerability of their nuclear forces, these new nuclear powers will be faced with the constant incentive to preempt. The combined effect of such incentives, of course, is a condition of extreme instability for each new nuclear power, its nuclear weapon capability notwithstanding.

And, once again, there is the problem of misperception. Even if all of the new nuclear powers were actually able to maintain secure nuclear retaliatory forces, prospective aggressors might, through errors in information, still perceive insecurity. Here, nuclear deterrence could fail in spite of the fact that each new nuclear power had "succeeded" in protecting its nuclear retaliatory forces.

We have already observed the dynamics of these problems in the foregoing scenario, wherein the Indian preemptive strike was impelled, in part, by India's perception of vulnerable Pakistani nuclear forces. For additional insight into these dynamics, let us construct another scenario, one which focuses our attention on another trouble spot in the world: The Middle East.

During a seventy-eight-hour period at the start of the 1973 October War, Israel—it is now widely believed—hastily assembled a small arsenal of atomic bombs which could have been dropped on

enemy targets from Kfir and Phantom fighters or
launched from Jericho missiles. Although a Treaty
of Peace was signed between Israel and Egypt on
26 March 1979, the ensuing difficulties surrounding
transference of the Sinai, purchase of Arab oil by
Israel, and moves toward Palestinian self-rule on
the West Bank and Gaza Strip occasion a return to
mutual suspicion and siege mentality. Frustrated
by what it regards as a continuing pattern of Israeli
intransigence, and goaded by pressures from the
PLO and other Arab states, Egypt feels compelled
to develop nuclear weapons of its own. The Israeli
leadership group, which learns of the Egyptian
plans, is reinforced in its suspicions that Egypt's
commitment to peace is illusory. Within a few
years, it becomes evident that Egypt—by diverting
foreign assistance funds from the United States
and Saudi Arabia—is progressing quickly in the
manufacture of a small number of bombs, and is
preparing to secure these weapons from enemy attack. This development is paralleled by growing
bellicosity toward Israel within the concentric
webs of pan-Arabism and Islam. Rather than risk
having its own still vulnerable nuclear forces destroyed by a preemptive Egyptian strike, the
Israelis choose to preempt themselves. The basic
rationale of the Israeli action, supported by bitter
memories of unpreparedness in 1973, can be stated
simply: Destroy the opponent's nuclear forces
while they are still vulnerable, or lose forever the
initiative to protect Israel.

What would happen next is anybody's guess. What would
be the American reaction? How would the Soviets respond?
At a minimum, Egyptian nuclear weapons would not only
have failed to provide a credible deterrence posture, they
would actually have supplied the overriding impetus for
Israeli preemption.[16] At worst, a chain reaction of interstate
nuclear conflict would ensue.

To guard against preemption, new nuclear powers are apt
to turn to the hazardous strategies of attaching hair-trigger
launch mechanisms to nuclear weapon systems and/or
adopting launch-on-warning measures with predelegations

of launch authority. Regrettably, as discussed earlier, even if such strategies can succeed in producing security from disarming first-strike attacks, they will surely increase the likelihood of accidental or unauthorized use of nuclear weapons.

For example, in terms of the recently mentioned rivalries between India and Pakistan, and between Israel and Egypt, let us imagine that both Pakistan and Egypt equip their nascent nuclear forces with a system that processes electronic warnings by computer, and launches a nuclear retaliation before the attacking weapons can reach their targets. And let us also suppose that Pakistan and Egypt delegate authority to launch a nuclear retaliation to a specified number of field commanders who would be able to act on warnings of an impending attack. Assuming that both India and Israel recognize these developments, it is extremely likely that they would recalculate the costs and benefits of the first-strike option. More exactly, it is likely that the two prospective attackers would be deterred in most instances.

At the same time, however, the Pakistani and Egyptian adoption of hair-trigger launch mechanisms and predelegations of launch authority would make it much more likely that the nuclear forces of these states could be unleashed by accident, by unauthorized use, or by miscalculation. These forces might be unloosed as a consequence of electronic or computer failure; as a result of incorrect readings of radar warning systems; as the outcome of a mutiny or takeover in nuclear-armed units; as a consequence of deliberate false warnings by individuals with psychopathic or insurrectionary motives; or as a result of the mistaken interpretation of orders by commanders in the field.

How might such a scenario end? Most likely, Pakistan and Egypt would still find themselves embroiled in a nuclear exchange, albeit one initiated not by an Indian or Israeli first strike, but by the hair-trigger controls that had been placed over their own nuclear forces to prevent such a strike. Consider the following possibility, which could just as easily be written around the India-Pakistan case as the Israel-Egypt rivalry:

In order to prevent Israeli preemption, Egypt equips its developing nuclear forces with hair-trigger launch instrumentation and predelegates launch authority to certain field commanders. Recognizing this situation, Israel decides against a preemptive strike. At the same time, however, a cabal of Egyptian colonels backed by pan-Arabic forces in other countries, and Islamic fundamentalists in their own country, with predelegated launch authority conspires to initiate a nuclear attack upon Israel without headquarters approval. The conspirators launch their attack, and the Israelis—upon discovering what is taking place—act swiftly to unloose their own nuclear weapons before they are destroyed. The Israeli defense minister urgently signals the premier: "This is the end of the third temple," whereupon the latter immediately authorizes the fullest possible retaliation. Less than twenty-four hours later, the better part of both countries lies in rubble, a mirror-image of Hiroshima and Nagasaki.

Multiple Nuclear Arms Races

The effort to create and maintain secure nuclear retaliatory forces will generate pressures for a relentless and system-wide nuclear arms race. In response to these pressures, the new nuclear states—as microcosmic reflections of today's superpowers—will begin to engage in increasingly intense qualitative and quantitative nuclear arms competition with each other. The net effect of such competition will not only be a heightened risk of nuclear war, but also a massive diversion of wealth and scarce resources from human and social services.

The existence of such a "nuclear crowd"[17] could wreak havoc on the idea of a stable balance of terror in world politics. There would be too many "players" and too much ambiguity.

Further, the present symmetry of strategic doctrine that exists between the superpowers would surely be upset. Some of the new nuclear powers might shape their strategies along the lines of "minimum deterrence" or "assured destruction" capabilities. Others might seek more ambitious objectives, including a "nuclear-war-fighting" capability. As a result, nuclear weapons might lose their current image as instruments of *deterrence,* a situation that would surely be accelerated by the first actual use of nuclear weapons by a secondary nuclear power. If, for example, the nuclear "firebreak" were crossed in the Middle East, by Israel or an Arab state, other antagonistic states might follow suit. Argentina might contemplate preemption against Brazil, China against India, and South Korea against North Korea.

An expanded number of nuclear powers could ultimately create the conditions whereby first-strike attacks could be unleashed with impunity, regardless of the intended victim's willingness to retaliate or the security of its retaliatory forces. This is the case because, in a world of many nuclear powers, it would become possible for a nuclear armed aggressor to launch its weapons against another state without being identified. Unable to ascertain the origin of the attack, the victim state might lash out blindly, thus triggering a worldwide nuclear war. Consider the following scenario:

It is 1985. Some fifty countries have nuclear energy programs, each producing several dozen nuclear explosives every year. A crisis exists in the Middle East between Israel and her Arab neighbors, Egypt and Saudi Arabia. In the midst of all the saber rattling, a deadly series of nuclear-tipped missiles strikes deeply into Egypt and Saudi Arabia. The victim states, believing this to be the first wave of a no-holds-barred Israeli assault, unleash a retaliatory strike against Israel employing both nuclear and conventional weapons. Israel, which is startled by the speed and destructiveness of these events, *because the initial strike against Egypt and Saudi Arabia was not the work of Israeli forces,* has no choice but to respond in kind. After the Israeli strike, which the Arab states view as a counterretaliation and the Israelis see as a retaliation, Syria, Jordan, Libya, Lebanon, and Iraq join in a concerted, final assault on Israel. When the smoke has cleared, only one major power in the area remains

> unscathed and in undisputed control—Iran—*the*
> *country responsible for the original, anonymous*
> *strike against Egypt and Saudi Arabia.*

This is, of course, a relatively optimistic way to end the
scenario. It would not be unreasonable to speculate that
once all of the countries in the region were embroiled in a
nuclear struggle, both the United States and the Soviet Union
would intervene on behalf of their respective "clients." In
this case, the scenario would end not with regional destruction, but with the cacaphony of worldwide calamity.

The existence of a "nuclear crowd" could also create the
conditions for a disastrous "chain reaction" of nuclear exchanges. Even before it becomes possible to launch a nuclear
attack anonymously, a strategic exchange might take place
between two or more new nuclear weapon states which are
members of opposing alliances. Ultimately, if the parties to
such a clash were clients of either or both superpowers, the
ensuing chain reaction might consume the United States and
the Soviet Union along with much of the rest of the world.

Another major threat is that proliferation could lead to
"microproliferation," whereby groups or organizations such
as terrorists might attain nuclear weapon capabilities. This
could allow not only for nuclear terrorism per se (see chap.
3), but it might also allow for a situation in which an anonymous terrorist detonation could be mistakenly blamed upon
another state by the victim, thus sparking regional or systemwide nuclear war between states. Consider the following
scenario:

> It is 1982. The government of South Africa is sit-
> ting on a powder keg, clinging desperately to its
> beleaguered racial policies and facing new threats
> from Namibia (formerly South West Africa). In
> the meantime, South African guerrilla groups are
> escalating insurgency operations, sustained by
> several neighboring black African countries, and
> inspired by the knowledge that Mozambicans,
> Namibians, and Zimbabweans have achieved their
> goals through armed force. In this tinderbox sit-
> uation, a series of huge nuclear explosions rock

Pretoria, killing upwards of 100,000 persons. Meeting in a shocked emergency session, government leaders feel compelled to respond in kind. But against whom? A few hundred indigenous guerrilla leaders? Such a response would be too limited. Instead, South Africa strikes against guerrilla strongholds in neighboring black African countries employing both nuclear and conventional weaponry. After unleashing these strikes, black Africa responds as one, generating a concerted military retaliation that is bent upon nothing less than total and final liberation for black residents of South Africa. Within the year, the government of South Africa falls, and an interim government is established by the "victorious" black African powers. All states in the area now lie devastated and must be rebuilt. The regional nuclear war that produced these conditions was sparked not by any one of the participant countries, but by a small insurgent group within South Africa.

A similar scenario could be conceived for the Middle East:

Early in the 1980s, Israel and her Arab-state neighbors finally stand ready to conclude a comprehensive peace settlement, one that extends the Egyptian-Israeli agreement to the entire region. Only the interests of the Palestinians, according to the PLO, still seem to have been left out. Several hours before the proposed signing of the peace agreement, a number of crude nuclear explosives in the one-kiloton range detonate in half a dozen Israeli cities. Public grief is overwhelming. In response, the government of Israel initiates selected strikes against terrorist strongholds in surrounding Arab countries, whereupon the governments of these countries retaliate against Israel. Before long, the entire region is embroiled in nuclear conflict. By resorting to nuclear terrorism, the PLO has not only achieved its overriding objective of blocking the intended peace settlement, but has reduced the entire region to rubble.

The expanded number of nuclear powers would create major asymmetries in power between rival states. Where one rival would find itself in possession of nuclear weapons, and another rival would be denied such possession, the new nuclear state might find itself faced with an overwhelming incentive to strike. The cumulative effect of such inequalities of power created by the "uneven" spread of nuclear weapons would be an elevated probability of nuclear aggression against nonnuclear states. For example, consider the following scenario:

> It is 1982. The United States has completed its staged withdrawal of ground forces—27,000 combat soldiers of the Second Infantry Division—from South Korea. In anticipation of this situation, South Korea has been working steadily over the past five years to develop its now completed modest nuclear weapon capability.[18] The North Koreans have signaled repeatedly that, very soon, they too will have nuclear weapons. Thus, South Korea, truculent and ever-fearful of a North Korean lightning thrust against Seoul, calculates that it can no longer rely on America's security "umbrella." Instead it decides to counter the geographic effect of a natural invasion corridor from the north by directing a preemptive nuclear strike against North Korean forces. With their temporary and significant military advantage the South Koreans attack with relative impunity.

It is not inconceivable that, given such a scenario, Russia and China, with their influence in this area so delicately balanced for years, would also enter the fray. Thus, the South Korean adventurism, sparked by a temporary nuclear weapon advantage, could ultimately produce systemwide nuclear catastrophe.

Accidental Nuclear War and Nuclear Weapon Accidents

The proliferation of nuclear weapon states would also increase the probability of accidental nuclear war and nuclear weapon accidents. As we have already seen this could occur not simply as a function of number (i.e., the more nuclear weapon states, the greater the number of existing risks), but also as a consequence of the need to compensate for vulnerable nuclear forces by utilizing risky command/control measures. In addition, all of the new nuclear powers are unlikely to invest the time and expense needed to equip the nuclear weapons themselves with interlocking safety mechanisms.

As discussed earlier, American (and almost certainly Soviet) nuclear forces are safeguarded from accidental firings by a considerable array of features built into both the chain of command and the weapons themselves. These features include the "two-man" concept whereby no single individual has the capability to fire nuclear weapons; a control system whereby each individual with nuclear weapon responsibility is certified under the Human Reliability Program; the use of secure, split-handled codes; the employment of coded locking devices which prevent firing in the absence of specific signals from higher command; and the use of environmental sensing devices which prevent unwanted detonations through the operation of switches that respond to acceleration, deceleration, altitude, spin, gravity, and thermal forces.

It would be the height of folly to expect all new nuclear powers to undertake similar precautions against inadvertent firings of nuclear weapons. To be effective, safety measures would have to apply to all available nuclear weapons and to all pertinent nuclear weapon operations throughout the stockpile-to-target sequence, i.e., storage, maintenance, handling, transportation, and delivery. Moreover, specific provisions would be needed for all unique nuclear-weapon-system operations, such as alerts, operational posturing, maneuvers, exercises, and training.

Considering both the complexity and cost of such safety systems and the fact that new nuclear powers will find it necessary to disavow certain safeguards in the interest of preventing preemption, the prospect of accidental nuclear war is great in a proliferated world. So, too, is the prospect of a catastrophic nuclear accident which while it may not give rise to nuclear war, may still produce a nuclear yield.

Since even the American record of "broken arrows" or nuclear weapon accidents has included a number of very close calls, one can't help anticipating many more broken arrows among forces of new nuclear powers. What will happen when their bombers crash; when the nuclear payloads which they carry are accidentally dropped or intentionally jettisoned; or when these nuclear bombs or missiles are burned in a fire on the ground? With the proliferation of nuclear weapons, such accidents can be expected to occur at an increased rate.

Unauthorized Use of Nuclear Weapons

As with accidental nuclear war and nuclear weapon accidents, nuclear proliferation would also increase the probability of the unauthorized use of nuclear weapons. This is the case, again, not only because of the expanded number of existing risks, but because the new nuclear powers would almost certainly lack the safeguards now in place in superpower arsenals. In response to the need for a quick-reaction nuclear force which can be fielded as soon as possible, new nuclear powers will inevitably turn to automatic or nearly automatic systems of nuclear retaliation which are not "encumbered" by complex and costly command/control checks.

The new nuclear weapons states will also be more likely to have a greater number of national decision makers who are properly authorized to use nuclear weapons. As long as their early-warning networks are not very good, and as long as concern exists that field commanders might not be able to respond to a first-strike attack if central authorization is required, these secondary nuclear powers will be apt to predelegate launch authority to selected field commanders. As already noted, such launch-on-warning strategies would increase the probability of all forms of both authorized and unauthorized nuclear attacks. In this connection, we must include the prospect of *intra*national nuclear weapon seizures via coup d'etats, a prospect that has particularly ominous overtones in such coup-vulnerable potential proliferators as Iraq, South Korea, Egypt, and Pakistan.

The probability of unauthorized use of nuclear weapons resulting from nuclear proliferation can also be expected to increase because of premeditated false warnings. The larger the number of nuclear weapon states, the greater the likelihood that personnel who man early-warning satellite or radar systems will deliberately falsify information about hostile action, especially since the new nuclear powers may enforce less than the highest standards of human and mechanical reliability. The results of such falsification, of course, might well be nuclear first strikes that are disguised as "retaliation."

Irrational Use of Nuclear Weapons

Finally, the spread of nuclear weapons increases the prospect of irrational use. The greater the number of nuclear powers, the greater the probability that irrational national leaders will have nuclear options. This is the case not only because of the increase in the number of nuclear powers per se, but also because many of the new nuclear powers are apt to select their leadership elites in a fashion that precludes all forms of public scrutiny.

Should a new nuclear weapon state fall under the leadership of a person or persons suffering from madness, severe emotional stress, or major physiological impairment, this state might initiate nuclear first strikes against other nuclear states, despite its anticipation of retaliation. Since the logic of nuclear deterrence is based upon the assumption of rationality—that states above all value self-preservation—irrational leadership would undermine that logic.

Today, dictatorships, which provide the most limited formal safeguards on abuses of authority and which generally are led by the most reckless of personality types, greatly outnumber democratic states. In the words of Sean MacBride, who received the Nobel Peace Prize of 1974:

> Have we reasons to hope that the governments and men who now wield power are more responsible than those in the past? Can we believe that there will be no more Hitlers in the world? What kind of a world are we living in nowadays?
> It has been said that there are thirty governments in the world today that are not dictatorships, that enjoy democratic processes in the ordinary sense of the word.

Since, however, there are a hundred or so dictatorships around the world, do we really believe that there is no danger that some dictator will not use these [nuclear] weapons? Have we ground to think that other leaders of the world are more responsible than the head of state of the biggest conventional democracy in the recent past?[19]

In answer to these questions, consider the following scenario:

It is 1982. Egypt and Libya continue to coexist in a hostile atmosphere marked by border skirmishes, frontier infiltrations, and espionage attempts. The man former Egyptian President Anwar Sadat once described as a "mental case"—the erratic strongman Muammar el-Qaddafi—is still at the helm of his country. Sadat, who had often been reviled by Tripoli spokesmen and other Arab rejectionist as a "Zionist tool," is no longer president. Both countries (Libya, largely as a consequence of a continuing rise in world oil prices) have succeeded in transforming new wealth into a modest number of nuclear bombs. Bolstered by the highly destructive weapons technology now at his disposal, el-Qaddafi—who first began to "shop around" for nuclear weapons more than four years ago— delivers an ultimatum to the Egyptian President: "Abrogate the peace settlement with Israel, and surrender all military forces to Libya or else suffer an all-out assault, including nuclear force." In reply, the Egyptians condemn the ultimatum as "boldfaced extortion" and "totally unacceptable," adding that they will respond to any Libyan aggression with the full brunt of their own conventional and nuclear forces. Incensed at this reply, el-Qaddafi attacks, oblivious of the retaliatory consequences for his own country. As promised, the Egyptians respond in kind, creating a wasteland of death and devastation.

Then, too, irrationality may occur as a function of the system itself to which a leader must respond. President Kennedy's actions during the Cuban missile crisis of 1962 were rooted in the very dynamics of the nuclear threat system. To operate "successfully" within these dynamics, even the coolest, most peace-loving, and careful of leaders must occasionally issue threats during crises which indicate a willingness to cross the nuclear threshold, thereby incurring the risk that this threshold will indeed be crossed. To date, with only two major nuclear antagonists, such threats have always met with retreat and reasoned reevaluation rather than with obstinacy and intransigence. In a world of many more nuclear antagonists, however, the odds are that, sooner or later, a country will choose to exercise the nuclear option rather than suffer humiliation. Should this happen, the devastating consequences will result from the competitive nuclear risk-taking that is at the very heart of nuclear deterrence doctrine. For example, consider the following scenario:

It is 1982. Taiwan, which has succeeded in "going nuclear," is in the midst of a crisis with China. The United States, although it continues to maintain unofficial ties to Taiwan since the transfer of diplomatic recognition to Peking, expects China to leave Taiwan unmolested but refuses to commit itself to Taiwan's defense. China, which has never ruled out the use of force against Taiwan, issues an ultimatum to Taipei: "Surrender your forces, terminate your rule, and return to the fold, or we will commence an invasion and take the island by military means." Undaunted, Taiwan announces that it will use all available force, including its newly acquired nuclear weapons, to repel an invasion by PRC forces. Within forty-eight hours, the PRC mounts its promised assault and Taiwan responds with its promised nuclear defense. In short order, China unleashes its own nuclear forces against Taiwan, decimating the island and ending the fighting. Taiwan, or more correctly, what is left of Taiwan, will be returned to the control of mainland China. The damage that it, and PRC forces, have suffered during the bitter exchanges of conventional and nuclear weapons can be regarded as a predictable outcome of the game of nuclear "chicken" in which each side stands firm in the belief that the other side will back down. In this case, it is adherence to the "rules of the game" rather than erratic behavior that brings about nuclear conflict.

The Treaty on the Non-Proliferation of Nuclear Weapons

The foregoing analyses and scenarios may seem to ignore the existence of the Treaty on the Non-Proliferation of Nuclear Weapons (NPT), which became effective in March 1970, and the International Atomic Energy Agency (IAEA), whose safeguards program is designed to prevent the diversion of nuclear material to nuclear weapon manufacture.[20] Moreover, these analyses and scenarios appear to reflect unconcern for other major elements of what one prominent writer has called the "non-proliferation regime."[21] These elements include the Limited Test Ban Treaty (Treaty Banning Nuclear Weapons Tests in the Atmosphere, in Outer Space, and Under Water), which entered into force on 10 October 1963; the Outer Space Treaty (Treaty on Principles Governing the Activities of States in the Exploration and Use of Outer Space, Including the Moon and Other Celestial Bodies), which entered into force on 10 October 1967; the Treaty of Tlatelolco (Treaty for the Prohibition of Nuclear Weapons in Latin America), which entered into force on 22 April 1968; the Seabed Arms Control Treaty (Treaty on the Prohibition of the Emplacement of Nuclear Weapons and Other Weapons of Mass Destruction on the Seabed and the Ocean Floor and in the Subsoil Thereof), which entered into force on 18 May 1972; and the treaties, interim agreements, and protocols that are connected with the Strategic Arms Limitation Talks (SALT).

In light of these major international treaties and agreements, wouldn't it be more appropriate to adopt a somewhat more sanguine posture on the proliferation problem? After all, the NPT binds nuclear weapon states not to transfer nuclear weapons to any other country and commits non-nuclear weapon states not to acquire such weapons by any means. These obligations extend to "other nuclear explosive devices" because of the overlap between peaceful and military nuclear explosion technology.

Regrettably, there is not really any cause for optimism. There is no evidence in the history of international relations and international law that states feel themselves bound by international agreements that are deemed contrary to their own immediate judgments of self-interest. And, however incorrect they may be, a steadily increasing number of states in world politics can now be expected to regard nuclear weapon capability as an important, even vital, national preference.

Whether the overarching motive is increased security, enhanced prestige, improved economic status, or some combination of the three, a panoply of states that are not yet nuclear are intent upon "getting a piece of the action." Whatever incentives present nuclear powers may offer these states to change their minds, be they offers of effective security guarantees or assurances of available fissile materials for energy purposes, they are bound to be outweighed by the perceived advantages. Like it or not, the states in world politics can be expected to continue to act as they have acted since the modern world system took form in the seventeenth century; that is, in conformity with the repeatedly discredited principles of *realpolitik*. In so doing, these states will fail to understand that the combined effects of their nuclear-competitive searches for security and well-being will bring only unparalleled insecurity.

Even if we ignore the cardinal fact that many critical countries have not, and will not, choose to become parties to the NPT, the proliferation problem is aggravated by the technological overlap between peaceful and military uses of nuclear technology. This point was made most succinctly by Fred C. Iklé, former director of the U.S. Arms Control and Disarmament Agency, at a conference sponsored by the Arms Control Association on 9 April 1975:

> Today, the spread of nuclear weapons capability is riding on the wave of peaceful uses of the atom. The world's first five nuclear weapons states clearly started out with a *military* program. Now it is *peaceful* technology that provides not only the means, but also the

cover, in all cases where we fear that a new weapons program might be on the way.[22]

Consider the Indian nuclear explosion of 18 May 1974. Officially described as a "peaceful nuclear explosive experiment," the Indian test in an underground site 100 miles from Pakistan's border signaled that country's entry into the nuclear club. Notwithstanding its alleged peaceful purposes, no peaceful uses have yet been found for the kind of explosion that blew a huge hole in the earth under the Rajasthan desert. Rather, the only conceivable uses for the Indian device, which is estimated to have been in the 15- to 20-kiloton range (the same order of destructiveness as the Hiroshima and Nagasaki bombs), are military ones.

It would be foolish, therefore, to speak of India, or any other country that has exploded a nuclear device, as a peaceful nuclear power, and not a nuclear weapon power. Since all nuclear explosives can be used as nuclear weapons, and since there are really no other agreed upon purposes for such explosives, every country that conducts a successful nuclear explosion must be recognized to possess a nuclear weapon capability. Today, any country that wishes to develop such a capability can follow the Indian example of "peaceful purposes." And like India, it can manufacture nuclear explosives from plutonium that is obtained from a civilian nuclear program. This is the case not only for nonparties to the NPT but for countries that are parties as well.

According to the terms of the treaty, any party can legally withdraw on three months notice if it believes that continued adherence constitutes a threat to its vital national interests. Most obvious of all, perhaps, any country can simply violate the treaty, and it can do so with impunity. As is the case with all treaties, there exist no appropriate sanctions to ensure broad compliance. A treaty without provision for affecting the prospective costs and benefits of compliance, as Pufendorf, a distinguished classical writer on international law, once observed, "makes no addition to the obligation of the natural law, that is, the convention does not add anything to which men were not already bound by the very law of nature, nor does it make the obligation more binding."[23]

There are other major difficulties with the NPT and its related international agreements. One such difficulty centers on the position of China, which has been to consider the NPT as a thinly veiled trick by the superpowers to maintain their bilateral dominance of the global system. Based on this position, China has effectively taken the "porcupine position" on nuclear proliferation, treating it as a legitimate and necessary means whereby the underdeveloped world can protect itself from the insatiable imperialist appetites of the United States and the Soviet Union.

A related difficulty concerns the attitude of the Third World countries in general. Many of these countries, now disappointed by the failure of the NPT to slow the superpower arms race or to spread the benefits of nuclear energy for peaceful purposes, have come to share the Chinese position on the treaty. They are impressed by the Chinese and Indian accomplishments in the nuclear field, feeling that nuclear weapons—like the six-gun in the American West—are essential "equalizers" in an otherwise unbalanced "struggle for existence."

Still another problem is the prevailing attitude of some of the nuclear supplier states.[24] Since the interests of these states, most notably West Germany and France, seem strongly oriented in the direction of profits and sales, there is little reason to believe that other prospective suppliers will choose to remain outside the lucrative nuclear market. At the moment, the West German-Brazilian deal represents the most prominent and hazardous transfer of sensitive nuclear technology and facilities. In this connection, it is sobering to point out that at the very time West German representatives were urging more effective controls on nuclear exports at the NPT Review Conference in May 1975, other West German officials were busily negotiating a multibillion dollar sale to Brazil of a complete nuclear fuel cycle.[25]

3 The Third Path
Nuclear Terrorism

The threat of nuclear terrorism is particularly serious today. There are five principal reasons why this is the case: (1) terrorists have increasingly easy access to nuclear weapons, nuclear power plants, and nuclear-waste storage facilities; (2) terrorists are known to have a penchant for indiscriminate violence; (3) many terrorists are insensitive to orthodox threats of deterrence; (4) there is, today, a developing pattern of cooperation among terrorist groups; and (5) many nations tolerate and support terrorism.

The individuals who comprise today's terrorist groups differ from one another in terms of their motivations and goals. Some are moved by a genuine desire to remedy the terrible inequalities of an unjust social-political order; others, in the fashion of bandits, are moved by the selfish search for material gain; while still others base their motives, consciously or unconsciously, on the need to escape from private anguish.

This tangled skein of participants and personalities is organized into approximately fifty major groups.[1] Ideologically, these groups include anarchists, separatists, black nationalists, New Left activists, Castroites, Trotskyists, and every conceivable brand of anti-imperialist. Their intellectual and spiritual mentors include a gallery of heroes featuring Bakunin, Marx, Lenin, Sorel, Marighella, Mao, Giap, Fanon, Marcuse, Malcolm X, Guevara, Debray, Trotsky, and Guillen. To the extent that all modern terrorism has its roots in the French Reign of Terror (1793–1794), the names of Robespierre, Marat, Saint-Just, and Fouché must also be added to the list. Today's terrorist groups may even draw sustenance from the romantic individualism expressed in the writings of Goethe and Schiller, and from the existential commitment to action associated largely with Camus and Sartre.

The Technological Problem: Terrorist
Access to Implements of Nuclear Destruction

Nothing can give greater cause for alarm than the access of terrorists to nuclear weapons, nuclear power plants, or nuclear-waste storage facilities. Today, it is widely recognized that determined, organized, and adequately funded terrorist groups could acquire nuclear weapons via the theft of assembled systems from military stockpiles or through self-development from pilfered weapons-grade nuclear material. Moreover, it is also widely understood that terrorists could attempt to exploit the unique destructive potential of nuclear technology by sabotaging nuclear reactors.

To acquire an assembled weapon, terrorist operatives might direct their efforts to any of the tens of thousands of nuclear weapons now deployed in more than seventeen different countries across the world. And in the future, with a greater number of nuclear weapon states in existence, their opportunities for stealing assembled nuclear weapons will increase, particularly since newer members of the nuclear club are apt to waver from demanding and expensive safeguards procedures.

This is not to suggest, however, that existing safeguards are adequate. In 1975, analysts at the Center for Defense Information in Washington, D.C. wrote: "U.S. Army Special Forces exercises have shown that nuclear weapons storage areas can be penetrated successfully without detection despite guards, fences, and sensors. Their example could obviously be followed by a daring and well-organized terrorist organization."[2] These fears have been shared by several members of Congress who looked into the problem of U.S. nuclear weapon security overseas during the period of 1973 to 1975, and who are currently examining security at nuclear storage sites.[3]

To fashion their own nuclear weapons, terrorists would

require both the special nuclear materials and the expertise to convert them into explosive devices or radiation dispersal implements. A growing body of literature on the subject suggests that both requirements seem well within the realm of terrorist capabilities.[4] The director of the Enrico Fermi Institute at the University of Chicago has reportedly become so pessimistic about terrorist theft of nuclear materials as to conclude that there is "essentially no escape from the road leading to nuclear disaster."[5] A recent discussion group report on "Nuclear Theft and Terrorism" issued by twelve leading experts indicates concern about "weak links" in national and international safeguards that could enable terrorist thefts of nuclear materials.[6] Remarks by NRC (Nuclear Regulatory Commission) Commissioner Victor Gilinsky concede that we must tighten our security control over nuclear materials.[7] And political scientist Forrest R. Frank has expressed particular concern about access to materials that can be used in the manufacture of radiological weapons.[8]

This body of literature is supported by the *Final Report of the Joint ERDA-NRC Task Force on Safeguards* which indicates that an immediate and significant increase in security is needed to protect special nuclear materials in licensed U.S. facilities. Pursuant to this finding, the report recommends

> initiating actions to upgrade the safeguards posture to a level affording high-confidence protection against theft of SNM (Special Nuclear Materials) by internal conspiracies or determined violent assaults. This recommendation is not based upon a perception of any imminence of threat to the nuclear fuel industry; rather, it is based upon the judgment of the task force as to what constitutes a prudent level of protection.[9]

There is some evidence to suggest that theft of special nuclear materials may already have occurred and that levels of protection of such material may be grossly substandard. In the fall of 1977, a number of members of both houses of Congress called for investigations following the release of a government report indicating that nuclear fuel plants were unable to account for *thousands of pounds* of special nuclear materials. Although the report stresses that there is no evidence of theft, the government is unable to account for 8,437 pounds of uranium and plutonium that have disappeared since World War II.[10] In terms of "weapons quantity" fissionable material, this represents an amount sufficient for the manufacture of a substantial number of crude nuclear weapons.

In its Annual Report to the Congress on *Domestic Safeguards* for Fiscal Year 1978, the U.S. Nuclear Regulatory Commission focuses on "inventory differences" concerning special nuclear material (SNM)—that is, uranium-235 (contained in uranium enriched to 20 percent or more in the U-235 isotope), uranium-233, or plutonium. These materials, of course, must be protected because of their use in fabricating nuclear weapons. According to the report: "During fiscal year 1978, inventory differences exceeding regulatory limits were experienced at three fuel cycle facilities."[11]

It is also disturbing to note that even if American safeguards against theft of nuclear materials were significantly improved in the future it would provide little assurance against theft, since, to be effective, the protection of fissionable material must be worldwide in scope. Moreover, the amount of special nuclear materials in other countries is almost certain to expand rapidly. The duality of nuclear power—its convertibility from peaceful to military purposes—signals very dangerous conditions. Unless immediate and effective steps are taken to inhibit the spread of plutonium-reprocessing and uranium-enrichment facilities to other countries, terrorist opportunities to acquire fissionable materials for nuclear weapon purposes, as well as fully assembled nuclear weapons, will reach unacceptable limits.

However, even if such steps are taken, the problems of smuggled nuclear material—i.e., fissionable material usable to make nuclear weapons—and assembled nuclear weapons, would remain. In the words of David Rosenbaum:

> One kilogram of uranium or plutonium is about the size of a golf ball. A typical one-kilogram brick of marijuana is about 12″ × 6″ × 2½,″ or about twenty times as large. If we intercept less than ten percent of the more

than 4,000 tons of marijuana smuggled into the United States each year, it is clear that we, or any country with reasonably open borders, has little chance of intercepting a few "weapons quantities" of SNM. Even Communist countries, which line their borders with electrified barbed wire, mine fields, search lights, and machine guns, have serious problems with smuggling. Thus, nuclear weapons or SNM stolen anywhere are a threat to countries everywhere.[12]

To fabricate its own nuclear weapons, a terrorist group would also require expertise. According to Willrich and Taylor, "The design and manufacture of a crude nuclear explosive is no longer a difficult task technically, and a plutonium dispersal device which can cause widespread radioactive contamination is much simpler to make than an explosive."[13] This point is seconded by David Rosenbaum:

> People with the skills needed to build crude nuclear weapons are easily found in the general technical community. Someone with experience in calculating fast neutron systems would be useful, as would a physical chemist and an explosives expert. There are thousands of people around the world with sufficient nuclear experience and tens of thousands of people with the appropriate skills in physical chemistry and explosives. Thus, most established organizations, given enough time, should be able to acquire appropriate people.[14]

Since the early 1950s, declassification and public dissemination of information about the design of fission weapons has been extensive. And terrorists who display an interest in constructing their own nuclear explosives or radiological weapons need not fulfill the same rigorous performance requirements that apply to professional weapons engineers. Dr. Forrest Frank, who has studied the problem in great detail, writes:

> While the amount of expertise needed to construct a nuclear bomb is perhaps no greater than college physics, chemistry, and perhaps engineering, the amount of expertise needed to construct a simple device for dispersing radioactive material is even less. Any container capable of dispensing liquid radioactive waste

under pressure would be sufficient; pouring liquid or particulate radioactive materials in air conditioning systems of large buildings or into urban water supplies might also represent highly effective methods of dispersing some radioactive materials.[15]

Terrorists might also achieve nuclear capability by means of sabotaging nuclear reactor facilities. Here, rather than acquiring assembled nuclear weapons or special nuclear materials for fabrication into explosives or radiation dispersal devices, terrorist groups would seek to penetrate the physical barriers between themselves and the fission material in the reactor. They might then threaten to disable the cooling systems to the reactor core (this would cause the reactor to melt through its protective shielding, releasing radioactivity into the atmosphere) unless stipulated demands were met. Or worse still, aiming at high levels of destruction for nihilistic purposes, they might simply proceed as saboteurs without making any demands.

Such choreographed acts of violence could pose monumental problems for responsible government authorities. Although a great many steps appear to have been taken in the United States during the past few years to diminish the vulnerability of nuclear power plants,[16] sabotage is certainly conceivable. In a recent interview, Kenneth R. Chapman, director of the NRC's Office of Nuclear Material Safety and Safeguards, indicated that while the risk of reactor sabotage is somewhat less than the risk of nuclear materials theft, the maintenance of effective security against reactor sabotage is "somewhat more difficult."[17]

Testifying before the Joint Committee on Atomic Energy in March 1974, a former U.S. Navy underwater demolitions officer stated that any three to five underwater-demolition or Green Beret officers could "sabotage virtually any nuclear reactor in the country."[18] Later in that same year, after improved security regulations had been implemented, the General Accounting Office stated: "Licensee and AEC officials agreed that a security system at a licensed nuclear plant could not prevent a takeover for sabotage by a small number—as few perhaps as two or three armed individuals."[19] A recent study prepared by the Sandia Corporation concludes: "It appears that a sufficiently determined and able group could perform acts of sabotage which could endanger the safety of the public surrounding the plant."[20] And one NRC official stated not long ago: "Several people with high explosives who really know how to use it can probably go through a nuclear facility like butter."[21]

In order to appreciate the urgency of the situation, these views of nuclear plant security must be coupled with the understanding that there have already been at least 175 instances of violence or threats of violence against U.S. nuclear facilities since 1969.[22] Several dangerous incidents have also occurred outside the United States. In 1975, a number of bombs exploded at nuclear plants in France. According to David Rosenbaum:

> Western Europe has already suffered a number of instances of nuclear-related sabotage. In 1975, in France, for example, two incidents of sabotage were reported. On August 15, two bombs exploded at the 70 megawatt Experimental Heavy Water Plant at Brennilis. The Breton Liberation Front-Breton Liberation Army claimed credit for the attack. More than three months earlier two bombs exploded at the nuclear power plant under construction at Fessenheim. The saboteurs put the bombs in exactly those places which would cause maximum delay in the construction. A French newspaper article said, "It is certain that the perpetrator of the crime must have been perfectly acquainted with the site and must have had experience and mastery of the explosives and some understanding of the technology of the installations at which he aimed." Seventy minutes before the bombs exploded, a telephone call gave warning and claimed credit for the Meinhof-Puig Antich Group. This group had never been heard of before.[23]

Terrorist sabotage of a nuclear reactor could result in extensive death and injury via radiation release. The latest major study sponsored by the Nuclear Regulatory Commission, WASH–1400—known popularly as the Rasmussen Report—cites, as consequences of such radiation release extensive fatalities, injuries, genetic defects, and property damage. The report of the NRC-organized Risk Assessment

Review Group, formed to "clarify the achievements and limitations of the Rasmussen Report," concludes that much of WASH–1400 is "conservative" in its conclusions.[24]

Nevertheless, experts seem to agree that the prospective societal costs of reactor core meltdown caused by sabotage are apt to be less than those costs associated with nuclear explosives or radiological weapons. According to Theodore B. Taylor's summation of the Stanley Foundation conference discussion group report on "Nuclear Theft and Terrorism":

> There was consensus among the group that if a terrorist group managed to take control of a nuclear power station, and caused the core to melt and release a substantial fraction of the radioactivity through the containment structure, the worst conceivable physical consequences would still be less than from a low-yield nuclear explosion in a highly-populated area, or the effective dispersal of a kilogram or so of plutonium throughout a very large office building.[25]

Presumably, the omission of any expressed concern for nuclear reactor sabotage in the *Final Report of the Joint ERDA-NRC Task Force on Safeguards* can also be attributed to the belief that the effects of sabotage would be comparatively small, and that the difficulties involved in sabotage would be comparatively great.[26]

Terrorist Orientations to Nuclear Violence

Exhibiting an orientation to violence that has been shaped largely by the preaching of Bakunin, Fanon, and Sorel, many of today's terrorist groups have abandoned the idea of distinguishing between combatants and noncombatants in the selection of victims. Rather, these groups are engaged in total war against various countries, religions, and ethnic groups, and their choice of targets is typically unaffected by considerations of age, sex, or innocence. As a result of this decisional calculus, terrorist activities have involved the killing and maiming of a great many people who have no particular part in the problems the terrorists seek to resolve.

In short, the imperative to create "boundaries" in the application of violence is ignored by many modern terrorist groups.[27] At the same time, the level of violence deemed appropriate by these groups is often constrained only by the limits of available weaponry.

To a certain extent, this no-holds-barred orientation to violence stems from the conviction that it is an expedient strategy. As long as war is still generally recognized as the final arbiter between countries, it is argued, so must untrammeled terrorist violence be treated as the final arbiter within countries.

The apparent randomness of terrorist target selection is designed to foster fear. If the enemies of terrorism can be made to feel that *everyone* is a potential victim of terrorist violence, they will be more likely to "cave in" under terrorist pressure. For example, German terrorists—in the aftermath of the murder of industrialist Hanns-Martin Schleyer and the successful German commando raid in Somalia—issued a threat to perpetrate "100,000 bombings to destroy the German economy."

Further, by extending the arena of conflict to include the entire world—exploiting the existence of a sophisticated global communications system—terrorists hope to focus worldwide attention on their demands. Terrorism is largely a propagandistic activity. This kind of activity involves the application of high levels of violence to virtually any segment of the human population.

At the moment, it is still unclear whether such methods are actually expedient. In certain instances, the willingness of modern terrorists to sacrifice virtually anyone for propagandistic purposes has been patently inexpedient. In these instances, opposition to terrorists has generally stiffened rather than softened, with counterterrorist strategies turning into a mirror image of terrorist cruelty.

Historically, it is worth noting that higher order acts of terrorist violence have often generated broad-based repulsion instead of support. As examples, we may point to the Stern Gang (especially the murder of Lord Moyne in Cairo in 1944, which inspired the Jewish agency to launch a counterterrorist campaign); the *Front de Liberation Québécois*, FLQ, (especially the killing of French-Canadian Cabi-

net Minister LaPorte); the Turkish People's Liberation
Army; the U.S. Weathermen; and the Netherland's South
Mollucan terrorists.

However, the practice of terror and cruelty has occasionally elicited support and admiration as well. In writing
about the history of bandits, for example, Eric Hobsbawm
has indicated that these sorts of terrorists have often become
heroes not in spite of their terrible cruelty, but because of it.
Their hero image stems not from their presumed ability to
right wrongs, but from their acknowledged ability to *avenge*.
In describing the Colombian *violencia* during the peasant
revolution of the years after 1948, Hobsbawm points out that
bandits who chopped prisoners into tiny fragments before
whole villages and ripped fetuses from pregnant women became instant heroes to the local population.[28]

Thus, in certain circumstances, terrorist calculations that
excessive violence is expedient may prove correct. In such
circumstances, the incentive to escalate to nuclear terror
may be great.

Terrorists often possess a romantic attitude toward bru-
tality. Even where it is doubtful that excessive and arbitrary
violence will produce their desired goals, terrorists are
sometimes moved by Bakunin's statement, "The passion for
destruction is a constructive passion,"[29] and by the equally
cathartic remark of Franz Fanon: "Violence is a purifying
force. It frees the native from his inferiority complex and
from despair and inaction. It makes him fearless and re-
stores his self-respect."[30]

Fused with Sartre's existential idea that "irrepressible
violence . . . is man recreating himself,"[31] such romanticization breeds a cold-blooded view of the role of force. The ultimate expression of this view is a blind and nihilistic devotion to the "creativity" of violence. In the United States, the
Weathermen best exemplified this attitude; they were
judged by their peers not according to the political effectiveness of their actions, but according to the degree of their
commitment to violence as an end in itself.

This nihilistic view of violence is subscribed to not only by
the so-called romantics, but also by psychopaths and socio-

paths within terrorist groups who enjoy carnage for its own sake. In this case, the complete inversion of the Judeo-Christian notions of conscience and compassion results neither from a means-ends calculation, nor a devotion to the "creativity" of violence, but from a purely psychotic motive. Such suicidal schizophrenics exacerbate the problems of effective counterterrorist activity, since their motivation is nihilistic rather than political, and they are apt to regard the threat of death as a stimulus rather than a deterrent.

Another aspect of the no-holds-barred orientation to violence that characterizes modern terrorists is the belief of many of them that the overwhelming righteousness of their objectives justifies any means whatsoever. Such a stance makes these groups susceptible to what political theorist Hannah Arendt called the "banality of evil" problem, whereby individuals are capable of engaging in evil without experiencing it as evil. This is particularly evident when terrorists displace responsibility for their own violent acts onto their victims. Witness, for example, the statement by the leader of the Black September band concerning responsibility for the helicopter deaths in Munich: "No Israelis would have been killed if the Germans had not trapped the operation. No one at all would have been killed if the Israelis had released their prisoners." Thus, following terrorist reasoning, by not succumbing to blackmail, the victim countries, West Germany and Israel, must assume responsibility for terrorist acts.

The principle that the ends justify the means also enables terrorists to avoid individual responsibility for their acts by displacing this responsibility onto the terrorist groups themselves. By transforming persons into members of a group—into servants of a "higher cause"—feelings of individual responsibility are submerged by the "psychology of the cell." The effects of this "psychology," which are best illustrated by the clandestine cell structure of Canada's Quebec Liberation Front (FLQ), Algeria's National Liberation Front (FLN), and Uruguay's Tupamaros, aggravate the "banality of evil" problem and hence increase the likelihood of nuclear terrorism.

Terrorist Insensitivity to Traditional
Threats of Deterrence

While it would be unreasonable to suggest that all terrorists are mad and irrational and therefore not capable of being deterred by threats of physically punishing retaliation, it does appear that terrorist groups tend to operate under a different meaning of rationality than do states. Indeed, as the name of one group, *Fedayeen* (meaning self-sacrificers) indicates, terrorist operatives are sometimes willing to "die for the cause." As a result, terrorists are often insensitive to the kinds of retaliatory threats that are the traditional mainstay of order between states.

There are numerous examples of this type of terrorist "rationality": In May 1972, two Red Army terrorists, during their attack on Israel's Lod International Airport, killed themselves; Holger Meins, of the Baader-Meinhof group, succumbed to self-inflicted starvation in 1974; Arab terrorists, in April 1974, seized an apartment building in northern Israel, and ultimately accepted death rather than capture; and SLA members, during the widely publicized California shootout in May 1974, preferred death to incarceration.

On 18 October 1977, three imprisoned West German terrorists, upon learning of the failure of a hijacking that was intended to secure their release, reportedly committed suicide. A fourth terrorist is also alleged to have tried to kill herself in her cell, but survived in critical condition. After a daring Entebbe-style operation at Mogadishu, Somalia, in which a West German commando force (Federal Border Guard GSG-9 Unit) rescued all eighty-six of the surviving hostages on the hijacked Lufthansa airliner, Andreas Baader, Gudrun Ensslin, and Jan-Carl Raspe took their own lives in jail, while the fourth imprisoned terrorist—Irmgard Moeller—slashed her wrists unsuccessfully. Baader and Ensslin were leaders of the West German Baader-Meinhof terrorist group.

Quite plainly, the most significant implication of this kind of behavioral pattern is that, should terrorists obtain access to nuclear explosives or radioactivity and calculate the prospective costs and benefits of use, the fear of retaliatory destruction might not figure importantly in their calculations. In effect, this means that traditional threats of deterrence might have little or no bearing on terrorist decisions concerning the use of nuclear force.

Before terrorists can be made to believe that violent acts are counterproductive, however, steps will have to be taken to weaken public tolerance and support of such acts. Presently, terrorist groups throughout the world enjoy considerable support in certain quarters. In some cases, sympathy for terrorist objectives is so great that all potentially effective terrorist means are judged acceptable. This problem is aggravated by the activities of certain states for whom considerations of human rights are overshadowed by the presumed requirements of power politics.

Another reason why threats of physically punishing retaliation are not apt to deter nuclear terrorism is the fact that harsh and repressive countermeasures often work in the terrorists' own interests. Indeed, with this understanding, terrorists have even been known to goad authorities deliberately into undertaking highly destructive countermeasures. In Algeria, FLN strategy was designed to provoke the kind of countermeasures which would make compromise impossible. More recently, the Irish Republican Army (IRA) in Northern Ireland and the Tupamaros in Uruguay deliberately prodded government repression in an attempt to alienate moderates' support of the government and erode faith in the political system. From the standpoint of effective counter-nuclear-terrorism strategies, these points suggest that governments give careful scrutiny to the prospective costs of harsh physical countermeasures before implementing them. Contrary to the facile conventional wisdom on the subject, fighting fire with fire is not always effective. Sometimes, it is much better to rely on water.

A final reason for terrorist insensitivity to the usual threats of deterrence lies in the relative safety of certain terrorists from retaliatory assaults. Since many terrorist groups operate from bases in states that are outside the target societies—e.g., Palestinian terrorists in Israel—these groups enjoy a certain level of security from reprisal. Because retaliation requires infringement upon the sovereignty of "host" countries, it inevitably creates problems under international law. Hence, unless the target states of terrorists are willing to turn their backs on legal niceties and initiate preemptive or retaliatory strikes on terrorist bases, it is these states—rather than the terrorists—who are placed on the defensive. The net effect of this condition, of course, is to embolden terrorist behavior.

Cooperation between Terrorist Groups

Venezuelan terrorist Illich Ramirez-Sanchez ("Carlos the Jackal") has ties to a Latin American coordinating junta founded in 1974 by revolutionary groups in Argentina, Bolivia, Chile, Paraguay, and Uruguay and heads a group comprised of Germans, Latin Americans, and Arabs who have undertaken operations in Austria, the Netherlands, Britain, and France.

Members of the Japanese Red Army terrorist group receive weapons training in Lebanon.

Joint training programs and arms transfers take place between the Turkish People's Army and Black September.

Members of the American Weathermen and Northern Ireland's IRA are trained in Palestinian camps.

Black September operatives demanded the release of German insurgents who had been involved in the killing of German policemen.

Liason between the Popular Front for the Liberation of Palestine (PFLP) and Japanese Red Army agents produced the Lydda Airport massacre, an attack on the American Embassy in Kuala Lumpur, Malaysia, the hijacking of a JAL flight, an assault on the Japanese Embassy in Kuwait, and a takeover of the French Embassy at The Hague.

Arab terrorists hijacked a Boeing 737 belonging to Lufthansa Airlines, and demanded the release of German members of the Baader-Meinhof gang from West German prisons in exchange for the release of their hostages.[32]

These are only a few of the most glaring examples of a new phenomenon in world politics—systematic cooperation and collaboration between terrorist groups. Terrorists have always formed alignments with sympathetic states, as we shall soon see, but they are now also beginning to cement patterns of alliance and partnership with each other. The result of such behavior patterns is a terrorist adaptation of Trotsky's theory of "permanent revolution."

It seems unlikely, however, that the existence of terrorist cooperation signals the beginnings of a genuine, system-wide organization of terrorists. The basic informality of terrorist activities and the diversity of terrorist ideologies and objectives mitigate against such an organization. Nevertheless, a pattern of cooperation has been established which is nurtured and sustained by a number of national leaders. Despite the fact that such cooperation has not always been successful, without it, transnational terrorist ventures would cease altogether.

Interterrorist cooperation facilitates nuclear terrorism in several ways. First, it increases the opportunities for acquiring nuclear weapons and for acquiring the "raw" fissionable material—along with the capital and expertise—for the design and self-development of such weapons. Second, it is likely to facilitate the proliferation of "private" nuclear weapons throughout the world, creating a network whereby such weapons can be exchanged and transmitted across national frontiers. Third, cooperation among terrorists is apt to spread the "benefits" of advanced training in the use of nuclear weapons and the techniques of nuclear plant sabotage. Fourth, and finally, terrorist cooperation is likely to provide such reciprocal privileges as forged documents and safe havens, which are necessary for both preattack preparations and postattack security.

The Phenomenon of Support
for Terrorists

It is an irony of modern world politics that while terrorists are engaged in "total war" with broad and diverse segments of humanity, the prevailing attitude in many countries is one of tolerance or even outright support for them. Consider just one recent example: In the wake of the 4 July 1976 Israeli commando raid in Uganda which freed 105 hostages taken by pro-Palestinian skyjackers, African members of the Security Council proposed a resolution to condemn the raid as a "flagrant violation" of Uganda's sovereignty. The

Ugandan supporters also refused to participate in the vote of a rival resolution under joint American-British sponsorship that would have condemned airline hijacking in particular and terrorism in general.

This attitude is manifested at both *intra*national and *inter*national levels. Within countries, two factors may contribute to this attitude: (1) sympathy for terrorist goals is so great that there is no longer any concern for "proportionality" between these goals and the violent means adopted for their implementation; and (2) fear of terrorists is so great that capitulation to their demands is judged necessary for survival. In the first case, terrorists are seen as the impressive vanguard of a new and more promising social order, locked in necessary and protracted combat with the forces of injustice and oppression. In the second case, terrorists are seen as intractable deliverers of unspeakable agony. In both cases, the concluding effect is a favorable environment for terrorist violence.

Between countries, the tolerance and support of terrorism by certain states stems from the belief that terrorist groups often work in their own national interests. Here, issues of morality and reasonableness are overshadowed by the presumption that terrorists, however inadvertently, are useful surrogates in the ongoing struggle for international power and influence.

At the moment, a number of countries—e.g., Libya, Saudi Arabia, Kuwait, Iraq, Syria, Algeria, China, Vietnam, the Soviet bloc, and Cuba—are committed sponsors of alignments with terrorist groups, and can be counted upon by terrorists for continuing safety and support. As long as this situation prevails, and history is replete with examples of states supporting terrorist efforts in other states, many terrorist groups will continue to interpret succor from sponsor states as an invitation to violent action.

Cooperation between state and terrorist actors allows the former to influence world politics at a safe distance. Such cooperation encourages terrorist inclinations to nuclear violence not only through direct assistance to terrorist groups (e.g., weapons, material aid, safe havens), but also through the progressive strengthening of states which support terrorism. Since the use of terrorists as surrogates by certain states may significantly alter prevailing patterns of global power in favor of these states, the long-term effects may also include the progressive strengthening of the surrogates themselves.

Tolerance and support of international terrorism are also increased to the extent that terrorists influence the foreign policies of "host" states. For example, the host states, sometimes in combination with allied countries, may act as advocates of the terrorist groups before the "tribunal" of the state system itself. Such advocacy further legitimizes terrorists as actors in world politics, extending their juridical arena of acceptance and influence. The recent Arab-backed resolution, sponsored by eighteen nations, which admitted the Palestine Liberation Organization (PLO) into the UN's Economic Commission of Western Asia (ECWA), is a case in point. Such action, which has the effect of making a terrorist organization a "juristic person," heightens terrorist incentives to nuclear violence.

Proposals to sever the bonds between states and terrorist groups are often based on the idea that all states share a common interest in obstructing terrorism. After all, it is argued, terrorists are clearly *hostes humani generis*, enemies of mankind. Like pirates, their interests can never really coincide with the long-term interests of states.

These proposals rest on the mistaken assumption that all states will always value the proper functioning of the international diplomatic system more highly than any goal that might be obtained through terrorist surrogates. It is, therefore, an erroneous argument, very much like the one that all states will agree to halt the proliferation of nuclear weapons because it is clearly in their common interest to do so. Sadly, everything that is known about the power-politics orientation to foreign policy mitigates against accepting that states will combine to counter terrorism in an anarchic world system.

In the absence of cooperative counterterrorism among states, the continuance of tolerance and support for terrorist groups suggests a propitious opportunity for such groups to step up their virulent activities. The support of nations might on the one hand enable terrorists to achieve their ends without having to resort to nuclear weapons or nuclear sabotage, or it might on the other hand serve as encouragement to do so (perhaps even in the form of assistance) should the terrorists perceive it to be necessary. In either case, to avert this second potential outcome counterterrorist nations would have to also avert the first as well, aiming at instilling a sense of "balance" among sympathizers between the ends and means of terrorism and requiring an international commitment to counterterrorist measures.

International Law and Terrorism

Initially, it would appear that our pessimism about preventing nuclear terror must be tempered by the structure of international legal agreements that have been formed to counter international terrorism. In the areas concerning protection of diplomats and international civil aviation, states *have* engaged in cooperative legal measures.

In December 1973, the U.N. General Assembly adopted a resolution supporting a Convention on the Prevention and Punishment of crimes against Internationally Protected Persons, including Diplomatic Agents, reinforcing the principles of diplomatic security codified in the Vienna Convention of 1961.

In the area of antihijacking, three major agreements—the 1963 Tokyo Convention, the 1970 Hague Convention, and the 1971 Montreal Convention—have now been ratified or are respected by more than seventy countries.

At the regional level, the Organization of American States (OAS) adopted a convention to prevent and punish acts of terrorism against diplomats and international civil servants in February 1971, and in January 1976, the Council of Europe adopted a Convention on the Suppression of Terrorism. Presently, there is a continuing initiative in the United Nations toward a convention against the taking of hostages, although a U.S. proposal for a convention to prevent the export of terrorism perished in the 1972 General Assembly.

Unfortunately, as is the case in the problem of international legal solutions to the problem of nuclear proliferation, the essential problem of effective counterterrorism is not the absence of relevant norms. Rather, it is the split sympathies of states on the question at issue and the resultant unwillingness of many of these states—even signatories to the various agreements—to abide by appropriate conventions. Nothing is apt to prove less productive than an attempt to prevent nuclear terrorism through excessive reliance on international conventions. The problem is not the absence of relevant law, but the absence of appropriate sanctions to enforce widespread compliance. And as long as the anarchic character of the world legal system remains intact, which is likely to be as long as the present system survives, such sanctions will never make an appearance.

In certain instances, the split sympathies of states on the question of terrorism have impaired extant norms. This impairment is best illustrated by the 1973 Report to the General Assembly of the Ad Hoc Committee on International Terrorism and the 1974 General Assembly Definition of Aggression.[33] Both documents exempt from the definition of prohibited acts those activities that are generated by principles of "self-determination" and "national liberation." According to Article 7 of the Definition of Aggression:

> Nothing in this definition, and in particular Article 3 (an inventory of acts that qualify as aggression) could in any way prejudice the right to self-determination, freedom, and independence, as derived from the Charter, of peoples forcibly deprived of that right and referred to in the Declaration on Principles of International Law concerning Friendly Relations and Co-operation among States in accordance with the Charter of the United Nations, particularly peoples under colonial and racist regimes or other forms of alien domination; nor the right of these peoples to struggle to that end and to seek and receive support, in accordance with the principles of the Charter and in conformity with the above-mentioned Declaration.[34]

While such exemptions may serve to protect the "just cause" of certain forms of insurgency, they inevitably provide a legal justification for virtually any acts of violence that are cloaked in appropriate juridical terms. In this sense, their amenability for abuse parallels the earlier distinctions in international law between just and unjust wars.

Yet, international law must not be allowed to serve the interests of counternuclear terrorism at the expense of international justice. Although unambiguous norms must serve to sustain international order, they must not be put in the position of supporting the status quo at all costs. But who is to determine the appropriate balance? What criteria can be applied by states in particular circumstances to distinguish between legitimate claims for human rights and/or national liberation and illegitimate acts of terror?

The answer to these questions lies in an abiding concern by states for *discrimination* and *proportionality* in their assessments of insurgent uses of force. These principles, which are an integral part of the laws of war of international law, support the understanding that even when the use of force is morally justified, there are boundaries that must be respected. Once these boundaries are violated—either through gratuitous excesses in the use of force or through the targeting of innocents—insurgency can no longer be tolerated by the international legal order.

Part Two

The Consequences of Nuclear Catastrophe

4 The Consequences of Nuclear War between the Superpowers

In Elie Wiesel's novel, *The Oath*, an old wanderer named Azriel tells a story about the destruction of the small town of Kolvillàg, somewhere in the Carpathian Mountains of Eastern Europe, in the 1920s:

> What I saw in Kolvillàg, not only during its last night, was the eruption of total violence, the rule of madness in the absolute sense, as though the Creator, in a fit of joyous and destructive rage, had granted full freedom to His creatures, from the greatest to the most insignificant; and these creatures, crazed by their burden of divinity, driven to madness and nothingness, suddenly resembled one another in their passionate hatred and vengefulness.

The "violence," "madness," and "rage" characterizing the final hours of Kolvillàg would be absent in the aftermath of a nuclear war between the superpowers. The devastation would be too great. Nor would these words characterize the motivations of the superpowers in initiating such a war. There would be an absense of the usual flesh and blood hatreds associated with this kind of rivalry. The overwhelmingly destructive consequences of nuclear war would stand in vivid contrast to the dehumanized and unfeeling execution of it.

Similarly, images of war as a temporary, albeit unhappy, interruption of the peace would also no longer be appropriate. Although such images have their roots in the ancient Greek view of war—a view which coupled the outcome of military campaigns with a return to the harvest and the

121

gathering of grapes and olives—they are no longer meaningful. The historian Thucydides' idea that war is a violent
preceptor, teaching some things that are good and some
that are evil, can no longer be taken seriously. A nuclear war
between the superpowers would have effectively permanent,
irreversible consequences. Its only lesson would be to show
the confirmed ability of human beings to magnify the suffering of individual persons to previously inconceivable levels,
and to lay waste to the human habitat in ways that would put
Rome's degradation of Carthage to shame.

While we can supply facts, tables, and charts to lend substance to what might lie ahead in the event of a nuclear war
(and, indeed, that is what I will do in this and the following
two chapters), such information can never satisfactorily
dispel the realization that we really do not *know*—that we
really cannot *feel*—the measureless dread and deprivation
that would be experienced by a "survivor" of Armaggedon.
As Freud observes in his *Civilization and its Discontents:*

> No matter how much we may shrink with horror from
> certain situations—of a galley slave in antiquity, of a
> peasant during the Thirty Years' War, of a victim of
> the Holy Inquisition, of a Jew awaiting a pogrom—it
> is nevertheless impossible for us to feel our way into
> such people, to divine the changes which original ob-
> tuseness of mind, a gradual stupefying process, the
> cessation of expectations, and cruder or more refined
> methods of narcotization have produced upon their
> receptivity to sensations of pleasure and unpleasure.

The same point is made succinctly in Stephen Vincent
Benét's "Nightmare for Future Reference," which offers a
retrospective view of life after the third world war:

> You've been to the Broken Towns? Yes, they
>   take you there. They show you the look of
>   the tormented earth.
> But they can't show the smell or the gas or
>   the death
> Or how it felt to be there, and a part of it.

This incapacity for a genuine experiential "link" to survivors of a nuclear war is merely an extension of a more

basic incapacity, the inability of human beings to imagine
their own deaths. According to Freud's "Thoughts for the
Times on War and Death": "It is indeed impossible to imagine our own death: and whenever we attempt to do so we
can perceive that we are in fact still present as spectators."

By "standing outside" and hence being unable to concep-
tualize the mortal consequences of nuclear war, we are not
likely to take appropriate prophylactic measures to avert
such a disaster. This "natural" complacency stands in ironic
contrast to the imagery of extinction surrounding us in our
art, literature, and politics that is intended to define the
unimaginable.

Perhaps we can come close to understanding what it
would be like to endure a superpower nuclear conflict by
studying the anatomy of life in the death camps of Nazi
Germany and the aftermath of atomic holocaust in Hiroshima. Although the analogies are certainly imperfect, there
are no other darkly visionary sources of human experience
to which we can so safely turn. The extraordinary immersion
in death; the olfactory stimulation provided by tens of
thousands of burning bodies; the overwhelming imagery of
unending terror, disintegration, and loss that were the central features of these two atrocities, offer us the clearest
human picture of life in a postapocalypse world.

Of the two experiences, of course, Hiroshima provides
the better rendering. After all, it was the site of a genuine
nuclear attack by one country upon another, although the
bomb itself—a weapon with the mere force of less than
20,000 tons of TNT—was certainly a pygmy by today's standards. The bomb created an area of total destruction which
extended about two miles in all directions, destroying
60,000 buildings and killing between 78,000 and 200,000
people.[1] At points close to the hypocenter, all metal and
stone were melted, and human beings were completely incinerated. According to Robert Jay Lifton, the distinguished
Yale psychiatrist:

> The area was enveloped by fires fanned by a violent
> "firewind;" these broke out almost immediately within
> a radius of more than three thousand meters (up to two
> miles). The inundation with death of the area closest to

the hypocenter was such that if a man survived within a thousand meters (.6 miles) and was out of doors (that is, without benefit of shielding from heat or radiation), more than nine tenths of the people around him were fatalities. . . . Those closest to the hypocenter could usually recall a sudden flash, an intense sensation of heat, being knocked down or thrown some distance, and finding themselves pinned under debris or simply awakening from an indeterminate period of unconsciousness. *The most striking psychological feature of this immediate experience was the sense of a sudden and absolute shift from normal existence to an overwhelming encounter with death.*[2]

After the initial shock, Lifton points out interestingly, the prevailing atmosphere was one of "deathly silence" rather than wild panic. Amidst an aura of wierdness and unreality, the "survivors" described a ghastly stillness in which the normal line between life and death was blurred beyond distinction. In the words of M. Hachiya's classic *Hiroshima Diary:*

Those who were able walked silently toward the suburbs in the distant hills, their spirits broken, their initiative gone. When asked whence they had come, they pointed to the city and said, "That way:" and when asked where they were going, pointed away from the city and said, "This way." They were so broken and confused that they moved and behaved like automatons. Their reactions had astonished outsiders who reported with amazement the spectacle of long files of people holding stolidly to a narrow, rough path when close by was a smooth, easy road going in the same direction. The outsiders could not grasp the fact that they were witnessing the exodus of a people who walked in the realm of dreams.[3]

This sort of dreamlike, disoriented behavior was also reportedly characteristic of the Nazi death camp survivors upon their liberation. And in both cases, despite the apparent hopelessness of the situation, numerous survivors—however ineffectually—sought to help others, a factor that probably contributed a great deal to their own survival. This point, that compassion and concern for others in extreme situa-

tions is the key to one's own survival, is the main thesis of
Terrence Des Pres's account of Hitler's kingdom of death.[4]
There are, however, several accounts of the atomic bomb
experience which discount this thesis. For example, according to Takashi Nagai, a physician of Nagasaki (the second
target of American nuclear attack in August 1945):

> In general, then, those who survived the atom bomb
> were the people who ignored their friends crying out *in*
> *extremis;* or who shook off wounded neighbors who
> clung to them, pleading to be saved. . . . In short, those
> who survived the bomb were, if not merely lucky, in a
> greater or lesser degree selfish, self-centered, guided by
> instinct and not civilization . . . and we know it, we who
> have survived. Knowing it is a dull ache without
> surcease.[5]

This last remark points to the phenomenon of *survivor
guilt,* an inevitable and enduring consequence of nuclear
attack. Lifton's descriptions of the need of the *hibakusha*
(atomic bomb survivors), from the moment of atomic
bomb exposure, to justify their own survival in the midst of
death for so many others, are paralleled by the death camp
accounts of other literary intellectuals.

Survivor guilt, however, is not the only enduring personal
consequence of nuclear catastrophe, as the experience of
the "Hiroshima Maidens" points out. These twenty-five
young women, brought to the United States in 1955 for
plastic-surgical treatment of burn scars and hideous accu-
mulations of keloid scar tissue, are still ravaged by their
experience of many years ago. Initially tormented by catastrophic injuries that left them with eyes they could not close
and mouths that could not speak or eat, they still live in fear
that their exposure to radiation might produce deformed
children. One of the "maidens," Michiko Sako, expresses her
feelings in a poem entitled, "Bring Back My Smile:"

> Though flowers bloom again,[6]
>   Even after blossoms have fallen,
>   Once injured, the body never heals.

Now that some of the more terrible physical deformities
have been corrected or relieved, Mrs. Sako still feels that she

will never "be able to erase the nonphysical scars, even in the future."[7]

At the time of their suffering, the survivors of Auschwitz and Hiroshima, of Treblinka and Nagasaki, reacted to the otherworldly grotesqueness of their conditions with what Lifton describes as a profound sense of "death in life." Witnessing, in the one case, the thrusting of newly delivered babies, *alive*, into ovens, and in the other, the appearance of long lines of severely burned, literally melting, ghosts, the survivors found themselves, in Bruno Bettelheim's words, an "anonymous mass," or in the Japanese term, *mugamuchū*, "without self, without a center." Such a total disruption of individual and social order, of one's customary personal and community supports, produced consequences that went far beyond immediate physical and emotional suffering. Indeed, this understanding is incorporated in the Japanese term for atomic bomb survivors, *hibakusha*, which delimits four categories of victims. According to Dr. Lifton, these categories include

> those who at the time of the bomb were within the city limits of Hiroshima as then defined . . . those who came into the city within fourteen days and entered a designated area extending to about two thousand meters from the hypocenter; those who came into physical contact with bomb victims, through various forms of aid or disposal of bodies; and those who were *in utero* at the time, and whose mothers fit into any of the first three groups.[8]

The effects of Hiroshima, therefore, are not confined to the immediate or even long-term experiences of those who bore witness, but extend to their rescuers, their progeny, and even to the progeny of their rescuers. Perhaps it would not be unreasonable to expand the category of *hibakusha* to include the children of Japanese mothers who do not fit into one of the three above-mentioned groups, as well as several generations of Americans who, willingly or unwillingly, share the burden of national guilt.[9] Perhaps it would not even be unreasonable to include humankind as a whole, since the legacy of Hiroshima is an interloper that can never be fully excluded from our collective destiny.

Despite the lessons, memories, and lingering consequences
of Auschwitz and Hiroshima, it is still impossible for us, in
thinking about the effects of large-scale nuclear war, to follow Martin Buber's injunction to "imagine the real." Nevertheless, we must keep trying. As Robert Lifton has put it:

> The problem, then, is not only calling forth end-of-the-
> world imagery but in some degree mastering it, giving it
> a place in our aesthetic and moral imagination. It is
> not only futile to try, as so much of the world does, to
> dismiss images of Hiroshima and Auschwitz from hu-
> man consciousness. To attempt to do so is to deprive
> us of our own history, of what we are. In blocking our
> imaginations we impair our capacity to create the new
> forms we so desperately require. We need Hiroshima
> and Auschwitz, as we need Vietnam and our everyday
> lives, in all of their horrors, to deepen and free that
> imagination for the leaps it must make. . . . The vision of
> total annihilation makes it possible to imagine living
> under and beyond that curse.[10]

Facts and Figures

Even though facts, tables, and charts "don't bleed," they are
essential to an informed vision of the consequences of nuclear war between the superpowers. Fortunately, there are
now a substantial number of official and scholarly studies of
likely consequences. Most of these studies can be categorized
according to whether their primary concern is "limited"
conflict (confined to essentially military targets) or all-out
conflict, and to whether the audience is professional or
general.

At the general, nontechnical level, the Defense Civil Preparedness Agency of the Department of Defense has produced an information booklet entitled, *Protection in the
Nuclear Age*. Available widely in post offices and government
bureaus across the country, this publication concedes that a
nuclear attack upon the United States "remains a distinct
possibility," and recognizes that millions of Americans
would undoubtedly die in such an attack. On the more
optimistic side, however, it points out that tens of millions
who would survive the initial effects of blast and heat could
be saved through the erection of fallout shelters or by reloca-

tion to less vulnerable areas before an attack. Indeed, in reading from the introduction, one gets the reassuring impression that things might really not be all that bad, that good old-fashioned American know-how combined with neighborly cooperation would set things right within a tolerable time frame. According to the booklet:

> Much has been done to prepare for a possible nuclear attack. Public fallout shelter space has been located for millions. Civil defense systems also include warnings and communications networks, preparations to measure fallout radiation, emergency operating centers to direct lifesaving and recovery operations, emergency broadcasting stations, local governments organized for emergency operations, and large numbers of citizens trained in emergency skills.
>
> If an enemy should threaten to attack the United States, you would not be alone. The entire Nation would be mobilizing to repulse the attack, destroy the enemy, and hold down our own loss of life. Much assistance would be available to you—from local, State, and Federal governments, from the U.S. armed forces units in your area, and from your neighbors and fellow-Americans. If an attack should come, many lives would be saved through effective emergency preparations and actions.[11]

Nowhere is there any mention of incinerated flesh, psychological deformation, or of an enduring state of "death-in-life." Instead, the citizen-reader is presented with an elementary account of the effects of a nuclear bomb or missile ("intense light or flash, heat, blast, and radiation"), and an indication that the intensity of these effects depends upon a number of variable conditions—"the size and type of the weapon; how far away the explosion is; the weather conditions, sunny or rainy, windy or still; the terrain (whether the ground is flat or hilly); and the height of the explosion (high in the air, or near the ground)." These explanations are accompanied by two illustrative diagrams.[12]

Following the report, the fallout danger could be dealt with by good preattack planning and preparation. To protect themselves from these particles of pulverized earth and

DIRECT EFFECTS OF 1 MT. BLAST
(SURFACE BURST)

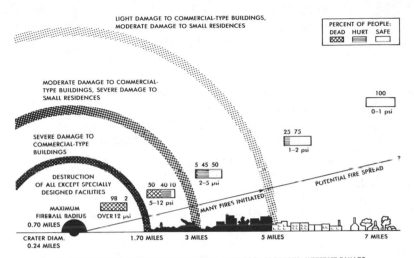

LIGHT DAMAGE TO COMMERCIAL-TYPE BUILDINGS,
MODERATE DAMAGE TO SMALL RESIDENCES

PERCENT OF PEOPLE:
DEAD HURT SAFE

MODERATE DAMAGE TO COMMERCIAL-
TYPE BUILDINGS, SEVERE DAMAGE TO
SMALL RESIDENCES

100
0–1 psi

SEVERE DAMAGE TO
COMMERCIAL-TYPE
BUILDINGS

25 75
1–2 psi

DESTRUCTION
OF ALL EXCEPT SPECIALLY
DESIGNED FACILITIES

5 45 50
2–5 psi

50 40 10
5–12 psi

MAXIMUM
FIREBALL RADIUS   98 2
0.70 MILES   OVER 12 psi

POTENTIAL FIRE SPREAD

MANY FIRES INITIATED

CRATER DIAM.
0.24 MILES   1.70 MILES   3 MILES   5 MILES   7 MILES

IF BURST IS ELEVATED TO ALTITUDE MAXIMIZING THE REACH OF BLAST DAMAGE, MODERATE DAMAGE
FROM BLAST AND INITIAL FIRES ON A CLEAR DAY ARE EXTENDED FROM 5 MILES TO 8 MILES.

DIRECT EFFECTS OF 25 MT. BLAST
(SURFACE BURST)

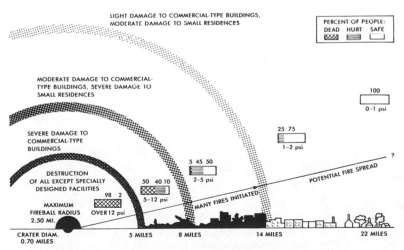

LIGHT DAMAGE TO COMMERCIAL-TYPE BUILDINGS,
MODERATE DAMAGE TO SMALL RESIDENCES

PERCENT OF PEOPLE:
DEAD HURT SAFE

MODERATE DAMAGE TO COMMERCIAL-
TYPE BUILDINGS, SEVERE DAMAGE TO
SMALL RESIDENCES

100
0–1 psi

SEVERE DAMAGE TO
COMMERCIAL-TYPE
BUILDINGS

25 75
1–2 psi

DESTRUCTION
OF ALL EXCEPT SPECIALLY
DESIGNED FACILITIES

5 45 50
2–5 psi

50 40 10
5–12 psi

MAXIMUM
FIREBALL RADIUS   98 2
2.50 MI.   OVER 12 psi

POTENTIAL FIRE SPREAD

MANY FIRES INITIATED

CRATER DIAM.
0.70 MILES   5 MILES   8 MILES   14 MILES   22 MILES

IF BURST IS ELEVATED TO ALTITUDE MAXIMIZING THE REACH OF BLAST DAMAGE, MODERATE DAMAGE
FROM BLAST AND INITIAL FIRES ON A CLEAR DAY ARE EXTENDED FROM 14 MILES TO 22 MILES.

other debris that have been sucked into the nuclear cloud and contaminated by the radioactive gasses produced by the explosion, Americans are urged to retreat to a fallout shelter. Detailed plans for building such a shelter are offered, as is advice for "shelter living."

A later chapter deals with what is described as "The Relocation Option," the temporary relocation of people from high-risk areas to safer areas during periods of international crisis. High-risk areas are defined as metropolitan areas of 50,000 or more in population or areas near major military installations. The safer areas, which would become the "host areas" during emergency relocation, are defined as the surrounding small-town or rural areas.

> Your Federal Government and many State and local governments are currently planning for the orderly relocation of people in time of an international crisis. These plans call for (1) allocating people from high-risk areas to go to appropriate low-risk host areas for reception and care, and for (2) developing and improvising fallout protection in the host areas.[13]

Moreover, citizens can take heart that a detailed set of instructions and a checklist for supplies is provided.[14] And in what is perhaps the most pathetically humorous prescription ever offered by a government to its citizens, the booklet cautions:

> If you get caught in a traffic jam, turn off your engine, remain in your car, listen for official instructions, and be patient. Do not get out of the line to find an alternate route. All routes will be crowded.[15]

To assist further in the full and rapid recovery of the nation, the Federal Preparedness Agency of the General Services Administration has made provisions for a National Defense Executive Reserve (NDER)—"a corps of talented citizen leaders ready to answer the President's call to serve in the event of emergency." The NDER, with about 3,500 designated members and an ultimate goal of 5,000 members, comprises executives selected from various sectors of the civilian economy and from government. It is assumed that in the event of a major national emergency such as a nuclear war, the Federal departments and agencies that sponsor Executive Reserve units would furnish each of their reservists with specific instructions indicating where and when to report as well as the nature of particular responsibilities. Moreover, in serving his country after a nuclear attack, the reservist would not even have to worry about receiving a proper salary for his extraordinary services. According to the FPA publication, *Ready to Serve the President: 5000 Executives*, when called to duty in an emergency, "the Reservist will become a Federal employee and may serve on a salary basis under the pay schedules then in effect."[16]

Such reassurances about contingency plans seem inappropriate in view of our knowledge of the effects of the very small Hiroshima bomb. Instead of building upon the understanding that a nuclear exchange with the Soviet Union would totally shatter the fabric of American society, these plans suggest it will be possible to continue business-as-usual under the direction of a "reservist" government.

Furthermore, to defend the reasonableness of civil defense measures, as is done in such government publications as *Protection in the Nuclear Age*, is a deception of the American people, since, in actuality, there is no real American civil defense program. In other words, citizens are encouraged to believe in the presence of procedures and personnel for postattack recovery and support that do not even exist. At the moment, the American civil defense "program" is merely a paper organization, tying a pitiful handful of command posts and underground federal regional centers into what is supposed to be a "lifeline network for survival" in the event of nuclear attack. The civil preparedness budget has become so paltry that the agency has not even been able to replace the millions of dollars worth of food now deteriorating in shelter areas. Hence, in the event of nuclear attack, Americans are being advised to run to whatever shelters may exist and *bring their own food.*[17]

It is folly to encourage public faith in a nonexistent civil defense effort.

With its ideas to evacuate "high-risk" metropolitan areas before any threatened nuclear missile attack, and by its claims that a well-coordinated plan for recovery would

WHAT TO DO BEFORE YOU LEAVE A HIGH-RISK AREA

1. Get ample supply of any prescription medicines and special foods.

2. Collect all your important papers and package them preferably in plastic wrappers in metal container (tool box, fishing-tackle box, etc.).

3. Check home for security; see that all locks are secure; store valuables being left behind (silverware, etc.,) in a safe place.

4. Close all window blinds, shades, and drapes to help prevent fires from the heat wave of a nuclear explosion.

5. If you use your car, be sure you have enough gasoline, and prepare to take shovels, picks, hammers, and work gloves—all will be needed to help improvise fallout shelter.

6. Stay tuned to your local TV or radio station for instructions on relocating if so directed by government officials.

7. Go over all instructions with your family so that all will understand what to do.

WHAT TO TAKE WITH YOU IN RELOCATING TO A SAFER AREA

(Take all these items if using your car. If using public transportation, take those marked "X.")

Clothing and Bedding
- ☐ X work gloves
- ☐ X work clothes
- ☐ X extra underclothing
- ☐ X outerwear (depending on season
- ☐ X rain garments
- ☐ X extra pair of shoes
- ☐ X extra socks or stockings
- ☐ sleeping bags and/or
- ☐ blankets and sheets

Food and Utensils
- ☐ Take all the food you can carry (particularly canned or dried food requiring little preparation.)
- ☐ water
- ☐ thermos jug or plastic bottles
- ☐ bottle and can opener
- ☐ eating utensils
- ☐ plastic or paper plates, cups, and napkins.
- ☐ plastic and paper bags.
- ☐ X candles and matches
- ☐ plastic drop cloth

Personal, Safety, Sanitation, and
Medical Supplies
- ☐ X Battery operated (transistor) radios, extra batteries
- ☐ X flashlight, extra batteries
- ☐ X soap
- ☐ X shaving articles
- ☐ X sanitary napkins
- ☐ X detergent
- ☐ X towels and washcloths
- ☐ toilet paper
- ☐ emergency toilet
- ☐ garbage can
- ☐ newspapers
- ☐ first aid kit
- ☐ X special medication (insulin, heart tablets, or other)
- ☐ X toothbrush and toothpaste

Baby Supplies
- ☐ X diapers
- ☐ X bottles and nipples
- ☐ X milk or formula
- ☐ X powder
- ☐ X rubber sheeting, etc.

Tools for Constructing a Fallout
Shelter
- ☐ pick ax
- ☐ shovel
- ☐ saw
- ☐ hammer
- ☐ broom
- ☐ ax
- ☐ crowbar
- ☐ nails and screws
- ☐ screw driver
- ☐ wrench

Important Papers
- ☐ X Social Security Card
- ☐ X Deeds
- ☐ X Insurance Policies
- ☐ X Stocks and Bonds
- ☐ X Will
- ☐ X Saving Accounts Books
- ☐ X Credit Cards and Currency

WHAT NOT TO TAKE WITH YOU IN RELOCATING TO SAFER AREA

Do not Take
- ☐ FIREARMS—(guns of any kind)
- ☐ NARCOTICS
- ☐ ALCOHOL BEVERAGES

quickly transfuse normalcy into the veins of a nuclear devastated body politic, the government of the United States
reveals a severe misunderstanding of both what is feasible
and what the postwar environment would be like. For any
New Yorker who has known the traffic of his city and the
cynicism of his fellow citizens, the claim that an effective
and orderly evacuation of Manhattan could take place during a crisis situation would produce side-splitting laughter.
When such claims are joined with "Relocation Checklists"
urging the transport of sanitary napkins and credit cards,
they descend to the level of absurdity.

The civil defense situation in the Soviet Union appears
vastly superior. While we, according to General Daniel Graham, former head of the Defense Intelligence Agency, would
lose "110 million in a first strike nuclear attack," the Soviets
could be expected "to lose about 10 million." In short, says
Graham, the Soviets "have a civil defense system well on the
way to protecting all but 10 percent of the population."[18]

In Moscow, Col. Gen. Alexander Altunin, a deputy minister of defense, heads what looks like an extremely sophisticated civil defense program that blankets the immense area
of the Soviet Union. There, civil defense training is manda-
tory, and plans for evacuation and sheltering-in-place are
supported by enormous amounts of money. If deterrence
fails, the Soviets will be able to fall back on a civil defense
program that has absorbed more than $1 billion a year, and
which supports a permanent organization of 72,000 people
engaged in devising measures for dispersing populations,
constructing blast resistant buildings, stockpiling food ra-
tions, and providing training for emergencies beginning in
grade school.[19]

Nevertheless, despite the superior Soviet civil defense system, the consequences of an American nuclear retaliation
would still be intolerable to them, since the damage that
surviving U.S. forces could inflict would involve not only
blast effects, but also thermal radiation and ionizing radiation. The fact that the population and economic resources
of the Soviet Union are concentrated in a very small number of major urban centers (about one-third of the population and two-thirds of the industrial capacity are concen-

trated in the country's 200 largest cities), makes the Soviets more vulnerable to such effects. Indeed, even if Soviet evacuation could reduce the number of prompt fatalities, the American retaliation would still destroy the entire industrial structure of the Soviet Union as well as that nation's essential medical, technical, social, political, legal, and educational bases.[20]

In the United States, civil defense spending has declined from a high point of $207.6 million during the 1961 Berlin crisis to $97 million in 1979. The director of the Civil Defense Preparedness Agency, John F. Davis, would like the figure raised to $123 million to give the Americans a greater chance of survival.[21] Of course, such a chance can never be afforded by civil defense, however generously funded.

Not only are the prescriptions for American civil defense hopelessly off the mark, they are also inconsistent with this country's avowed strategic doctrine, according to which a general nuclear war between the superpowers is unthinkable; we cannot fight and win such a nuclear war; and mutual deterrence is the only rational strategy for survival.

The prescriptions for Soviet civil defense, on the other hand, while based on grievous underestimates of U.S. retaliatory capabilities, are entirely consistent with their view that superpower nuclear war would not necessarily be total in its destructiveness, and that such war could be fought and won. According to Richard Pipes, professor of history at Harvard University and chairman of "Team B"—a committee appointed in 1976 by the President's Foreign Intelligence Advisory Board to prepare an alternative to the CIA estimate of Soviet strategic objectives—the classic dictum of Clausewitz (war is politics pursued by other means) is still at the heart of Soviet strategic doctrine. Says Pipes, this doctrine, which spells the rejection of the whole basis on which U.S. strategy has come to rest, stipulates that "thermonuclear war is not suicidal, it can be fought and won, and thus resort to war must not be ruled out."[22]

The Soviet view of "unacceptable damage," it is suggested, is different from that of the United States. Soviet decision makers appear prepared to absorb much higher levels of nuclear devastation. This is due in part to the Soviet's primary concern for the protection of "cadres"—political, military, industrial, and labor leaders—rather than of ordinary civilians, and they believe these cadres could be protected even if the USSR's cities sustained total destruction. This Soviet willingness to absorb greater degrees of nuclear punishment must also be understood in the light of that country's historical uniqueness. In the second world war, Russia lost 20 million people, 12 percent of its total population. Yet, it emerged, as we well know, in stronger form than before. According to Professor Pipes:

> Allowing for the population growth which has occurred since then, this experience suggests that as of today the USSR could absorb the loss of 30 million of its people and be no worse off, in terms of human casualities, than it had been at the conclusion of World War II. In other words, all of the USSR's multimillion cities could be destroyed without trace of survivors, and, provided that its essential cadres had been saved, it would emerge less hurt in terms of casualties than it was in 1945.[23]

Although Professor Pipes's conclusions may be technically correct, they ignore the wider implications of the effects of nuclear war. Even if the Soviet Union were to emerge from a strategic exchange with the United States "less hurt in terms of casualties than it was in 1945," this does not mean that it would emerge "less hurt" in other terms. Today's Soviet economic and industrial base is almost immeasurably more complex and vital than it was in 1945; hence, the Soviet capacity for postwar recovery would be far more limited. Since the centrally planned economy of the Soviet Union today is concentrated in a limited number of facilities, it has many vulnerable "choke points." Should these facilities be destroyed by American missiles, the return to status quo ante bellum would be much more difficult than it was after World War II. Indeed, even disregarding these choke points, recovery from a nuclear war with the United States would entail a return to far more advanced conditions of development than was necessary in 1945. There was, in short, far less of an advanced industrial base to restore after the second world war than there would be today.

More Facts and Figures

What, exactly, could be expected in the wake of a nuclear exchange between the superpowers involving the direct targeting of civilian populations? In a recent article, Bernard T. Feld, the distinguished professor of physics at MIT, calculates that even if SALT II ceilings prevail, the amount of explosive power deployed in strategic nuclear weapons by the superpowers will amount to some 15,000,000,000 tons of TNT (approximately 3,000 megatons in 15,000 warheads for the United States, and about 10,000 to 15,000 megatons in 8,000 to 10,000 warheads for the Soviet Union). According to Dr. Feld:

> An exchange involving some substantial fraction of these could promptly destroy some 75 and 60 percent, respectively, of the populations (the urban fractions) of the United States and the Soviet Union, and upwards of 50 percent of the remaining rural inhabitants through the subsequent fallout.[24]

Dr. Feld goes on to describe the effects of fallout:

> Fallout is, of course, not confined by national boundaries. Nations bordering on the antagonists would be profoundly damaged as well, although they might escape the total annihilation that would be the lot of the superpowers in the case of a full-scale strategic nuclear exchange. But the rest of the world would not escape either. There would be worldwide contamination of the atmosphere in the event of such an exchange, as a consequence of the fission products and induced radioactivity that would be distributed both in the elemental form and on dust carried aloft in the expanding fireball and which would be widely dispersed by normal atmospheric circulation.[25]

In one of the earliest authoritative treatments of the consequences of nuclear war, biologist Tom Stonier asked the question, "What would happen if a 20 megaton thermonuclear weapon were exploded on New York City?" His answer is summarized as follows:

> As mass fires raze the destroyed city below, fallout be-

gins to descend from above, poisoning the surrounding countryside. One bomb might endanger the lives of people in a 4000 square mile area. Such a large thermonuclear device exploded in midtown Manhattan, for example, would probably kill 6,000,000 out of New York City's 8,000,000 inhabitants, and produce an additional 1,000,000 or more deaths beyond the city limits.[26]

Dr. Stonier also considers the probable effects of a full-scale nuclear attack on the nation as a whole. He forecasts the following scenario:

Even before the threat of fallout radiation completely subsided the country could be thrown into a state of economic and social chaos—including serious outbreaks of famine and disease—and the ensuing shock, loss of morale, and weakened leadership would further hamper relief operations and impede rehabilitation. The effects of this disruption could persist for decades, just as would the somatic damage inflicted on people exposed to radiation. Even individuals who escape the hazards of the explosion and who are themselves uninjured by radiation might carry a legacy of genetic damage, which they would then pass from generation to generation. Perhaps most uncertain, and potentially most disastrous, are the ecological consequences, the imbalances in nature itself, which might well create the preconditions for the disappearance of American civilization as we know it.[27]

Fortunately, much of the uncertainty lamented by Stonier in 1964 has now been dispelled. In 1975, a study entitled *Long-Term Worldwide Effects of Multiple Nuclear-Weapons Detonations* was prepared by a special committee of the National Research Council, National Academy of Sciences, in response to a request by Dr. Fred C. Iklé, former director of the U.S. Arms Control and Disarmament Agency. Its point of departure, according to Dr. Philip Handler, president of the National Academy of Sciences, is

a horrendous calamity: a hypothetical exchange involving the detonation of many nuclear weapons. In the worst case considered, about one half of all nuclear weapons in current strategic arsenals, viz., 500 to 1000 weapons of yield 10 to 20 megatons each and 4000 to

5000 lesser [sic!] weapons with yields of 1 or 2 megatons each, i.e., a total of 10^4 megatons (10,000,000,000
tons) of TNT-equivalent are exchanged among the participants. No report can portray the enormity, the utter
horror which must befall the targeted areas and adjoin-
ing territories. Nor does this report so attempt.[28]

What the report does attempt to portray are the long-
term, worldwide effects following the exchange of 10,000
megatons of explosive power in the northern hemisphere, in
a plausible mix of low- and high-yield weapons, and at a
variety of altitudes of detonation. Merely acknowledging
the "unimaginable holocaust" that would occur in the primarily afflicted nations, the report confines its attention to
possible long-term effects on more distant populations and
ecosystems, with special reference to the atmosphere and
climate, natural terrestrial ecosystems, agriculture and animal husbandry, the aquatic environment, and both somatic
and genetic effects upon humans.

Although the report concludes that the biosphere and the
species, Homo sapiens, would survive the hypothetical strategic exchange,[29] it suggests that civilization as we know it
might not. The report deliberately does not address the social, political, or economic consequences of the hypothesized nuclear exchange, which it characterizes as "entirely
unpredictable" effects of "worldwide terror", but rather the
interrelated physical and biological aspects of such a
calamity.

The likely long-term physical and biological effects on
civilization would include temperature changes, major
global climactic changes; contamination of foods by radionuclides; worldwide disease epidemics in crops and domesticated animals because of ionizing radiation; shortening of
growing seasons in certain areas; irreversible injury to sensitive aquatic species; possible long-term carcinogenesis
due to inhalation of plutonium particles; some radiation-
induced developmental anomalies in persons in utero at the
time of detonations; an increase in skin cancer incidence of
about 10 percent, which could increase by as much as a
factor of 3 if the ozone depletion were to rise from 50 to 70
percent; severe sunburn in temperate zones and snow blind-

ness in northern regions in the short-term; and an increased incidence of genetic disease that would not be limited to the offspring of the exposed generation, but would extend over many generations.

The participants in the six separate committees who produced the NAS report caution their readers about the limitations of the data upon which their conclusions rest. Their predictions might, in fact, represent only the "tip of the iceberg." It may even be the case that the magnitude of the war postulated in their report is too small. Were the superpowers to exchange between 50,000 and 100,000 megatons of nuclear explosives, rather than the 10,000 megatons assumed by the report, global climatological changes would certainly imperil the very survival of humankind. Moreover, according to Professor Feld:

> It is becoming frighteningly plausible to consider the level of nuclear war that would represent the end of humankind: the detonation of one million megatons of nuclear explosives (which may be defined as one "Beach"[30]) would result in a global irradiation of around 5000 rad.[31] It is very difficult, in the present anarchic world, to be sanguine about the fact that we are now about one-tenth of the way toward the possibility of this ultimate insult (used also in its medical sense) that would certainly spell the end of humankind on planet Earth.[32]

Another factor which makes the consequences of nuclear war between the superpowers difficult to predict is the potential for interactions between individual effects. This point is skillfully summarized in a publication of the U.S. Arms Control and Disarmament Agency, *Worldwide Effects of Nuclear War . . . Some Perspectives:*

> In attempting to project the after-effects of a major nuclear war, we have considered separately the various kinds of damage that could occur. It is also quite possible, however, that interactions might take place among these effects, so that one type of damage would couple with another to produce new and unexpected hazards. For example, we can assess individually the consequences of heavy worldwide radiation fallout and in-

creased solar ultraviolet, but we do not know whether the two acting together might significantly increase human, animal, or plant susceptibility to disease. We can conclude that massive dust injection into the stratosphere, even greater in scale than Krakatoa, is unlikely by itself to produce significant climactic and environmental change, but we cannot rule out interactions with other phenomena, such as ozone depletion, which might produce utterly unexpected results. We have come to realize that nuclear weapons can be as unpredictable as they are deadly in their effects. Despite some 30 years of development and study, there is still much that we do not know. This is particularly true when we consider the global effects of a large-scale nuclear war.[33]

Limited Nuclear War:
The Strategy of Controlled Annihilation

During the past few years, a great deal of attention has been directed to the idea of "limited nuclear war," whereby nuclear exchanges are confined to military targets. Although formulations of nuclear strategy based on "flexible response" rather than "massive retaliation" are nothing new,[34] the idea of limited nuclear war received especially strong and expanded support on 4 March 1974. On that date, former Secretary of Defense James R. Schlesinger gave testimony before Congress supporting an American capability of reacting to a limited nuclear attack with selected "counterforce" strikes against enemy military installations. According to Schlesinger, such strikes would reduce the chances for escalation into all-out strategic exchanges, thereby producing fewer civilian casualties and increasing the credibility of American nuclear threats.

What are the probable effects of a limited nuclear war? What sorts of casualties might be expected in the wake of so-called "counterforce" attacks against military targets envisioned in this doctrine of flexible response? Would the costs of limited nuclear war really be "limited," or would they be as unacceptable as the expected consequences of general nuclear war between the superpowers?

In his 1974 Defense Department Report, Schlesinger remarked that nuclear attacks against American military installations might result in "relatively few civilian casualties." Subsequently, on 11 September 1974, the Subcommittee on Arms Control of the Senate Committee on Foreign Relations met in executive session with Dr. Schlesinger to look into the probable consequences of nuclear attacks against military installations in the United States. The former defense secretary took a remarkably sanguine view, claiming that as few as 800,000 casualties could result from an attack on U.S. ICBM silos.[35]

Since Schlesinger's conclusions generated considerable skepticism among several senators, the Office of Technology Assessment (OTA) of the U.S. Congress was asked to evaluate the Defense Department calculations. In response to this invitation, the OTA convened an ad hoc panel of experts,[36] chaired by Dr. Jerome Wiesner, which returned with the following summary of conclusions:

> The panel members examined the results of the analyses of nuclear attacks which were given the Senate Foreign Relations Committee by the Department of Defense, and the assumptions which went into these analyses, in some detail. They concluded that the casualties calculated were substantially too low for the attacks in question as a result of a lack of attention to intermediate and long-term effects. They also concluded that the studies did not adequately reflect the large uncertainties inherent in any attempt to determine the civilian damage which might result from a nuclear attack.
>
> The panel could not determine from the DOD testimony any consistent set of hypothetical Soviet objectives in the strikes analyzed. The attacks studied were evidently not designed to maximize destruction of U.S. ICBM's and bombers even though all ICBM's and large numbers of bomber bases were attacked. It seems apparent, however, even from the data now available, that if the Soviets used weapons now deployed or under development in an attack designed to maximize damage to U.S. strategic offensive forces, they would inflict massive damage on U.S. society. On the other hand, if the Soviet objective was something other than a desire to maximize damage to military targets, this objective

was never made clear. It is evident that a small number of nuclear weapons could be detonated over isolated areas in the U.S. without causing significant civilian damage. It is not clear, however, that the Soviet Union could benefit in any way from such an attack particularly since they would be running the risk of a massive U.S. response. The panel's assessment of the material presented does not, therefore, intend to imply that its members feel that the attacks analyzed are sensible or realistic.

The panel also noticed that the material examined did not contain any estimates of the intermediate or long-term effects of attacks smaller than a "comprehensive military attack" although this was requested in the original inquiries of the Foreign Relations Committee. The panel was informed that the Office of the Secretary of Defense had been contacted about this issue and had responded by saying that this analysis had not been done and would require several weeks or months to perform. To the extent that policy will be based on this analysis, the panel finds this to be a serious deficiency particularly since the secondary effects of limited attacks on relatively remote installations are likely to represent a more substantial fraction of the total effects of such an attack than would be the case in a large attack near population centers.

The panel did not feel that it had enough information about DOD techniques for determining long-term effects to comment on the adequacy of these techniques.

While the panel believes that it is important that a realistic assessment of civilian effects be available for analysis of proposed changes in our target strategy and our attitude toward counterforce, they wish to emphasize that such analysis is only one and perhaps not the most important element of a much larger set of considerations affecting policy in this area. Such issues include: the effect, if any, on U.S. weapons acquisition, particularly weapons for hard-target counterforce attacks; the extent to which the new strategies could be executed without escalating into general nuclear war; the effect on deterrence of nuclear war; the degree to which such policy increases or decreases our reliance on nuclear weapons; the extent to which it raises or lowers the threshold of nuclear first use; and the effect on the perception of our allies about the credibility of our commitment to them. The panel recommends, therefore, that the Foreign Relations Committee ask for the additional analysis of casualties outlined in the following section only if it intends to engage in a discussion of these other issues.[37]

To reconcile the differences between the former defense chief's estimates of the consequences of limited nuclear war and the views expressed by the OTA panel of experts, Senator John Sparkman—then chairman of the Commtitee on Foreign Relations—asked Schlesinger to "redo the analysis using more realistic assumptions."[38] In a cooperative effort, the Department of Defense joined with the Senate Subcommittee on Arms Control, International Organizations, and Security Agreements, and with the Office of Technology Assessment to reassess the estimates of expected casualties and damage resulting from postulated Soviet nuclear attacks on selected military targets in the United States. Ultimately, the Department of Defense completed new calculations which show that under certain circumstances, an attack upon U.S. ICBM silos could result in casualties of between 3 and 22 million as opposed to the 800,000 to 6.7 million previously cited by Dr. Schlesinger.[39]

What, exactly, would be the impact of this "limited" number of casualties on American society? According to Dr. James V. Neel, professor of human genetics at the University of Michigan and professor in the Department of Internal Medicine at the University of Michigan Medical School, one of the most unsettling components of this impact would be on medical facilities. Working with a figure of 10 million fatalities from an attack on American missile silos, the midpoint in the revised range of estimates provided by the Department of Defense, Dr. Neel has hypothesized a situation in which two-thirds of the estimated casualties die at once, leaving some 3 million persons with fatal injuries consistent with survival for weeks and months, and another 2 million persons with serious injuries who will survive with adequate medical care. To convey the impact of this many casualties upon the American medical establishment, Dr.

Neel, who worked at length with survivors of the atomic
attacks on Hiroshima and Nagasaki, and who served as
director of the Child Health Survey in Hiroshima from 1958
to 1959, underscores the lack of comparability between the
incidence of nonfatal injuries during peacetime and the
simultaneous occurrence of 5 million casualties from atomic
weapons. According to Dr. Neel:

> Most of you have some familiarity with the problem of
> severe burns. The major medical center with which I
> am associated at the University of Michigan has a special
> burn unit which receives referrals from all over the
> State; it can handle exactly 10 severe, acute patients at a
> time. Try to visualize the problem of distributing the
> burn casualties from atomic weapons throughout the
> United States so they will receive adequate care. You are
> less familiar with radiation sickness. Its principal mani-
> festations result from destruction of the blood-forming
> elements, resulting in hemorrhage and tendency to in-
> fection. Treatment is with antibiotics and transfusions.
> The need for whole blood will far, far outrun the supply,
> especially given the burn situation, and people will sim-
> ply die untreated. I cannot accept the DOD statement
> (page 51, hearings of September 11, 1974) that: "Na-
> tionally, the effect of the attack on medical care re-
> sources, facilities, doctors and supplies would be
> slight."[40]

Dr. Sidney D. Drell, deputy director of the Stanford University Linear Accelerator and a consultant at Los Alamos
Scientific Laboratory perceives the situation in these terms:

> The difficulties imposed on a society that is trying to
> recover in the face of vast casualty levels, with food and
> water shortages and insufficient medical attention, are
> simply unknown quantities. Our political and military
> leaders have much greater humility in predicting levels
> of destruction, devastation, and death in conventional
> non-nuclear conflicts than in nuclear ones because there
> is a vast body of experience to humble them. And as
> destructive as were the unforseen consequences of our
> Vietnam policy, in a nuclear conflict the scale of our
> errors will be much, much greater and their conse-
> quences ever so much graver.[41]

These prognostications and speculations pertain to a limited nuclear war. The question remains whether it is reasonable militarily to assume such a limited attack. Even if such attacks hold out the "promise" of relatively low casualty levels, there is little reason to believe that anything short of an all-out nuclear assault would make military sense to the Soviets. According to testimony by Dr. Drell, in order to carry out a militarily effective attack against American ICBMs, one that would destroy about 800 out of 1,054 or 80 percent, the Soviets would have to unleash an attack which would engender approximately 18.3 million American fatalities. And even so extensive a counterforce assault would not be entirely disabling, since the remaining American ICBMs would still constitute a "healthy robust retaliatory force."[42]

The United States has developed an elaborate "counterforce doctrine" that not only greatly understates the potential effects of limited nuclear war, but also ignores the primary fact that such war makes no military sense. There is, in fact, no clear picture as to what the Soviet Union might gain from the kinds of limited counterforce attacks cited in Department of Defense analyses. By attacking U.S. ICBMs and bomber bases, while leaving the still invulnerable SLBMs at sea untouched, the Soviets would be unable to prevent an assuredly destructive American strategic retaliation. That is why the first report of the Nuclear Effects Panel states: "The panel could not determine from the DOD testimony any consistent set of hypothetical Soviet objectives in the strikes analyzed."[43]

Indeed, everything we know about Soviet military strategy indicates that it has no concern whatsoever for the very idea of limited nuclear war. In the Soviet view, all nuclear conflict would necessarily be total. It follows that once the nuclear firebreak has been crossed, it is exceedingly unlikely that the conflict would remain limited. This point was hinted at by Henry Kissinger, when, in 1965, he wrote: "No one knows how governments or people will react to a nuclear explosion under conditions where both sides possess vast arsenals."[44] And it was understood by Robert McNamara, who claimed that once even tactical nuclear weapons are employed, "you can't keep them limited; you'll destroy everything."[45]

Yet, while the prudent course would be to assume that any onset of a nuclear exchange would quickly become total, the Department of Defense has been reluctant to abandon its flexible response policy, with its attendant emphases on limited nuclear war-fighting and counterforce targeting. Although it has now been widely acknowledged by large numbers of prominent scientists outside the government that once a nuclear exchange is commenced, it would become very difficult if not impossible to verify yields, sizes, numbers, and types of nuclear weapons employed,[46] the Department of Defense continues to cling to the notion of "limited exchanges" conducted in "a deliberate and controlled fashion."[47] In his Annual Defense Department Report for FY 1978, former Secretary of Defense Donald H. Rumsfeld insistently defends the idea that a full-scale strategic response would be distinguishable from direct attacks on populations, and that counterforce nuclear exchanges between the superpowers need not escalate to all-out attacks on cities.

> In every case considered, both the short-term and the longer-run collateral damage from attacks on a comprehensive list of military targets (including ICBM silos) has been dramatically lower than the fatalities from direct attacks on population targets. It must be emphasized, however, that the results, even in limited and controlled exchanges, could be appalling. [An improvement, at least, from the times of former Secretary Schlesinger's original estimates of the effects of limited nuclear war.] They could involve the potential for millions of fatalities, even though the distinction between 10 million and 100 million fatalities is great and worth preserving.[48]

On the basis of the evidence considered above there is surely nothing to support the contention that the distinction between limited and all-out nuclear war "is great and worth preserving." Not only would 10 million fatalities be totally outside the boundaries of "acceptability," it is a figure suggested by a military doctrine that is totally alien to the Soviet superpower.

NATO, Warsaw Pact, and the
Neutron Bomb

A wave of Soviet tanks and armored personnel carriers rolls across the northern German plain. Unable to stem the tide, NATO generals request permission to use tactical nuclear weapons. According to an alliance agreement, the President of the U.S. must give his assent before battlefield nukes can be fired. He does. Scores of heavy artillery pieces are aimed at the invaders. Nuclear devices, each packing the equivalent of ten kilotons (10,000 tons) worth of TNT, halt the aggressors. But in the process, West Germany's cities and factories are leveled, and civilian casualties run into the millions. An American military spokesman, paraphrasing another from the Viet Nam War era, explains, "We had to destroy Germany in order to save it."[49]

To avoid such a scenario, the United States has considered preparations for equipping NATO commanders with the neutron bomb, a nuclear weapon that can allegedly strengthen NATO nuclear deterrence because of its ability to destroy advancing forces without devastating property. Should deterrence fail, it is conceivable that a nuclear war between the superpowers could be fought by NATO and Warsaw Pact forces in Western Europe using neutron-bomb weapons.

The neutron bomb, deliverable by artillery shells or Lance missile warheads, is a relatively small thermonuclear weapon that is designed to minimize the fraction of energy going into blast and heat. Upon detonating, large quantities of radioactive neutrons would be released, killing people but leaving buildings and other structures unaffected. Far more than tactical nuclear weapons, the neutron bomb is regarded as a precision, battlefield weapon. Consequently, it has been described by the Pentagon as a significantly more credible NATO deterrent than the existing arsenal of tactical nuclear weapons.

Yet, as the West Germans, whose country would be the most likely site of enhanced radiation warfare, have indicated, the neutron bomb "is by far not as harmless as some of the planners for an atomic war are suggesting."[50] For many, the alleged benefits of a device that kills humans with particular gruesomeness, but preserves property, represents only the most perverse ideal of military progress. Enhanced radiation warheads would produce appreciable fallout from the fission trigger (the neutron bomb is triggered by a minimum-yield fission explosion), while blast and heat would not be eliminated entirely. But the critical effects of this weapon would be the deaths spawned by intense radiation.

The neutron bomb, or ER warhead, would release about 80 percent of its yield in the form of very high doses of neutrons and gamma radiation. Understood in terms of the U.S. Army's new radiation casualty criteria, this means that three basic categories of "incapacitation" would be created, with each category defined according to the extent of the absorbed dose of ionizing radiation. The basic unit of this absorbed dose is known as the *rad*.

For persons who receive between 17,000 to 19,000 rads, incapacitation would occur within five minutes and remain until death occurs within one day. For persons who receive between 7,000 and 9,000 rads, incapacitation would occur within five minutes and remain until death occurs in one to two days. All persons who have received between 7,000 and 19,000 rads would have suffered "Immediate Permanent Incapacitation (IP)."

For persons who receive between 2,500 and 3,500 rads, incapacitation would occur within five minutes of exposure, and remain for 30 to 45 minutes. Thereafter, they would "recover, but remain functionally impaired until death, which will occur within four to six days." Such persons would have suffered "Immediate Transient Incapacitation (IT)."

For persons who receive between 500 to 800 rads, "functional impairment" would occur within two hours of exposure, whereupon some would survive with medical treatment, but the majority would remain functionally impaired until death took hold in several weeks. Such persons would have been designated to have suffered "Latent Lethality (LL)."[51]

What all of this means in simple, human terms is agonizingly slow, painful, mass death.

Moreover, in estimating the effects of neutron bomb warfare between NATO and Warsaw Pact forces, we must also include the effects of "ordinary" nuclear exchanges that might ultimately ensue. This is the case because once enhanced radiation weapons have been used, it is extremely likely that escalation to strategic weapons could not be prevented. Indeed, the prospect of such escalation is probably much greater with the neutron bomb than with existing tactical forces because the former type of weapon is apt to have a more corrosive effect on the barrier between nuclear and conventional conflict. That effect is, after all, the basis of its presumably greater credibility as a theater nuclear deterrent. Or, as Bernard Feld put it:

> Therein lies the real objection to the neutron bomb. By contributing to the illusion that nuclear weapons are usable; by eroding the barrier against any first-use of a nuclear weapon; by increasing reliance on them and lowering the threshold of their introduction into possible conflict, the deployment of neutron bombs could greatly increase the chances of the nuclear war whose avoidance must be the raison d'etre of the most responsible diplomacy of the superpowers.[52]

Sapere Aude!

Sapere aude! "Dare to know!" This motto for the eighteenth century period of Enlightenment suggested by the philosopher Kant acquires a special meaning in the late twentieth century study of nuclear war. Just as repression of the fear of death by individual human beings can occasion activities that impair the forces of self-preservation,[53] so can nations impair their prospects for survival by insulating themselves from reasonable fears of collective disintegration. While it is true that the fear of death must be tempered in both individual and national drives lest it create paralysis, to deny the affect of such fear altogether is to make the threat of extinction *more imminent*. This point has been stated tersely by Ernest Becker, the distinguished author of *The Denial of Death:* "Reality and fear go together naturally."[54]

If it is to serve any useful purpose, the fear generated by our straightforward look at the consequences of nuclear war between the superpowers must lead us away from that rarified and bloodless brand of "realism" that is still dear to the hearts of "targeteers" and strategic savants. Instead of sanitized "think-tank" analyses of the effects of nuclear conflict that reek of the very unreality they seek to dispel, we must begin to prevent the "unthinkable" by highlighting its flesh and blood costs. Such euphemistic notions as "limited nuclear war," "collateral damage," "countervalue" and "counterforce" strategies, "enhanced radiation warfare," "incapacitation," and "functional impairment" are dangerous to the cause of peace, not only because they are deceptions, but because they also help to make the currency of nuclear war-fighting valid coin. To counter the strategic mythmakers whose thinking about the unthinkable has etherized an unwitting humanity into accepting the unacceptable, we must not only face the danger of superpower nuclear war squarely, but prepare to rail against it with rage and partisanship.

5 The Consequences of Nuclear War through Proliferation

At that moment ... there flashed into my mind a passage from the Bhagavad-Gita, the sacred book of the Hindus: "I am become Death, the Shatterer of Worlds!"

J. Robert Oppenheimer

If the consequences of a nuclear war between the superpowers seem beyond the pale of human endurance, then the consequences of nuclear war through proliferation call forth an entirely new paradigm of death. We must conceive not only *gigadeath* (death in the billions), but also the final triumph of meaninglessness and discontinuity. We need a framework for interpreting and absorbing the vision of nuclear obliteration because, with the proliferation of nuclear weapons, the consequences of a nuclear war could be effectively boundless.

Of course, the consequences of a nuclear war through proliferation need not necessarily signal worldwide devastation. While the spread of nuclear weapons makes such devastation much more probable, it also creates new arenas for local or regional nuclear conflict. What might happen in these new arenas, therefore, must be treated as one set of consequences of nuclear war through proliferation.

Indeed, in appraising the effects of nuclear war that might arise through proliferation, we must examine the entire spectrum of nuclear conflict possibilities, excepting only those exchanges which would be confined to members of the existing nuclear club. These possibilities range from a nu-

152

clear attack by a new nuclear power against a nonnuclear one, to a two-country strategic exchange involving secondary nuclear powers, to an all-out system-wide nuclear war. In between these possibilities, we must focus on nuclear exchanges among several secondary nuclear powers; nuclear exchanges between secondary nuclear powers and one of the superpowers; nuclear exchanges between secondary nuclear powers and both of the superpowers; and nuclear exchanges between secondary nuclear powers plus one of the superpowers on the one side and other secondary nuclear powers on the opposing side. Let us begin this appraisal with the most devastating possibility of all—worldwide nuclear war.

Exchanges of One Million Megatons of Nuclear Explosives, or "On The Beach"

If the proliferation of nuclear weapons should lead to a nuclear war involving the exchange of one million megatons of nuclear explosives, the world would probably experience what Nevil Shute described in his modern classic, *On the Beach*. Assuming a global irradiation of around 500 rads,[1] those who would not succumb immediately to the effects of blast and heat would survive no longer than a few weeks. Dwarfing even the "horrendous calamity" postulated in the NAS report, *Long-Term Worldwide Effects of Multiple Nuclear-Weapons Detonations*, the effects of such a war would defy not only our imaginations of disaster, but our customary measurements as well.

On the technical side, the consequences of system-wide nuclear war may be evaluated in terms of atmospheric effects, effects on natural terrestrial ecosystems, effects on managed terrestrial ecosystems, and effects on the aquatic environment. While it might be plausible, in principle, to also consider the somatic and genetic effects on humans, the probable absence of survivors would render such considerations meaningless.[2]

Atmospheric Effects

Three general kinds of atmospheric effects could be expected as consequences of system-wide nuclear war: global-scale transport and deposition of radionuclides; depletion of stratospheric ozone resulting in an increase in solar ultra-violet radiation in the lower atmosphere and at the earth's surface; and climatic change resulting from the ozone depletion and from surface dust injected into the stratosphere. The spread of radioactive atoms which decay by emitting energetic electrons or gamma particles would be extensive over the surface of the earth. The greatly reduced ozone concentrations would produce increased ultraviolet radiation and a drop in average temperature.

While such an increase in ultraviolet would cause human populations to suffer prompt and incapacitating cases of sunburn or snow blindness, the probable absence of survivors would make this particular effect academic. More importantly, since the nitric oxide produced by the exchange of strategic weapons could reduce worldwide ozone levels catastrophically (the exchange of 10,000 megatons postulated in the NAS study could be expected to produce as much as 30 to 70 percent ozone elimination in the northern hemisphere, and as much as 20 to 40 percent elimination in the southern hemisphere), significant drops in temperature could be anticipated. Indeed, the possibility of irreversible climatic shifts cannot be ruled out.[3]

Effects on Natural Terrestrial
Ecosystems

Natural terrestrial ecosystems would be affected by three principal stress factors resulting from a system-wide nuclear war: ionizing radiation, uv-B radiation, and climatic change. While the influence of uv-B would probably be the greatest of the three, current scientific understanding of uv-B effects on individual living organisms is meager.[4] Ionizing radiation, according to the NAS study, would produce "hot spots," or localized regions which could experience exposures in the range of 500 rads during a thirty-year period. This assessment was based on the NAS assumption of a *relatively* limited nuclear exchange; a system-wide nuclear war would render the entire planet a "hot spot." According to the study,

> ecosystems containing a major proportion of relatively sensitive species, such as the vast coniferous forests of

the north temperate zone, would show physiological and genetic damage, increased mortality, and decreased production. The timing of the early fallout with respect to the growing season in "hot spot" localities would further affect the response in many species within ecosystems.[5]

Climatic change could be expected to affect the production of crop species, but very little information exists on the nature of such effects.

Effects on Managed Terrestrial Ecosystems

In the wake of a worldwide nuclear war, the technology base for modern agriculture would disappear, foods would be contaminated by radionuclides to unacceptable levels, and ionizing radiation could cause disease epidemics in surviving crops and domesticated animals. Direct genetic effects on crops would include chromosome breakage and gene mutations, resulting in altered expressions of genes and loss of chromosome material from the cell's nucleus upon division of the cell. The effect of these changes would be yield-reducing sterility in seed crops. Moreover, according to the NAS report:

> There is the possibility of mutations in subsequent generations of the exposed plants causing abnormal plants or gametic or whole-plant lethals. These would not be important in most agricultural situations because man intervenes. However, mutations to disease susceptibility or inactivation of pathogen inhibitors in these plants might increase susceptibility to pathogens and affect agriculture.[6]

Indirect genetic effects on agricultural plants could arise from mutations in plant pathogens that would increase their virulence.[7]

Effects on the Aquatic Environment

The aquatic environment would be affected primarily by ionizing radiation from radionuclides in marine waters and fresh waters, solar ultraviolet radiation, and changes in water temperatures associated with climate. Irreversible injury to sensitive aquatic species could be expected during the years of large transient increase in uv-B isolation. And depending upon the extent of change in average temperature of the aquatic environment, the range of geographic distribution of sensitive populations of aquatic organisms could be reduced.[8]

Although such dispassionate, scientific examinations of the postapocalypse world are necessary, they tend to intrude upon the essential fact that such a world would be without human populations. Hence, we must ask ourselves: So what about atmospheric effects? So what about effects on natural and managed terrestrial ecosystems? And so what about effects on the aquatic environment? If we aren't even going to be around in such a world—a world which would deny us even our posterity—what purpose is there in scrutinizing its other properties?

Unlike the consequences of a nuclear war between the superpowers, a system-wide nuclear war would occasion no problems of "survivor guilt," no long-term physical or mental scars, no profound feelings of "death-in-life," no fourfold categories of victims. In the aftermath of such a war, there would be no advantages for populations that had burrowed themselves into fallout shelters or had dutifully relocated to "safe" areas. No benefits would accrue to those citizens who had heeded their government's warning to carry credit cards and sanitary napkins into relocation centers. In the United States, members of the reservist government would be unmoved by the commitment to place them on the federal payroll during the time of crisis. Even in the Soviet Union, the all-important "cadres" would fail to draw life-giving support from the system that sought to assure their survival.

The consideration of these environmental effects of a system-wide nuclear war reveals that, even if there were some survivors, the possibilities for a new beginning, for a general rebirth, for improved social and spiritual forms would be eliminated. Robert Lifton's idea of the survivor as creator, as one who can fashion a new self and world *because* he has known terrible disruption[9] would be alien in this context. With few if any survivors, there would be no continuity, no learning from lessons of the past, and no pos-

terity. Those who have known "the end" would take that
knowledge with them to their deaths.

Two-Country Nuclear War

Nuclear proliferation will enable an ever-increasing number
of antagonistic pairs of countries to engage in nuclear conflict. To evaluate the consequences of this type of conflict,
we must first consider such factors as the kinds of weapons
that might be used, their yields, their altitudes of detonation,
and prevailing weather patterns. In general, however, we
can say that two-country nuclear war would involve the
exchange of anywhere between several Hiroshima-yield
weapons (i.e., in the neighborhood of 10 to 20 kilotons) and
several dozen ballistic missiles carrying warhead yields of
up to 20 megatons each. At the moment, the higher limits
seem well beyond the capabilities of new nuclear weapon
states.

From what we already know about Hiroshima and the
probable effects of nuclear war between the superpowers, it
is evident that even the most limited nuclear exchange would
spell catastrophe for combatant parties. The immediate
effects of the explosions—thermal radiation, nuclear radiation, and blast damage—would cause wide swaths of death
and destruction. Victims would suffer flash and flame burns.
Retinal burns could occur in the eyes of persons at distances
of several hundred miles from the explosion. People would
be crushed by collapsing buildings or torn by flying glass.
Others would fall victim to raging firestorms and conflagra-
tions. Fallout injuries would include whole-body radiation
injury, produced by penetrating, hard gamma radiation;
superficial radiation burns produced by soft radiations; and
injuries produced by deposits of radioactive substances
within the body.[10]

In the aftermath, medical facilities that might still exist
would be taxed beyond endurance. Water supplies would
become unusable as a result of fallout contamination. Housing and shelter would become unavailable for tens or
hundreds of thousands of survivors. Transportation and
communication would break down to rudimentary or non-

existent levels. And serious food shortages would be inevitable.

Assuming that the combatant states were to enter into nuclear conflict as modern industrial economies, their networks of highly interlocking and interdependent exchange systems would now be shattered. Virtually everyone would be deprived of his or her basic means of livelihood. Emergency police and fire services would be decimated and stressed to thoroughly ineffectual levels. All systems dependent upon electrical power would cease to function. Severe trauma would occasion widespread disorientation and psychological disorders for which there would be no therapeutic services.

Normal society, in short, would cease to function. The pestilence of unrestrained murder and banditry would augment the pestilence of plague and epidemics. With the passage of time, many of the survivors could expect an increased incidence of degenerative diseases and various kinds of cancer. They might also expect premature death, impairment of vision, and an increased likelihood of sterility. Among the survivors of Hiroshima, for example, an increased incidence of leukemia and cancer of the lung, stomach, breast, ovary, and uterine cervix has been widely documented.[11]

Of the many delicately balanced relationships in nature that would be upset by extensive fallout, one of the most distasteful and potentially destructive concerns the size of insect populations. According to Tom Stonier:

> Mushrooming insect populations are likely to spread from the radiation-damaged areas in which they arose, and, like the locusts of biblical times, wreak havoc in previously undamaged areas. Accompanying the insect plagues would be the plant diseases transmitted by insects, particularly those diseases which attack plants that have been injured or weakened by insect or radiation damage. The combined assault of radiation, insects, disease, and fire could temporarily strip off the plant cover of vast areas. If the attack is sufficiently widespread, it is conceivable that a few years later almost all the forests would have been destroyed, and most of the countryside would have become converted into marginal grasslands, if not actually stripped, leaving a

naked earth to be ravaged by the ever-present forces of erosion.[12]

In all likelihood, certain of the biological and ecological effects of a nuclear war between two countries would be felt in other countries as well. Radioactive fallout does not respect political boundaries. Because of the way that nuclear explosions behave in the atmosphere, the altitude reached by the mushroom-shaped cloud would depend on the force of the explosion. For yields in the low-kiloton range, the cloud would remain in the lower atmosphere, and its effects would be entirely local. That is, they would not extend beyond the boundaries of the combatant countries. However, for yields exceeding 30 kilotons, part of the cloud of radioactive debris would "punch" into the stratosphere, affecting many non-combatant countries as well.[13]

At the international level, the political effects of a nuclear war between two countries would be enormous. Since the nuclear firebreak would have been crossed, every state in the system would fear that the long-standing inhibitions against nuclear war-fighting were no longer operative. Within the resultant atmosphere of suspicion and apprehension, every state would begin to fear that it might become the victim of a preemptive strike. And such fears would generate new incentives to preempt.

For those states that had not yet joined the nuclear club, the occasion of a two-country nuclear war would almost certainly mitigate *on behalf* of membership. Any previous inhibitions about "going nuclear" would most likely be cast aside in the wake of actual nuclear combat between two states. While such a scramble for nuclear weapon status might not be a rational reaction to the situation, history suggests it is a likely one.

In terms of international law, such a reaction would provide an inevitable deathblow to the entire nonproliferation regime. Whatever hopes had existed for enforcing the claims of the Treaty on the Non-Proliferation of Nuclear Weapons and its associated international treaties and agreements would almost surely disappear. Whatever incentives had been held out by present members of the nuclear club to discourage further membership would now be overridden by the presumed security advantages of nuclear weapon status. The principles of realpolitik would be embraced by even those states that had formerly shown an interest in worldwide cooperative searches for security, and the nuclear supplier states would be moved to step up their commercial activities in the transfer of sensitive nuclear technology and facilities.

Since the accelerated search for nuclear weapon status would cost vast sums of money, the increased impoverishment of much of the world would also have to be reckoned with as a consequence of nuclear war between two countries. Resources available for essential social/welfare sectors of national economies would be diverted to fuel an expanded and reactive nuclear arms race. "Security" needs would continue to outdistance human needs, and the poverty of human resources would spark even more hunger, illness, joblessness, and crime. Throughout the world, the expansion of nuclear-armed countries would be paralleled by an expansion of the desperately poor, the ill-fed, the ill-housed, and the uneducated.

All of this terrible waste of resources would take place in a world where the claims of military "security" already take priority over other basic human needs. Today, the world's military budget equals the annual income of 1,800,000,000 people in the thirty-six poorest nations. At present levels of military spending, the average person can expect to surrender three to four years' income over his lifetime to the production of weapons. The world's budget for military research is more than six times the size of its budget for energy research. The developed nations spend twenty times more for their military programs than for economic assistance to poorer countries. The developing nations import arms at the rate of more than $6 billion a year. In the developing world, 1,400,000,000 people have no safe drinking water; 520,000,000 suffer from malnutrition. In two days, the world spends as much on arms as is spent on a year's budget for the United Nations and its specialized agencies. The cost of one Trident submarine equals the cost of a year's schooling for 16,000,000 children in developing countries.[14]

Other political effects of a nuclear war between two countries would depend upon the nature of alignments in world politics, the reasons behind the war itself, and the reactions of unstable national leaders. The United Nations, too, would be a likely casualty of such a nuclear war.

If either one or both of the combatant countries had been party to a major alliance system, special tensions would develop throughout that system and within its opposite number. At a minimum, military forces of alliance countries would be placed on high-alert status, and a good deal of saber rattling could be expected. After a time, such saber rattling could have a self-fulfilling effect, bringing about the very conditions of extended nuclear conflict it was designed to prevent.

If it is generally believed that the two-country nuclear war had been initiated because the attacking party perceived vulnerability on the part of the victim's retaliatory forces, we could expect that other developing nuclear powers in the system would accelerate their construction of hair-trigger launch mechanisms and adoption of launch-on-warning measures. It follows that we could then expect an increased probability of additional strategic exchanges as a consequence of the accidental or unauthorized use of nuclear weapons.

All in all, the most important international political effect of a nuclear war between two countries would be a *psychological* one. With the actual use of nuclear weapons, states would become less inclined to think of such weapons as instruments of deterrence, and more inclined to think of them in orthodox military terms, as instruments of *warfare*. As a result of such changed orientations, what had once been in the realm of the "unthinkable" would now be entirely "thinkable," and national leaders would begin to take seriously the presumed advantages of striking first.

The danger of this effect, of course, would be greatest among those national leaders with a proclivity toward irrational behavior. In a world that already has more than its fair share of leaders who are mad, dictatorial, overstressed, or physically impaired, it is not unreasonable to expect that a nuclear war between two countries might set off the "spark" whereby one of these leaders would order the use of his own nuclear forces. The probability of such a scenario would be heightened should one or both of the parties to the two-state nuclear war be perceived as an ally or supporter by the irrational national leader.

Finally, the United Nations and its system of collective security would face the gravest crisis in its brief history. Divisions and alignments within the international organization would be hardened, and the expression of a genuinely global community interest would be well beyond the reach of members who had rededicated themselves to the competitive dynamics of power politics. Within this disintegrating system of international cooperation, the forces of anarchy would overwhelm the forces of collaboration, and every state would attempt to ensure its special claims on the foundations of military power.

Nuclear Attack by a Nuclear Weapons State against a Nonnuclear State

As noted, the spread of nuclear weapons could lead to situations wherein one rival state would possess nuclear weapons and another might not. The combined effect of such new inequalities in international power would be a greatly increased probability of nuclear attacks against nonnuclear weapon countries.

The consequences of this type of attack would, in all likelihood, parallel those already described in connection with two-country nuclear war. However, the actual scale and magnitude of injuries, fatalities, and physical destruction would probably be significantly smaller, since a nuclear strike against a nonnuclear country would almost surely be relatively limited in yield and counterforce in nature. It follows that as long as the purpose of the nuclear attack is a preemptive one, intended to destroy the victim side's future potential for striking first itself, something less than the total decimation of normal society could be expected.

Nevertheless, in spite of this relatively sanguine expectation, it is conceivable that the preemptive motive would be overshadowed by attitudes of national or ethnic hatred and personal bitterness. Here, rationality might give way to feelings of vengefulness, and the destructiveness of the nuclear strike could exceed levels needed for "rational" preemption. In such cases, gratuitous devastation might be meted out that comes close to, or even equals, the devastation associated with a full strategic exchange between two countries.

For example, in targeting its nuclear weapons, the attacking country might aim at population centers directly, thereby creating significantly greater levels of casualties and destruction than would be generated if only military installations and weapons were targeted. Moreover, in targeting cities, the attacking country might deliberately use greater yields than would be necessary for "minimum" destructiveness. Because of firestorm effects, one 10-megaton bomb, or about six one-megaton bombs, would suffice to destroy a megalopolis of 3,000 square kilometers.[15] Yet, an attacker interested in vengeance as well as preemption might intentionally employ higher-than-necessary levels of nuclear firepower.

Another possible act of gratuitous destructiveness might involve the use of "dirty" bombs. A fission-fusion fission bomb, or jacketed H-bomb, would add enormously not only to the power of the explosion, but to the degree of radioactive contamination as well. Of course, as soon as yields exceeded approximately 30 kilotons, a portion of the distinctive mushroom cloud would penetrate into the stratosphere. With yields exceeding 2 to 5 megatons, virtually all of the cloud of radioactive debris and fine dust would enter into the stratosphere. The lighter particles would penetrate to altitudes of twelve miles or more, spreading around the world for months or even years with stratospheric circulation and diffusion.[16] Hence, the consequences of a nuclear attack against a nonnuclear country might even have long-term, worldwide effects.

At another level, a nuclear attack against a nonnuclear country would have dramatic international political consequences. Even more than a nuclear war between two countries, such an attack would generate fears of victimization on the part of weak states, and hasten the spread of nuclear weapons throughout the world. Together with a weakening of the claims of the NPT in particular and the United Nations in general, this kind of crossing of the nuclear firebreak would almost certainly accelerate military spending in poorer countries, further reducing resources that are desperately needed for social welfare services in those lands.

Furthermore, if the attacked country were a member of a major alliance system such as NATO, other weak states would discover the unreliability of the collective-defense or alliance approach to security and would quickly turn to every-man-for-himself strategies. These strategies would be founded upon the presumption that each state must have its own nuclear weapons for effective protection.

With more and more states becoming captives of "porcupine" thinking, membership in the nuclear club would soon swell as would the likelihood of further nuclear conflict. New nuclear wars could be triggered by the following: incentives to preempt; errors in perception; vulnerable nuclear forces; accidental or unauthorized use of weapons, the belief that an attack could be carried out anonymously; or by irrational national leaders. Furthermore, the spread of nuclear weapons that might be accelerated by a nuclear attack against a nonnuclear country would enlarge the opportunities for microproliferation and nuclear terrorism. We see, therefore, that even a single nuclear assault against a nonnuclear country could generate conditions which would have profoundly destabilizing, long-term implications for world political affairs.

Nuclear War among Several New Nuclear Powers

Should the proliferation of nuclear weapons lead to a nuclear war involving several new members of the nuclear club, the effects would most likely be more severe than those associated with a two-country nuclear war, but less severe than those resulting from nuclear war between the superpowers. Blast damage from the nuclear bursts would be extensive. Radiation would produce wide areas of radiation sickness, horrible skin burns, and huge fires.

The actual extent of these effects, of course, would depend upon the degree to which the full nuclear inventories of the combatant countries were involved. At a minimum, however, colossal destruction would be suffered in all of the target areas, and the biological/ecological aftereffects would almost certainly be global. Fallout hazards, which depend on such factors as weapon design, explosive force, altitude and latitude of detonation, time of year, and local weather conditions, would affect both local and worldwide populations.

For example, a single nuclear weapon with a fission yield of one megaton, exploded at ground level in a 15-mile-per-hour wind, would produce fallout in an ellipse extending hundreds of miles downwind from the burst point. At a distance of 20 to 25 miles downwind, a lethal radiation dose would accumulate in persons who did not find shelter within 25 minutes of the initial fallout. Those at a distance of 40 to 45 miles would have no more than three hours to find shelter. Immediately downwind of the burst point, therefore, persons who could not be sheltered or evacuated would have slim prospects for survival.[17]

In a nuclear war among several secondary nuclear powers, the use of 100 one-megaton-fission-yield weapons would kill more than 20 percent of each country's population immediately through blast, heat, ground shock and instant radiation effects. A war involving 1,000 such weapons in each combatant country would destroy immediately more than half of the affected populations. And these figures do not include deaths due to fires, lack of proper medical care, starvation, or lethal fallout downwind of the burst points.[18]

As to worldwide effects of fallout, if a war of this type were to involve the detonation of as much as 10,000 megatons of nuclear force, radiation-induced cancers and genetic damage together could be estimated to range from 1.5 to 30 billion for the world population as a whole over thirty years. This would mean one additional case for every 100 to 3,000 people, or about one-half percent to 15 percent of the estimated peacetime cancer death rate in developed countries. Moreover there might well be potential effects that we do not at present even anticipate.[19]

A war of this type would also profoundly affect international political affairs. In addition to the effects associated with other forms of strategic exchanges that might arise through proliferation—increased incentives to "go nuclear," increased incentives to preempt, the breakdown of the non-proliferation regime, diminished resources for social-welfare needs, weakened collective defense and collective security processes—such a war would probably greatly increase the chances for superpower nuclear conflict. With so widespread a use of nuclear weapons, military planners in the Soviet Union and the United States would almost certainly doubt the prolonged effectiveness of mutually assured destruction as a basis for their own national security. Faced, therefore, with the presumed inevitability of nuclear war, each side would strive for conditions under which preemption would be "rational."

On the other hand, there is always the chance that a nuclear war among secondary nuclear powers might provide a critical incentive for cooperation or even collaboration between the superpowers. In this connection, we may consider the possibility that a nuclear war among secondary nuclear powers involving China could spark a form of collaboration between the superpowers, united by their common fear of a third party. Should this fear be great enough, it could even generate the conditions for a joint Soviet-American first strike against China. Indeed, if one can believe H. R. Haldeman's claim in his Watergate book, *The Ends of Power*, the Soviet Union actually asked the United States to take part in a nuclear first strike against China in 1969.

Nuclear War between Secondary Nuclear Powers and One of the Superpowers

The spread of nuclear weapons could also produce a nuclear exchange involving secondary nuclear powers on the one side, and one of the superpowers on the other. Some of the anticipated effects of this kind of war would be the same as those discussed in regard to other nuclear conflicts. These include death and devastation resulting from the blast, and thermal and nuclear radiation. Radiation sickness, characterized by initial nausea, vomiting, and diarrhea, would then cause spontaneous bleeding from the mouth, bleeding of the intestinal tract, and loss of hair, and would ultimately affect the immune mechanisms of the body, allowing the development of an overwhelming and irreversible infection.[20]

The degree and extent of the damage, however, would
depend upon a number of factors including the following:
the number of secondary nuclear powers involved in the
exchange; the destructive power at their combined disposal;
the degree of cooperation and alignment among these powers; the vulnerability of the combined secondary nuclear
forces to retaliatory blows on the part of the superpower;
and, finally, how "limited" the goals are of the combatant
countries. Would they all be content to aim solely at enemy
military targets, or would some or all of them be inclined
to "all-out" nuclear war? This last factor would depend to
a considerable extent on the combatants' perceptions of the
still-peaceful superpower. It goes without saying that all
parties to the war would have serious concerns about the
prospective entry of this other superpower into the conflict.

The international political consequences of a nuclear war
between secondary nuclear powers and one of the superpowers would be largely determined by the actions of the
remaining superpower. Should the still-peaceful superpower
throw the weight of its influence and perhaps even its military forces on the side of the warring superpower, an entirely new structure of international relations could ensue.
Here we might have the kind of situation once envisioned
by former French President Charles de Gaulle, a situation
in which the United States and the Soviet Union actually
join forces and collaborate in the establishment of a new
pattern of global dominance.[21] Impetus for such collaboration in the years ahead could come from a shared fear of
another country such as China and from a combined reluctance to permit expansion of the superpower club to three
members.

Alternatively, should the still-peaceful superpower throw
its influence and perhaps its military forces on the side of
the secondary nuclear powers, there would be little to prevent the onset of a worldwide nuclear conflagration. Here
we would be confronted with the prospect of death and
devastation at a level somewhere between that of a superpower nuclear war and a system-wide conflict of *On The
Beach* proportions. The rearrangement of world power patterns that might emerge from the wake of such conflicts is

both unpredictable and absurd to contemplate, since it is not clear that any normally functioning human societies would survive.

Finally, it is worth considering that the still-peaceful superpower would choose to stay out of the existing war altogether. Here, depending upon the precise outcome of the war, that superpower could find itself in a position of either "collecting the spoils" and embarking upon a new period of singular global dominance, or of having been weakened further in comparison with the victorious superpower.

Nuclear War between Secondary Nuclear Powers and Both of the Superpowers

We have already considered that a nuclear war between secondary nuclear powers and one of the superpowers could ultimately involve both superpowers fighting together. Could such a strange partnership ever come to pass? Before discounting it altogether, we should keep in mind that even stranger bedfellows have been discovered during the perplexing history of international affairs. We would be prudent to consider *especially* those situations in world politics that are, on the surface, least likely to take place.

Consider, for example, a scenario in which China and a number of Third World nuclear powers are arrayed on one side with the Soviet Union on the other. Here, the United States, feeling that its interests would be better served by a Soviet victory, might well decide to join forces with the Soviet effort. Or it might even find itself on the Soviet side unintentionally. This could happen if a first strike were launched against the United States or its military installations abroad by the secondary nuclear powers.

An alternate scenario could be developed from a situation wherein China and her allies are on one side, and the United States is on the other. Here, the Soviet Union, feeling that its security would be better served by removing the Chinese threat than by weakening the American one, might decide to join forces with the American effort. Or, as in the original scenario, the decision might effectively be made for the Soviets by a first strike originating with the Chinese side. Either scenario might precipitate a rapid cessation of hos-

tilities. However, the scale of lethal conflict would still be
great enough to ensure a large number of deaths and critical
levels of devastation. And as we already know from our
prior discussions of the consequences of multiple nuclear
weapon detonations, these effects would be long-term and
worldwide.

The political effects of a nuclear war between secondary
nuclear powers and both of the superpowers would be profound. For a limited time, at least, the Soviet Union and the
United States would fuse into a single "pole" of global
power, exercising a new hegemony over those societies that
still remain intact. Previous distinctions between NATO and
the Warsaw Pact would disappear as surviving members of
those alliance systems recognized a new and common enemy
—a *super* superpower. Indeed, the NATO and Warsaw Pact
countries might even coalesce into a new alliance, designed
to protect themselves from the combined threat of the Soviet
Union and the United States. After a time, therefore, the
world might witness a new bipolarity, with the Soviets and
the Americans at one pole, and the NATO/Warsaw Pact
countries at the other. *Credo quia absurdum.*

Alternatively, the partnership between two superpowers
might not outlast its original purpose. Here, the end of the
common fight against certain secondary nuclear powers
might only signal the beginning of a new war between the
two former partners. The plausibility of such a scenario is
underscored by the uncertainty that each side would feel
about the intentions of the other after vanquishing the common enemy, and by the predictable inclination of each side
to exploit the weakened position of the other. Depending
upon the condition of the other nuclear powers at the time,
such a superpower nuclear war could quickly spiral into a
worldwide exchange of nearly one million megatons of nuclear explosives.

Nuclear War between Secondary Nuclear
Powers Plus One of the Superpowers
and Other Secondary Nuclear Powers

The final case in the spectrum of nuclear conflict possibilities to be considered involves nuclear war between com-

peting coalitions of secondary nuclear powers, with one of the coalitions joined by one of the superpowers. As in the other cases already examined, such a conflict would surely bring a cauldron of horrors from which neither humankind nor its habitat would be spared.

The world political effects of such a conflict would depend, of course, upon the nature of the participants. If, for example, the conflicting coalitions were the NATO and Warsaw Pact countries, with the first coalition joined by the United States, we might expect a more isolated and less influential Soviet Union in the postwar world. However, should the United States suffer significant destruction of its civilian population and armed forces during the conflict, it might well emerge militarily weaker than the Soviet superpower. In such circumstances, the chances that the Soviets would seek to exploit the weakened American state with a first-strike attack would appear to be considerable.

If instead the conflicting coalitions were NATO and Warsaw Pact countries, but this time with the second coalition joined by the Soviet Union, we might expect a reverse situation. The United States would probably decline in influence as it became more and more isolated. At the same time, its military power could be expected to increase vis-à-vis the Soviet superpower, providing a new and possibly irresistible incentive to strike first.

Should these same conflicting coalitions be joined by their superpower allies, it is worth considering that the Russians and the Americans might refrain from targeting each other. Here, both superpowers would emerge intact, while the NATO and Warsaw Pact countries would be destroyed. According to a scenario once developed by Charles de Gaulle, such bizarre events could lead to an even stranger outcome:

> Who can say that if the occasion arises the two, [superpowers] while each deciding not to launch its missiles at the main enemy so that it should itself be spared, will not crush the others? It is possible to imagine that on some awful day Western Europe should be wiped out from Moscow and Central Europe from Washington. And who can say that the two rivals, after I know not what political and social upheaval, will not unite?[22]

Still another set of participants might involve China. If, for example, the conflicting coalitions were to include China and Pakistan on the one side and the Soviet Union and India on the other, we might expect the postwar world to resemble an earlier form of bipolarity. Here, in the manner of the simpler, two-bloc antagonism which characterized the period of the late 1940s and the decade of the 1950s, Russians and Americans might resume the clear-cut hostility that had prefigured the Sino-Soviet split. All of this speculation, of course, assumes the victory of the Soviet-Indian side.

If, on the other hand, the Chinese were to emerge reasonably intact from their war with Russia (an admittedly unlikely possibility), it is conceivable that the United States would consider the possibility of "finishing the job" against the Soviet Union. Such consideration, of course, would require the conviction that an American first-strike could be undertaken against a seriously weakened Soviet state without entailing unacceptably damaging retaliation. Should the United States ever undertake such a strike, the resultant pattern of world affairs would again be based upon competition and rivalry between two superpowers. Only this time the preeminent players would be the United States and the People's Republic of China.

The Effects of New Weapons

Before concluding this exploration of the consequences of nuclear warfare that might occur because of proliferation, we should also consider how these probable consequences could be affected by the development and introduction of new weapons. With so great a proportion of the world's wealth currently being spent on military research and development, and with roughly half of the world's total scientific and technical manpower engaged in weapons-related work of some kind, we can expect a future with increasingly more sophisticated weapons.

These "improved" weapon systems can be counted on to find their way into the arsenals of new members of the nuclear club. Just as today's latest members of this club took their original strategic cues from superpower development of ICBMs, SLBMs, and tactical nuclear weapons, so will tomorrow's nuclear powers base their deployment of cruise missiles, neutron bombs, and weapons for space warfare on Soviet-American models.[23]

Of special concern are long-range cruise missiles, since these weapons could provide new nuclear powers with a relatively cheap means of delivering nuclear warheads. Essentially small, highly maneuverable, low-flying pilotless aircraft,[24] these weapon systems would be well within the financial means of smaller countries. By bringing the cost of a nuclear weapon capability down to a point that can be afforded by even poor countries, the development of the cruise missile portends the end of an era when the exorbitant cost of nuclear weapons provided an important safeguard against proliferation.

These potentially cost-effective nuclear weapons, which resemble the German V-1 "buzz bomb" of World War II, can strike distant targets with great accuracy and can be launched from submarines, surface ships, or airplanes. Regrettably, these advantages suggest that their deployment by the United States will spark a new escalatory cycle involving not only the Soviet Union, but other countries as well. In this connection, England, France, Japan, India, Sweden, West Germany, Italy, and Israel are especially likely candidates, since they possess the necessary technological infrastructure in electronics, airframes, and jet engines. The net effect of this escalatory cycle, as with all such cycles, will be higher military expenditures and a diminished level of security for all concerned.[25]

The neutron bomb, which falls under the category of "enhanced radiation weapons," releases large quantities of radioactive neutrons which are effective in killing people while leaving buildings intact. Exploded 130 yards in the air, a neutron bomb would kill instantly anyone within a half-mile radius, and cause delayed deaths for people within a one-mile radius. Because of its extraordinary precision, the neutron bomb erodes the distinction between conventional and nuclear conflict, thereby increasing the chances for large-scale nuclear war. It goes without saying that the potential danger of this particular weapon increases with every new addition to the nuclear club.

And then there is space warfare. Today, both of the super-powers are hard at work on developing weapons for war in space, weapons that will put an end to humankind's last sanctuary. Like the oceans, space is regarded by the Soviet Union and the United States as a proper medium for military purposes. Any hopes that it might remain an unmolested territory have already been shattered.

Since satellites are now central to the national security of both superpowers, both countries are now embarked on a program to develop and deploy antisatellite weapons. Notwithstanding the 1967 UN outer-space treaty and the 1972 anti-ballistic-missile agreement between the United States and the Soviet Union, it now appears certain that both sides will build satellite killers. Russia is already reported to have successfully tested its killer satellite, and the U.S. Air Force has recently awarded a $58.7 million contract to build its own satellite killer.

Other far-out weapons that must be considered in an assessment of proliferation prospects fall under the heading of "environmental modification techniques." Some of these "doomsday weapons" are now well within the range of technical possibility. Included in this category are weapons that can generate earthquakes or tidal waves, "cook" target countries with ultraviolet radiation by punching holes in the atmosphere's ozone layer, or steer storms toward an enemy. Although the superpowers, together with thirty-two other nations, signed a Convention on the Prohibition of Military or Any Other Hostile Use of Environmental Modification Techniques on 18 May 1977, it is doubtful that the prospect of environmental warfare can be effectively eliminated.

Perhaps the most remarkable new weapon of all is the so-called death beam, a directed-energy beam weapon that could destroy nuclear ballistic missiles in flight. According to Maj. Gen. George J. Keegan, the retired head of U.S. Air Force intelligence, the Soviet Union is currently developing a charged-particle beam weapon, while the United States has abandoned its effort to create such a weapon.[26] The beam would focus and project atomic particles near the speed of light, and could be used for defense against nearly simultaneous multiple attackers. It follows that a state which possesses this kind of weapon could conceivably attain a first-strike capability.

Finally, there are other weapons of mass destruction that are neither new nor nuclear, but which could affect profoundly the consequences of a nuclear war that occurs through proliferation. These are "CBW" weapons, or weapons of chemical-biological warfare. Such weapons, of course, might also be used in the absence of nuclear weapons altogether and pose a significant proliferation hazard themselves.

Rethinking the Unthinkable

Six hundred or so years ago, the Black Death of plague decimated the population of Europe, claiming at least twenty-five million people. Since that time, only the present moment has been so pregnant with "end of the world" possibilities. Yet, while the dangers of nuclear proliferation actually pose infinitely greater hazards for humankind than did the Black Death, there is no general awareness of this fact. Indeed, while those who lived through the plague years existed amidst a universal fear of imminent death, no such fear exists today. Rather than creating a nightmare of paralyzing panic, the current crisis of human survival has only barely interfered with our everyday lives. And such interference has been limited to occasional, painless reminders, in the newspapers or news magazines or on television, that all is not well with the world.

As we already noted in the preceding chapter, the essential first step in changing this situation must be based upon a wider awareness of what we now face. Proliferation *does* carry the seeds of an all-destructive nuclear war. The effects of such a war, or of any of the other more "limited" nuclear conflicts to which proliferation might give rise, *would be* of great consequence. What is more, these effects would include the most significant enlargement of human suffering that humanity has ever experienced.

6 The Consequences of Nuclear Terrorism

In modern world politics, the leading actors have always been states. Their leaders, accorded the authority to galvanize military forces in the name of national interest and purpose, have only been able to exert such influence in their official capacities.

Today, however, we are faced with the unprecedented situation wherein individual human beings—*privately and without governmental function*—are capable of exerting a profound and destructive influence on world affairs. This capability is enhanced by the ability of individuals to exploit the uniquely destructive potential of nuclear technology. The threat of nuclear terrorism is real.

Nuclear terrorism might manifest itself in three ways: (1) through the use of nuclear explosives; (2) through the use of radiological weapons; and (3) by sabotage of nuclear reactors.

Explosive Nuclear Weapons

As we have already seen, a terrorist group could design and build a crude nuclear device. This could be done without a great deal of technological equipment and with financial resources that do not exceed a fraction of a million dollars. To construct a device that would produce a significant nuclear yield,[1] the terrorist group would require modest machine-shop facilities, persons capable of understanding and implementing the open technical literature, and sufficient quantities of fissile material.[2]

The nuclear yields of such low-technology nuclear explo-

175

sives could range anywhere from a few hundred tons to several kilotons. Indeed, using low-neutron background materials (i.e., U^{235}, U^{233}, and weapons-grade plutonium), terrorist groups could design devices that would produce yields up to the equivalent of 10 or even 20 thousand tons of TNT.[3] A weapon having a yield equivalent of around 10 kilotons of TNT might also be manufactured using highly enriched uranium. Such a weapon would present fewer fabrication problems than a plutonium weapon. However, there is presently very little highly enriched uranium available in commercial channels that would be suitable for weapons.[4]

To estimate the power of such weapons, consider that the largest conventional bombs of World War II contained about 10 tons of high explosives, while the Hiroshima and Nagasaki bombs had yields of approximately 14 and 20 kilotons respectively. (As mentioned earlier, the Hiroshima bomb involved the fission of about 700 grams of uranium-235, while the Nagasaki bomb fissioned about 1.3 kilograms of plutonium-239.) Moreover, devices with yields ranging down to the equivalent of one ton of chemical high explosive could cause major destruction.[5]

Nuclear explosions are generally more damaging than chemical explosions of equivalent yield, because a nuclear explosion releases large quantities of penetrating radiation as well as energy in the form of blast wave and heat. The damage potential of nuclear explosions depends upon such factors as the size of the explosion, the design of the explosive, and the characteristic features of the target area. For example, a nuclear explosion with a one-ton yield might have only limited effects in a sparsely populated area, but might lethally irradiate thousands of people if it were detonated on a busy city street.[6] A one-kiloton bomb exploded in or near the Capitol during a State of the Union address by the president of the United States could obliterate the heads of all branches of government.

Although the effects of nuclear explosions vary according to whether they are produced in the air or on the ground,[7] and according to the structural characteristics of buildings in the target area, there is good reason to believe that a terrorist bomb could yield at least as much destruction as the wartime bombings of Hiroshima and Nagasaki. The number of people killed by Little Boy and Fat Man, those two bombs, has been estimated to exceed a quarter of a million, a death rate of over 40 percent of the population. Approximately 97 percent of those persons within 500 meters of the hypocenters died by the end of 1945. About 60 percent of those persons within 2 kilometers died, most of them within the first twenty-four hours. Roughly 3 percent of those persons between 2 and 5 kilometers of the hypocenters died by the end of the year.[8]

Most of those who were killed right away were either crushed or burned. In Hiroshima, an area of 13 square kilometers was reduced to rubble and ashes by blast and fire. In Nagasaki, the comparably affected area extended 6.7 square kilometers.[9] Firestorms raged in both cities. Thermal radiation burned exposed human skin at distances of up to 3.5 kilometers from the hypocenter in Hiroshima and 4 kilometers in Nagasaki.

As moisture condensed around rising ash particles that came into contact with cold air, a "black rain" of radioactivity descended upon the two cities. Of the approximately 76,000 buildings that had existed before the bombing in Hiroshima, about 63 percent were destroyed by fire and 5 percent by blast. Twenty-four percent were very seriously damaged. About 25 percent of Nagasaki's 51,000 buildings were destroyed, and another 11 percent very seriously damaged.[10]

A more human picture of the devastation is provided by the written account of Kataoka Osamu, a teenage schoolboy in Hiroshima when the atomic bomb hit.

> I looked out of the window at the branch of a willow tree. Just at the moment I turned my eyes back into the old and dark classroom, there was a flash. It was indescribable. It was as if a monstrous piece of celluloid had flared up all at once. Even as my eyes were being pierced by the sharp vermillion flash, the school building was already crumbling. I felt plaster and roof tiles and lumber come crashing down on my head, shoulders, and back. The dusty smell of the plaster and other strange smells mixed up with it penetrated my nostrils.

I wonder how much time passed. It had gradually become harder and harder for me to breathe. The smell had become intense. It was the smell that made it so hard to breathe.

I was trapped under the wreckage of the school building. . . . I finally managed to get out from under the wreckage and stepped out into the schoolyard. It was just as dark outside as it had been under the wreckage and the sharp odor was everywhere. I took my handkerchief, wet it, and covered my mouth with it.

Four of my classmates came crawling out from beneath the wreckage just as I had done. In a daze we gathered around the willow tree, which was now leaning over. Then we began singing the school song. Our voices were low and raspy, with a tone of deep sadness. But our singing was drowned out by the roar of the swirling smoke and dust and the sound of the crumbling buildings.

We went to the swimming pool, helping a classmate whose leg had been injured and who had lost his eyesight. You cannot imagine what I saw there. One of our classmates had fallen into the pool; he was already dead, his entire body burned and tattered. Another was trying to extinguish the flames rising from his friend's clothes with the blood which spurted out of his own wounds. Some jumped into the swimming pool to extinguish their burning clothes, only to drown because their terribly burned limbs had become useless. There were others with burns all over their bodies whose faces were swollen to two or three times their normal size so they were no longer recognizable. I cannot forget the sight of those who could not move at all, who simply looked up at the sky, saying over and over, "Damn you! Damn you!"

Our gym teacher had come to the swimming pool too. Though he was moving about energetically, the sight of his burned and swollen body and his tattered clothes made everyone's heart sink. We all began to cry. But he gave us directions and encouraged us in a firm voice, urging us to gather together our friends who had lost their sight or were badly injured and to leave the burning school building behind.

There were others who could not move at all and

there were probably many who were still trapped beneath the burning wreckage of the school. Were we to
run away and leave them behind without caring at all?
No. . . . But there was nothing we could do. Friends,
please forgive us.[11]

Those who survived beyond 1945 began to develop a variety of illnesses, including eye diseases, blood disorders,
cancers, and psychoneurological disturbances. The mortality
rate for leukemia reached a level about thirty times higher
among survivors than among nonexposed Japanese. A
higher incidence of malignant tumors of the thyroid, breast,
lung, salivary gland, bone, and prostate is still in evidence
among survivors. And children born to women who were
pregnant when the bombs exploded show a greater incidence
of certain congenital malformations, especially disorders
resulting in mental retardation.[12]

The social and psychological effects upon the survivors
are also significant. According to Frank Barnaby, director
of the Stockholm International Peace Research Institute:

> The social and psychological effects of the atomic
> bombings were extremely severe. The communities dis-
> integrated. The social services collapsed. Many people
> went mad or committed suicide. Thousands of children
> became orphans.
> Some of the effects of the bombs are still apparent.
> There is a disproportionate number of aged among the
> survivors. Fear of malformed offspring often prevents
> marriages, and unusual susceptibility to disease and
> fatigue often threatens employment.
> The ratio of sick and injured among the survivors is
> almost twice the national average. Disease and poverty
> among the survivors are continuously aggravated by
> aging and failing health.
> Thirty-two years have passed since the atomic bomb-
> ings, yet we are still unable to grasp the totality of the
> disaster. The destruction produced by nuclear weapons
> may simply be incomprehensible.[13]

These, then, are the kinds of effects that might be expected
in the wake of a terrorist nuclear assault involving explosions in the 10 to 20 kiloton range. Of course, there would

be certain mitigating circumstances which could make the
terrorist assault more tolerable than the Hiroshima/
Nagasaki blasts. For one, terrorist use of explosive nuclear
weapons would almost certainly be localized, allowing unaffected parts of the victim country to extend far-reaching
patterns of aid. For another, many countries now have
operational plans for dealing with such emergencies. In
the United States, the Federal Preparedness Agency of the
General Services Administration has prepared a *Federal
Response Plan for Peacetime Nuclear Emergencies*.[14] This
document is designed to:

1. Provide policy and planning guidance for the preparation of Federal and State operational response
   plans for peacetime nuclear emergencies;
2. Facilitate a complete and coordinated Federal planning effort that will cover all peacetime nuclear
   emergencies;
3. Provide the basis for compatibility between Federal
   and State plans related to peacetime nuclear emergencies; and
4. Identify responsibility for implementing and coordinating the efforts of Federal agencies responding to
   peacetime nuclear emergencies.[15]

Such mitigating circumstances, however, would prove to
be of little comfort to those tens or even hundreds of thousands of affected persons. For them, the effects that flow
from terrorist use of nuclear explosives would surely transcend the importance of all past events. Even if these effects
were essentially "local," the ensuing predicament of the
survivors would not only strain the outer limits of human
tolerance, but would also create permanent, impenetrable
barriers between afflicted and unafflicted elements of the
population.

Radiological Weapons

Less understood, perhaps, than nuclear explosives, but
equally ominous in their potential effects, are radiological
weapons. Placed in the hands of terrorists, such weapons
could pose a lethal hazard for human beings everywhere.
Radiological weapons are designed to disperse radioactive

materials, produced a substantial time before their dispersal (e.g., not in a nuclear explosion) for any of the following purposes:

  a. Killing people within a short time (less than a few weeks).
  b. Killing people, or causing severe illness, after a long time (weeks to many years).
  c. Damaging property through short-term contamination to levels that require evacuation to prevent severe effects on occupants.
  d. Damaging property through long-term contamination, to low levels that would deny access to or use of an area if present occupancy or use standards for the general population were enforced.[16]

The targets against which terrorists might choose to use radiological weapons are many and varied. For example:

  a. High concentrations of people inside buildings; dispersal as aerosol introduced into air-conditioning or ventilation systems.
  b. High concentrations of people outside (e.g., crowded urban streets or sports events).
  c. Urban areas as a whole, with high population density, to affect people and property inside and outside buildings.
  d. Large urban, suburban, or rural non-agricultural areas, primarily to deny access and require expensive decontamination. The dispersal might even be designed specifically *not* to produce any significant acute health effects.
  e. Agricultural area, primarily to deny access and use.[17]

In principle, radiological weapons could be fashioned from any radioactive material. In fact, however, terrorists would most probably turn to plutonium, which—in the form of very minute particles suspended in air—is extraordinarily toxic. Indeed, in terms of the total weight of material that represents a lethal dose, its toxicity is at least twenty thousand times greater than cobra venom or potassium cyanide, and one thousand times greater than heroin or modern nerve gases. The inhalation of between 10 and 100 *millionths* of a gram would very likely produce death by lung cancer. For predictive purposes, it is ordinarily assumed that 50 micro-grams of plutonium-239 represents a lethal dose.[18]

The ways in which this elixir of death could pose a serious threat to society are already well known. Simpler to make than a fission explosive, and capable of distributing lethal effects without even the awareness of exposed populations, a plutonium dispersal device could take the form of an aerosol in a building's air conditioning intake or a strategi-cally placed "package" combined with chemical explosives. With only a few grams of dispersed plutonium, a terrorist group could pose a serious danger to the headquarters of a large corporation or—during the President's annual address on the State of the Union—the entire leadership sector of the government of the United States. With only a few dozen grams of plutonium, terrorists could contaminate several dozen square kilometers to an extent requiring evacuation and decontamination.[19]

Thus, the threat of nuclear terrorism involving radiologi-cal weapons is potentially more troublesome than the threat involving nuclear explosives. In fact, the threat is so great, it would be easy to perpetrate a hoax, whereby responsible national authorities throughout the world could find them-selves resorting to increasingly repressive policies to cope with the presumed threat. In the long run, the policies themselves could pose a severe danger to national and inter-national society.

Nuclear Reactor Sabotage

The sabotage of nuclear reactors provides an already famil-iar avenue for terrorism.[20] Such sabotage would involve pre-cipitating core meltdown and breach of containment. Incidents involving violence or threats of violence at nuclear facilities are already a matter of record, both at home and abroad.

In the United States, between 1969 and 1975, the Atomic Energy Commission (AEC) and later the Energy Research and Development Administration (ERDA) recorded 288 threats or incidents of violence directed at nuclear facilities or offices related to such facilities. Of these, 240 were bomb threats, 14 were bombings or attempted bombings, 22 were incidents involving arson or attempted arson, and 12 involved forced entry or other breaches of security. To date, however, the only known casualty in an adversary nuclear incident in the United States was the wounding of a night watchman by an intruder at the Vermont Yankee plant in 1971.[21]

The incidents that have occurred abroad are of a more serious nature. While there has been no complete chronology of such incidents, we do know of at least several major episodes. In March 1973, Argentina's Atucha reactor was actually overrun and temporarily occupied by a Trotskyist urban guerrilla group. The attackers, armed with machine guns and hand grenades, overpowered the guards, painted slogans on the walls, stole weapons, but did not attempt to damage the reactor itself. In separate incidents that took place in France during 1975, bombs were detonated at nuclear plants at Fessenheim and Mt. D'Arree. Responsibility for the attacks was claimed by the Meinhof-Puig Antich group (an offshoot of the Baader-Meinhof group) and the Breton Liberation Front respectively. Expensive fires ensued, but little damage was done to the reactors themselves.

The fact that none of these nuclear incidents has been truly catastrophic should be no cause for complaisance. As nuclear industry expands worldwide, so will the use of nuclear reactors. Taken together with the steady growth of international terrorism, this expansion of nuclear power poses new and more serious hazards of nuclear reactor sabotage. In Europe, widely circulated underground publications are already giving consideration to attacks on nuclear power plants.[22] These ideas are bound to be echoed in similar publications in other parts of the world, thus further encouraging violence-prone groups to attempt reactor sabotage.[23]

In the United States, fear of such sabotage has even been cited by New York City in a legal argument seeking to block use of a 250-kilowatt research reactor by Columbia University on its Morningside Heights campus. In an affidavit arguing for a different site for the research reactor, Dr. Leonard R. Solon, director of the Health Department's Bureau for Radiation Control, noted: "In the past few years, the city has become a target for urban terrorists using diverse and highly sophisticated weaponry." Moreover, said Dr. Solon, the Columbia reactor's location "makes it a prime focus for terrorist activity," and any sabotage "has the potential for causing thousands of latent cancer deaths" in New York City.[24]

In developing countries and the Third World, with their instability manifested in frequent coups, guerrilla wars, insurgent movements, and military regimes, the risk of sabotage would be even greater than elsewhere. Struggles would surely ensue over the control of nuclear reactors, and the potential for sabotage would be increased by the fact that these countries are unlikely to provide adequate security around their newly acquired nuclear facilities.[25]

The Consequences of Attacks on Nuclear Reactors

By now, a good deal is known about the probable consequences of nuclear reactor sabotage. In comparison to low-yield nuclear explosions, the meltdown of a nuclear reactor core and loss of containment would release only a small amount of energy and radiation.[26] Nevertheless, the amount of radioactive material released, much of it gaseous, would be sufficient to expose the neighboring population to the risk of death or radiation injuries such as cancer and genetic defects.[27]

In 1957, the Atomic Energy Commission issued a report, known as WASH-740 or the "Brookhaven Report," estimating that a serious nuclear reactor mishap could result in 3,400 immediate deaths, 43,000 acute injuries, and $7 billion in damage. By 1964, when it became apparent that larger reactors were being developed, these figures were revised upward. Most importantly, estimated fatalities were increased to 45,000.[28] A 1973 AEC estimate refers to the same number of fatalities (45,000), 100,000 injuries, and $17 billion in property damage.[29] And an even more recent study by the Ford Foundation's Nuclear Energy Policy Study Group reports that a single major nuclear incident could produce "as many as several thousand immediate fatalities and several tens of thousands of latent cases of cancer that would be fatal within thirty years."[30]

But the most important and well-publicized report on the danger of nuclear power plants is the so-called Rasmussen Report, named after Professor Norman C. Rasmussen, who headed a team of sixty persons assembled by Saul Levine, deputy director of the Nuclear Regulatory Commission's Office of Nuclear Regulatory Research.[31] Culminating a three-year study, the thirteen- volume report deals with the chances of a large-scale *accident* in a nuclear-fueled reactor of present-day design. Since the consequences of such an accident would resemble those of a terrorist-induced meltdown and breach of containment, they are worth considering.[32]

According to the report, the accident consequences are substantially smaller than those estimated in earlier reports. More specifically, an extremely serious accident could be expected to produce 3,300 prompt fatalities, 45,000 instances of early illness, 240,000 thyroid nodules over a thirty-year period, 45,000 latent cancer fatalities over a thirty-year period, and 30,000 genetic defects spanning 150 years. The economic loss due to contamination over an area of 3,200 square miles is estimated at $14 billion.[33] In 1978, a NRC panel directed by University of California Professor H. W. Lewis challenged the reasonableness of the Rasmussen Report's relatively low evaluation of meltdown/breach of containment consequences.[34]

The technical problems in blowing up a reactor would be easier to handle than those involved in the manufacture of a nuclear explosive.[35] Should these problems be tackled and overcome by a determined terrorist group, the consequences would depend greatly upon the density of population and prevailing weather patterns in the vicinity of the reactor. The latent consequences could affect populations hundreds of miles from the incident site.[36]

Overall, the most serious health effect of reactor sabotage, and the consequent release of radioactivity, would be fatalities from latent cancer.[37] According to a major analysis of these potential cancers on an organ-by-organ basis, 83 percent of the eventual latent cancer deaths would result from exposure during the first week after the accident.[38] This points up the fact that health consequences would vary greatly according to the promptness of evacuation measures. It also suggests the inherently limited value of any long-range decontamination programs following an incident.[39]

The types of radiation effects resulting from the release of some of the radioactive inventory from a large sabotaged reactor would also depend upon the kinds of fission products released and the degree to which individuals are protected against irradiation. According to the Rasmussen Report, the most unfavorable configuration of conditions could involve 45,000 individuals developing radiation sickness and 3,300 persons becoming prompt fatalities. The cancers, which were projected over a thirty-year period of distribution and expected to represent approximately a 9 percent increase above the naturally occurring incidence in the exposed population, were attributed largely to irradiation of the lung.[40]

Other Forms of Nuclear Terrorism

We have, to this point, focused upon the three principal avenues available for nuclear terrorism: use of nuclear explosives, use of radiological weapons, and nuclear reactor sabotage. There are, however, other avenues that terrorists could exploit. These might include sabotage of spent fuel and sabotage of fuel reprocessing plants.

The sabotage of irradiated fuel could result in the spread of radioactivity. In order to achieve an effective way to distribute the radioactivity contained in the spent fuel, the terrorist saboteur would have to focus on certain specific points along transportation routes. This means that consequential sabotage of casks used for spent fuel transportation would probably occur in cities, at river crossings, or in switch yards.[41]

Fuel reprocessing plants might also present an attractive target for terrorist sabotage. Here, the objective would also involve the spread of fission products beyond site boundaries. Since it is in reprocessing plants that the plutonium is separated from the irradiated fuel and purified, highly radioactive waste material is present for possible terrorist exploitation. All in all, however, the most likely results of such exploitation would be far less serious than those of other forms of nuclear terrorism. Indeed, in view of the

structure of a fuel reprocessing plant, its compartmentaliza-
tion, and its multiple backups for radioactivity removal systems, the most probable result of a major sabotage attempt
would be closing of the plant, with little radioactivity released to the outside.[42]

Political Effects of Nuclear Terrorism

Should nuclear terrorism take place, its effects would be not
only biological and ecological, but social and political as
well. These social and political effects would be experienced
internationally as well as domestically. And they would be
displayed not only by nations and governments, but by
insurgents themselves.

Once terrorists had crossed the threshold from conventional forms of destructiveness to the higher-order mode of
nuclear technology, strategies of counterterrorism would
almost certainly become more severe and repressive. Faced
with what would appear to be the primordial cell of a malignant growth, citizens of many countries throughout the
world would call upon their governments to take all necessary steps to arrest the "cancer" before it spread beyond the
reach of possible therapy. To implement these steps, governments would be compelled to adopt measures that trample
upon basic human and civil liberties.

The terrorists themselves would most likely act in a
manner that coincides with these fearful expectations. Not
only the group that perpetrated the original act of nuclear
terrorism, but many kindred groups as well, would be apt
to lose their inhibitions about "going nuclear." Subject to
technical, financial, and ideological limitations, several of
these other terrorist groups could be expected to exploit the
potential of nuclear explosives, radiological weapons, or
reactor sabotage.

In many ways, the ensuing situation between terrorists
and governments would resemble the one between states
after a nuclear exchange had taken place. Both situations
would create an atmosphere of fear and suspicion that nur-
tures a mutual incentive to preempt. Confronted with a
newly plausible threat of nuclear terrorism, governments
would begin to take seriously the advantages of "prophy-

lactic" measures against terrorist groups. At the same time, these groups, recognizing that such measures were on the way, would begin to move toward the very forms of destruction that generated these measures in the first place. Whether by conscious design or because of the conviction that the conflict had escalated through the out-of-control momentum of recent events, terrorists would find themselves under enormous pressure to strike first.

As in the case of a nuclear exchange between countries, the most important social and political effect of nuclear terrorism would be a psychological one. With the actual advent of nuclear terrorism, terrorists would become inclined to think of nuclear weapons use as distinctly "thinkable." This changed orientation would have its most dangerous effects among those particular groups of terrorists that are characterized by nihilistic or psychopathic tendencies. Here, governments would be confronted with essentially the same problem that is involved in deterring nuclear attacks by irrational national leaders.

Alignment Effects of Nuclear Terrorism

Once terrorists demonstrate an intimacy with nuclear weapon technology, new patterns of cooperation are likely to develop, first among states bent upon countering nuclear terrorism; second, amongst terrorist groups themselves; and third, between states that "sponsor" terrorism (states that would use terrorist groups as surrogate warriors) and certain terrorist groups. The combined effect of such alignments would depend, of course, on the relative power and influence of the participants.

Countering nuclear terrorism would necessarily require countries to cooperate in protecting nuclear weapon stockpiles, fissionable materials, and nuclear reactors. On a political level, international cooperation would almost certainly focus on the exchange of intelligence on terrorist groups, agreements dealing with extradition, mutual judicial assistance on matters of terrorism, collaborative infiltration of terrorist organizations, expanding and improving border checks, manipulation of the media for counterterrorist purposes, and combined negotiations with terrorist groups to project an image of common purpose and collective power.

Accelerating a process that is already well under way (see chap. 3), terrorist groups could be expected to cement new and more far-reaching patterns of cooperation among themselves after an incident of nuclear terrorism. Already, links have been established between such groups as the Palestinian organizations, the Tupamaros, the FLQ, the IRA, the Basque Liberation Front, the Baader-Meinhof group, the Turkish Popular Liberation Front and the Japanese Red Army. Occasionally, joint operations have even been staged, as in the case of the Lod Airport Massacre in May 1972, which was carried out for the PFLP by Red Army agents who had been trained in Syria. By strengthening the ties between them in response to nuclear adventurism by one or more of their number, terrorist groups would find it much easier to acquire a nuclear capability and to exploit reciprocal privileges in the form of safe havens for preattack preparations and postattack security.

Finally, since several terrorist groups operate from bases in states that are external to the target societies (most notably, the Palestinians in their ongoing "war" against Israel), and since these groups often carry out their violent activities with the blessings of these and certain other states, alliances between states and terrorists would surely become more common. As a result, many terrorist groups would experience an additional incentive to explore the "benefits" of nuclear terrorism. History is replete with such examples of states supporting terrorist efforts under way elsewhere. For example, during the period of their insurgency, FLN terrorists in Algeria received vital support from Tunisia, Morocco, and Egypt.

Although it is difficult to predict the precise combined effect of these different patterns of alignments, it would almost certainly harden existing cleavages in world politics as well as create new differences and divisions. As a result, some fundamental alterations and realignments of power might develop among states, possibly producing a wholly transformed system of international relations. It is even possible that the new ties and alignments would spark major wars between certain states. Such wars could involve terrorist surrogates on one or both sides, and might escalate from conventional to nuclear modes of conflict.

Effects of Nuclear Terrorism on Civil Liberties

No account of the political and social effects of nuclear terrorism would be complete without a careful look at the effects of such terrorism on civil liberties. Both employees in the nuclear industry and the general public would be affected.

Those in the nuclear industry would be subject to security checks, physical searches, and surveillance activities. While these restrictions would be subject to careful constitutional guarantees under normal circumstances, the onset of a genuinely grave crisis could create pressures to "be realistic" and "temporarily bypass" the Constitution. Under these conditions, industry employees might be detained or searched without probable cause, while ordinary citizens might become the object of warrantless surveillance, forced evacuations, or detention and interrogation without counsel or probable cause.[43]

Such curtailment of civil liberties has already taken place in democratic states under conditions far less threatening than nuclear terrorism. A good example of this is former Canadian Prime Minister Trudeau's response to FLQ tactics of bombing and assassination in 1970. Taking steps to put his government on a genuine wartime footing against its internal insurgents, Trudeau invoked the War Measures Act on 16 October 1970, authorizing the government to do anything "it deems necessary for the security, defense, peace, order, and welfare of Canada."[44]

Any government that feels itself faced with a potentially "lethal" threat to the state's very survival is capable of resorting to strategies that are injurious to social justice and human rights. If, in the years ahead, nuclear terrorism becomes a reality, any state could find itself turning to counter-nuclear-terrorism measures that would ordinarily be judged inconceivable. Such measures might involve a total, no-holds-barred military-type operation aimed at "prophylaxis," or a protracted campaign against insurgents employing informers, infiltrators, and perhaps even assassins.

Left unchecked, these measures could represent so great an assault on civil liberties that they would destroy the very values the strategies of counternuclear terrorism are designed to protect. Examples of such measures abound. When General Massu, head of the French Paratroop Division, was called in to deal with the FLN in Algeria in January 1957, his concern for efficient counterterrorist measures so outweighed his concern for civil liberties that he quickly abandoned measures of interrogation and intelligence-gathering in favor of torture and murder raids (*râtissages*). Similarly, under the guise of counterterrorism, right-wing vigilante groups have been allowed to run amok in Brazil, Argentina, and Guatemala.

Nuclear terrorism could also affect the civil liberties of citizens in states that harbor terrorists. In this case, those states that are the targets of terrorists' activities might act to curtain the civil liberties of citizens in the state harboring the terrorists. For example, in March 1978, Israel attacked PLO strongholds in southern Lebanon in reprisal for the Palestinian terrorist killing of thirty-three Israeli civilians near Tel Aviv. Civilians in southern Lebanon not only suffered physically, but their rights and privileges as citizens also had to be curtailed as a consequence.

It should not be assumed, however, that strategies of counternuclear terrorism which severely infringe upon civil liberties would necessarily be effective. The adoption of severe measures to curtail terrorism could impair civil liberties without providing any counterterrorist benefits. Indeed, such measures might even incite the very terrorist excesses they are designed to prevent.

Harsh and repressive measures aimed at terrorists could stiffen rather than weaken terrorist resolve, creating a condition wherein the terrorists take on the appearance of underdogs rather than criminals. In this case countermeasures would generate a symbiotic relationship between opposing "armies," with government and insurgents each "feeding" upon the other. Inevitably, this relationship would create incentives for escalation of violent action by both sides. An example of this phenomenon is the case of FLN terrorism in Algeria (1954–62) and the "mirror image" response of the OAS.

To date, virtually everyone concerned about the prospect of nuclear terrorism has sought a mechanical or technological "fix" for what is intrinsically a social-psychological and political problem. Nuclear terrorism, however, cannot be prevented by additional guards, higher fences, and other increasingly sophisticated protection devices. Sooner or later, a determined terrorist group will be able to bypass these measures and gain access to fissionable materials, assembled nuclear weapons, or nuclear power plants. Indeed, this emerged as the primary theme at the International Atomic Energy Conference held in Salzburg, Austria in May 1977. After considering numerous "black-hatting" ways of overcoming protective measures, Rudolf Rometsch, director of the IAEA Safeguards Program, offered the following conclusion: "If technological safeguards are the only protection, the system can be beaten."[45]

What *can* work to prevent nuclear terrorism are strategies directed toward affecting the *behavior* of terrorists. Such strategies must be differentiated according to the particular type of terrorist group in question (there is no such thing as "the terrorist mind") and must include promises of rewards as well as the usual threats of punishment. It may very well be that we can influence terrorists more effectively with carrots than with sticks. After all, if we take a cue from studies of behavior modification in child-rearing, positive sanctions can be more effective than negative ones.

Psychology offers other cues to behavior modification in terrorists. First, terrorists must be made to believe that their use of nuclear technology would be self-defeating. If, for example, a terrorist group displaying the self-sacrificing traits of many of today's Palestinian insurgents were to threaten nuclear violence (or were known to be considering such violence), it would be pointless to try to prevent such violence by threatening physical retaliation. Here, physical punishment, in the form of armed response, is bound to be ineffective unless it is devastating enough to ensure wholesale annihilation. Indeed, such punishment could even act as a stimulus to terrorist nuclear violence.

Instead, preventive measures should take the form of threats to obstruct the terrorist group's political objectives. To support such threats, steps would have to be taken to convince the terrorist group that nuclear violence would generate broad-based repulsion rather than support. As long as the threatened act of nuclear violence stemmed from propagandistic motives, terrorists associating such violence with unfavorable publicity would be inclined to less violent strategies.

Second, terrorists must be made to believe that their resort to nuclear violence would be met with disfavor by all of the states in world politics. Presently, of course, terrorists owe their very existence to the sympathies of certain states which sustain their efforts and encourage their excesses. As long as this situation persists, so will the incentives for terrorist acts of violence. To change this situation, states must be made to understand that they have a common interest in curbing terrorist adventurism that overrides any short-term interest in terrorist success.

Third, terrorists must be made to believe that their use of destructive nuclear technology would be countered by a united front of collaborating governments. To accomplish this objective, states must begin to create special patterns of counterterrorist cooperation of the sort outlined earlier in this chapter. In the absence of such cooperative strategies, states will soon experience a painful understanding of the consequences of inaction.

Part Three

Preventing Nuclear Catastrophe in World Politics

7 Preventing Nuclear War between the Superpowers

The existing balance of terror between the superpowers cannot last indefinitely. At one point or another, for one reason or another, the strategy of peace through nuclear deterrence must fail. The alleged rationality of mutually assured destruction (MAD) notwithstanding, this strategy promises only a temporary reprieve.[1]

What is to be done? At one level, the answer is obvious. We must put an end to the nuclear arms race. And ultimately, we must attempt to rid the American and Soviet arsenals of their existing nuclear stockpiles.

At another level, we must transform the characteristic behavior of the superpowers in world politics. As Henry Kissinger once urged (in his now famous *Pacem in Terris* speech of 8 October 1973), we must create the conditions whereby the United States and the Soviet Union "consider cooperation in the world interest to be in their national interest." While such a proposal reminds one of a popular Aesop maxim—"It is easy to propose impossible remedies"—there is no other way. Only a joint understanding that the principles of realpolitik are strikingly unrealistic can offer enduring peace between the superpowers. Only a mutual renunciation and reversal of the long-cherished pattern of nuclear arms competition can give palpable form to the benefits of arms control and disarmament measures.

Arms Control and Disarmament

In his inaugural address, President Jimmy Carter expressed his hope that "nuclear weapons could be rid from the face of the earth." On 22 March 1978, the president, in transmitting to the Congress the Seventeenth Annual Report of the U.S. Arms Control and Disarmament Agency, underscored the importance to the United States of "arms control as an essential means of promoting its security." He stressed that the "most urgent" task in this regard is "ensuring the stability of the nuclear relationship between the United States and the Soviet Union."[2] This belief is shared by Soviet President Leonid Brezhnev, who continues to warn of thermonuclear war unless the superpower arms race is curtailed.

To sustain a stable nuclear relationship, the United States and the Soviet Union have entered into a series of arms control agreements, beginning with the Limited Test Ban Treaty of 1963 and continuing through the Strategic Arms Limitation Talks (SALT) agreements of 1972 and 1974[3] and the SALT II Agreement signed in Vienna on 18 June 1979. The SALT agreements, which concern the restriction of U.S. and USSR strategic weapon systems, are the primary focal point of superpower arms control efforts. In view of their centrality to American and Soviet security, these agreements warrant a brief historical overview.

SALT

Preparations for the first Strategic Arms Limitation Talks were initiated during the administration of President Lyndon Johnson. The talks opened formally in 1969 during the administration of President Richard Nixon. The first phase, generally known at SALT I, produced both the ABM Treaty and the Interim Agreement on Strategic Offensive Arms in 1972. The ABM Treaty and the supplementary Protocol of 1974 limit ABM systems to one site per superpower, and define low limits on the number of permitted ABM interceptor missiles and radars. This treaty is of unlimited duration, subject to review by each side every five years. The particular importance of the ABM Treaty has been summed up by the U.S. Arms Control and Disarmament Agency in its Seventeenth Annual Report:

> The ABM Treaty reflected a decision on the part of both the United States and the Soviet Union to avoid a massive arms race in ballistic missile defenses that in the

end could not prevent destruction of both societies in a nuclear attack. Had the United States and the Soviet Union gone ahead with plans to deploy ABM systems, both nations would also have built more numerous and more advanced offensive weapons to insure penetration of these defenses, with consequent reduced stability, heightened political and military tensions, and substantially greater costs.[4]

The Interim Agreement Limiting Offensive Strategic Arms placed separate ceilings on land-based intercontinental ballistic missiles (ICBMs) and submarine-launched ballistic missiles (SLBMs), with the disparity in favor of the Soviet Union. This agreement froze the number of ICDM and SLBM launchers for five years, and expired on 3 October 1977. Nevertheless, both the United States and the Soviet Union, in an effort to maintain the status-quo during their negotiations toward a SALT II agreement, consented to continue their compliance with the Interim Agreement.

SALT II negotiations began in November 1972. Designed to achieve a comprehensive agreement limiting strategic offensive arms that would replace the Interim Agreement, these negotiations experienced a first major breakthrough in November 1974 at the Vladivostok meeting between President Ford and General Secretary Brezhnev. At this meeting, the two superpower leaders agreed on the following basic guidelines for a SALT II agreement:

—The duration of the new agreement would be through 1985;
—The sides would be limited to equal aggregate totals of 2,400 strategic nuclear delivery vehicles;
—The sides would be limited to 1,320 MIRVed (multiple, independently targetable reentry vehicles) systems;
—Forward-based systems (i.e., nuclear-capable U.S. systems based in Europe such as fighterbombers) would not be included.[5]

Soon after the delegations in Geneva resumed negotiations based on these guidelines, serious disagreements began to surface. The essential stumbling block lay in the inability of the Soviets and the Americans to agree on what weapons should be limited under the proposed 2,400 ceiling. More specifically, the two major issues centered on the problem of American precision-guided, long-range cruise missiles,[6] and on the new Soviet Backfire bomber.

The Vladivostok aide mémoire placed limitations on air-launched missiles with ranges that exceed 600 kilometers. The American position, however, stipulated that this referred to air-launched *ballistic* missiles and not to cruise missiles. The Soviets insisted that the cruise missile in all its variants had to be limited in any new agreement.

On the matter of the new Soviet bomber known by its NATO code name of Backfire, the arguments were reversed. The Americans insisted that the Backfire be counted in the 2,400 ceiling on overall launchers. The Soviets resisted these demands, maintaining the Backfire was primarily a theater weapon system.[7] Ultimately, stalemate was reached on these contentious issues, and the negotiations shifted to other areas, namely provisions for MIRV verification, bans on new strategic weapons, and missile throw-weight limitations.

Taking office amidst a renewed spirit of dedication to Soviet-American strategic arms control, President Jimmy Carter consciously moved to isolate SALT from other elements of superpower relations. Moreover, an effort was undertaken to strive for a cessation of strategic weapons deployment instead of merely preserving the stability of a strategic relationship. The Vladivostok stumbling blocks were placed on a back burner, and attention was focused on new goals: reducing launcher numbers from the 2,400 ceiling, limiting the testing of new missiles, installing a new set of limits on Soviet "heavy" ICBMs, and banning a number of new systems altogether.[8] These moves stemmed from a detailed interagency review of unresolved SALT issues, which stressed adding significant reductions in strategic arsenals, placing restrictions on both qualitative and quantitative aspects of the strategic arms race, and emphasizing limits on the most destabilizing strategic systems.

The result of these moves took the form of a comprehensive proposal presented to the Soviets by Secretary of State Vance and Ambassador Warnke in March 1977. This pro-

posal called for major reductions in the Vladivostok ceilings,
limits on the number of land-based, MIRVed ICBMs, limits
on the number of very large or "heavy" ICBMs, and restric-
tive limits on the testing and deployment of new types of
ICBMs. It was also proposed, as an alternative, that both
superpowers could enter into the Vladivostok arrangement
and defer the tricky cruise missile and Backfire issues until
a later time. Not only were both proposals rejected by the
Soviets, but Foreign Minister Andrei Gromyko denounced
the comprehensive proposal with particular acerbity, calling
it an attempt by the Carter Administration to achieve "unilateral advantages" through the SALT process.

Following the March 1977 debacle, a compromise arrangement was formulated by the Administration. This SALT II
Agreement Framework accommodated both the Soviet wish
for retaining Vladivostok guidelines and the American desire for most comprehensive limitations. The principal elements of the SALT II framework were outlined as follows
by the U.S. Arms Control and Disarmament Agency:

—A treaty lasting until 1985, based on the Vladivostok
  guidelines;
—A protocol which would on an interim basis deal with
  the remaining contentious issues not ready for long-
  term resolution; and
—A statement of principles for SALT THREE.

The SALT TWO treaty will establish equal limits for
the Soviet Union and the United States on each side's
aggregate number of strategic nuclear delivery vehicles
—ICBMs, SLBMs, and heavy bombers. The numerical
level specified in the treaty will be the same as the level
agreed to at Vladivostok, with provision for reduction to
a lower level.

Specifically, the treaty includes the following major
provisions:

—An initial aggregate level of 2,400 strategic systems,
  to be reduced to an agreed number between 2,160 and
  2,250 during the term of the treaty.
—A 1,320 sublimit on MIRVed ICBM and SLBM
  launchers and aircraft equipped with long-range
  cruise missiles.

—A sublimit of an agreed number between 1,200 and 1,250 on MIRVed ballistic missiles.

—A sublimit of 820 on MIRVed ICBM launchers.

Within the numerical limits set by the Treaty, each side may determine its own force structure. In other words, the sides would have "freedom to mix" among these strategic systems. This combination of equal numerical limits, with the freedom to choose the force mix within overall ceilings, resolves the otherwise difficult problem of providing for equivalence given differences in the composition of U.S. and Soviet strategic forces.

The treaty's subceilings on MIRVed ballistic missiles, and on ICBMs equipped with MIRVs, will place an upper limit on the deployment of the most threatening of the Soviet strategic weapons.

In addition, the treaty will include detailed definitions, restrictions on certain new strategic systems, and provisions designed to improve verification.

Certain issues not ready for longer term resolution, such as restrictions on new types of ICBMs, cruise missiles, and mobile ICBMs, will be included in the protocol. These issues will be topics for discussion in SALT THREE.

Specifically, the proposed protocol includes the following provisions:

—A ban on deployment of mobile ICBM launchers and on the flight testing of ICBMs from such launchers.

—Limitations on the flight testing and deployment of new types of ballistic missiles.

—A ban on the flight testing and deployment of cruise missiles capable of a range in excess of 2,500 km, and on the deployment of cruise missiles capable of a range in excess of 600 km on sea—or land-based launchers.

The third element of the SALT TWO package will be a Joint Statement of Principles for SALT THREE. These agreed upon principles will serve as general guidance for the next stage of SALT. The principles will include commitments to further reductions, more comprehensive qualitative constraints on new systems, and provisions to improve verification.[9]

On 18 June 1979, the SALT II Agreement was signed in

Vienna by Presidents Carter and Brezhnev. This agreement is composed of the text of the treaty, with its agreed statements and common understandings; the Protocol to the treaty, with its agreed statements and common understandings; the Memorandum of Understanding Regarding the Establishment of a Data Base on the Numbers of Strategic Offensive Arms; the Joint Statement of Principles and Basic Guidelines for Subsequent Negotiations on the Limitation of Strategic Arms; and the Soviet Backfire Statement.

The basic features of the treaty, which would be in force until the end of 1985, are as follows:

An equal aggregate limit on the number of strategic nuclear delivery vehicles—ICBM launchers, SLBM launchers, heavy bombers, and air-to-surface ballistic missiles (ASBMs) with ranges over 600 km. Initially, this ceiling is 2,400, but it will be lowered to 2,250 by the end of 1981.

An equal aggregate limit of 1,320 on the total number of MIRVed ballistic missile launchers and heavy bombers equipped for launching cruise missiles with ranges over 600 km.

An equal limit of 1,200 on the total number of MIRVed ballistic missile launchers and a limit of 820 on the number of launchers of MIRVed ICBMs.

Ceilings on the throw-weight and launch-weight (i.e., total missile weight) of light and heavy ICBMs.

A ban on the testing and deployment of new types of ICBMs with one exemption for each side (including a definition of a new type of ICBM based on missile parameters).

A freeze on the number of RVs on current types of ICBMs, a limit of 10 RVs on the one exempted ICBM for each side, a limit of 14 RVs on SLBMs, and a limit of 10 RVs on ASBMs.

A limit of 28 on the average number of ALCMs with ranges over 600 km deployed on heavy bombers.

A ban on the testing and deployment of ALCMs with ranges over 600 km on aircraft other than those counted as heavy bombers.

A ban on construction of additional fixed ICBM launchers and on any increase in the number of fixed heavy ICBM launchers.

A ban on heavy mobile ICBMs, heavy SLBMs, and heavy ASBMs.

A ban on certain types of strategic offensive systems not yet employed by either side, such as ballistic missiles with ranges over 600 km on surface ships.

An agreement to exchange data on a regular basis on the numbers deployed for weapons systems constrained in the agreement.

Advance notification of certain ICBM test launches.

The Protocol, which is an integral part of the treaty, sets forth limitations of shorter duration on certain systems which will remain in force until 31 December 1981. Consisting of a preamble and four Articles, the Protocol provides for the following temporary limitations:

A ban on the flight-testing of ICBMs from mobile launchers and on the deployment of Mobile ICBM launchers. Since the MX missile will not be ready for flight-testing prior to the expiration of the Protocol, this limitation will not affect the development of an American mobile-based MX missile.

A ban on the testing and deployment of air-to-surface ballistic missiles (ASBMs).

A ban on the deployment of ground-launched cruise missiles (GLCMs) and sea-launched cruise missiles (SLCMs) having ranges greater than 600 km.

The Memorandum of Understanding, signed by Ambassadors Earle and Karpov (chiefs of the United States and Soviet SALT delegations) on 18 June 1979, fulfills paragraph 3 of Article XVII of the treaty, under which the parties are required to maintain an agreed data base consisting of the numbers of strategic offensive arms of each party by specific categories. The Memorandum of Understanding establishes such an agreed data base and stipulates that the parties, have, for the purposes of the treaty, agreed on the number of arms in each category for each party as of 1 November 1978.

The Joint Statement of Principles, also signed on 18 June 1979, sets forth the intent of the parties concerning subsequent negotiations on strategic arms limitations. In its three preambular paragraphs and four sections, the Joint Statement commits the parties to continue to negotiate limitations on destabilizing strategic arms; to subject further limitations and reductions of strategic arms to adequate verification by national technical means; to perfect the operation of the Standing Consultative Commission in order to promote assurance of compliance with treaty obligations; to pursue significant and substantial reductions in the numbers of strategic offensive arms; and to consider other steps to enhance strategic stability, to ensure the equality and equal security of the parties, and to implement the aforementioned principles and objectives.

The Soviet Backfire Statement stems from the following written statement handed to President Carter by President Brezhnev on 16 June 1979:

> The Soviet side informs the U.S. side that the Soviet "Tu-22M" airplane, called "Backfire" in the USA, is a medium-range bomber, and that it does not intend to give this airplane the capability of operating at intercontinental distances. In this connection, the Soviet side states that it will not increase the radius of action of this airplane in such a way as to enable it to strike targets on the territory of the USA. Nor does it intend to give it such a capability in any other manner, including by inflight refueling. At the same time, the Soviet side states that it will not increase the production rate of this airplane as compared to the present rate.

President Brezhnev confirmed that the Soviet Backfire production rate would not exceed thirty per year. President Carter stated that the United States enters into the SALT II Agreement on the basis of the commitments contained in the Soviet statement and that it considers the carrying out of these commitments to be essential treaty obligations.[10]

The success of the SALT II Treaty will depend in part on how it deals with developing inequalities in strategic balance. At the moment, critics of the new treaty contend that proposed ceilings on Soviet land-based MIRVed missiles are unlikely to have any meaningful effect on Soviet military capabilities. Whatever the constraints laid down by the treaty, the unprecedented buildup of Soviet capabilities is expected to continue.

A special cause of current concern is that, within the next seven years, the treaty will allow the Soviet Union to develop the capacity for a successful first strike against the

American Minuteman ICBM force. To counter this threat, the United States will move ahead unilaterally with deployment of MX mobile missiles. Sometime in the late 1980s, approximately 200 of these missiles will be moved around 4,000 empty launching sites in random fashion, creating a strategic "shell game" in which land-based missile vulnerability could presumably be overcome. Under study for some time, the MX concept has emerged as the Pentagon's favored approach to coping with the silo-vulnerability problem.

Of course, the "shell game" approach to handling Soviet increases in deliverable megatons and throw-weight (a measure of how payloads can be exploited) harmonizes with the SALT agreements. American officials, concerned that the Air Force's 1,000 Minuteman and 54 Titan land-based missiles will become especially vulnerable by the mid 1980s because of Soviet advances in missile accuracy, feared that deployment of the mobile missiles would endanger a new strategic arms accord.[11] In balancing these two interests, the Carter administration, in July 1978, informed Moscow that any new accord limiting strategic nuclear arms must permit the United States to deploy the MX.

As political scientists are well aware, these problems of international bargaining and negotiation are complicated by *intra*national political and bureaucratic considerations. In the United States, the MX missile produced significant cleavages between the Pentagon and the Arms Control and Disarmament Agency (ACDA), and steps to go ahead with the MX were certainly motivated by the need for Senate approval of any SALT agreement. Similarly, the Carter administration rejected a Soviet proposal to test and deploy one new single-warhead missile (a replacement for the existing Soviet force of some 900 liquid-fuel SS-11 rockets) because of expected Capitol Hill opposition.

Another problem is the developing arms race in space. Although Soviet-American talks on controlling antisatellite weapons have taken place in Helsinki, Moscow continues to deploy hunter-killer satellites. While both superpowers have been using satellites for some time for early warning of attack and for communications, reconnaissance, and navigation, the new operational Soviet antisatellite capability is clearly destabilizing to strategic equilibrium. By perfecting techniques for intercepting satellites, the Soviets are upgrading their combat capabilities in space. A prospective problem in negotiating a ban on these "Star Wars" weapons concerns Pentagon reluctance to agree to an accord before the United States has demonstrated its own antisatellite capability.[12]

The prospects for a viable SALT II agreement are also endangered by an entire spectrum of political differences. Notwithstanding President Carter's explicit commitment not to allow SALT to become hostage to "linkage diplomacy," progress with superpower arms control has been steadily impaired by disagreements on Soviet maneuvering in Cuba and Africa, Soviet handling of human rights, American relations with China, and the Soviet invasion of Afghanistan. Despite President Carter's attempts to depoliticize SALT, it has become increasingly clear that arms control strategies have been affected by the general pattern of Soviet-American political relations.

The Soviet concern for "linkage" was clarified in late June 1978 by an article in the Communist party newspaper, *Pravda* which stated that "the present course of the United States is fraught with serious dangers, dangers for the United States, for all countries interested in peace, for the entire course of development of international relations."[13] This view signals current Soviet concern about a new Cold War hysteria in the United States, and reflects the continuing deterioration of political relationships between the two countries. It also suggests a major conceptual difference between Soviet and American ideas about detente whereby the Soviets adopt a narrow view of strategic arms control and war avoidance while the Americans adopt a broad perspective on limiting competition for international influence.

The Soviets are also particularly vexed by American interest in human rights within their country, which they view as an entirely domestic concern. In this connection, they are visibly upset by veiled American threats that SALT prospects are contingent upon the improvement of human rights conditions in Russia. And they are no less bothered by the

Carter administration's moves to "play the China card," moves involving American briefings to Chinese leaders on Soviet-American arms talks and a perceived pattern of American-Chinese alignment against Soviet interests.

In the *Pravda* article, the Soviets announced: "Alignment with China on an anti-Soviet basis would rule out the possibility of cooperation with the Soviet Union in the matter of reducing the danger of nuclear war and, of course, of limiting armaments." Coupled with their own moves in Cuba, Africa, and Afghanistan, this statement suggests that the Soviet search for parity with the United States involves not only strategic weapons, but also positions of influence throughout the Third World. Thus, it appears that the success of superpower arms control efforts will depend on joint attempts to improve general political relations. And these attempts may call for unpalatable compromises by both sides.[14]

This point was clearly understood by Paul C. Warnke, former director of the U.S. Arms Control and Disarmament Agency:

> A SALT II Treaty or any other arms control agreement between the Soviet Union and the United States certainly should not be a reward for Soviet good behavior. We should enter into any arms control agreement if— and only if—it advances U.S. security interests when viewed on its own merits. If it does so, we should not deprive ourselves of its benefits because the Soviet Union fails to meet our ideal of international conduct. And if an agreement does not advance our interests on its own merits, we should not accept it no matter how benignly the Soviet Union may conduct itself internationally.[15]

SALT and NPT

The benefits of a viable SALT II agreement between the superpowers would extend to the more general goal of nonproliferation. In fact, SALT was originally conceived, in large measure, as a necessary incentive to nonnuclear powers to accept the NPT. As Wayland Young (Lord Kennet), chairman of the International Parliamentary Conference on the Environment, put it: "SALT, be-all and end-all to the

superpowers, is to the non-nuclear powers just the son of
NPT. . . . SALT is there because the non-nuclear powers
would not accept the NPT unless the superpowers under-
took to try to reach nuclear disarmament."[16] According to
Article VI of the Treaty on the Non-Proliferation of Nuclear
Weapons:

> Each of the Parties to the Treaty undertakes to pursue
> negotiations in good faith on effective measures relating
> to cessation of the nuclear arms race at an early date
> and to nuclear disarmament, and on a treaty on general
> and complete disarmament under strict and effective
> international control.

In the absence of Soviet-American compliance with this
element of the NPT, it is difficult to imagine that non-nuclear-
weapon states would remain in their restricted conditions
indefinitely.[17] Should the superpowers fail to sustain an effective SALT II agreement, the resultant spread of nuclear
weapon countries would not only create new opportunities
for nuclear conflict, but would also heighten the probability
of a Soviet-American nuclear war. As discussed earlier, proliferation would increase the likelihood of catalytic war
(war provoked by a new nuclear power), war between new
nuclear powers with alliance or interest ties to the superpowers, and nuclear terrorism.

Catalytic war might be brought about through the accidental, unauthorized, or irrational use of nuclear weapons
by new nuclear powers against one or both of the superpowers. The danger would be particularly great should such
use be anonymous. Leo Szilard, one of the first scientists to
understand the physics of an atomic chain reaction, wrote
in 1961 a story which represents a fictional retrospective
look at the future. The story, entitled "The Voice of the
Dolphins," depicts the period 1980 to 1985 largely in terms
of the probable consequences of proliferation. The following segment illustrates the problem of an anonymous
attack:

> Fears were growing, both in America and in Russia, that
> one day a bomb might be launched from a German or a
> Japanese submarine and destroy, say, an American city.

Since the identity of the attacker would remain concealed, America might counter-attack Russia, with the result that Russia would counter-attack America. To what extent such fears were justified it is difficult to say, but it is certain that if Russia and America had mutually destroyed each other this would have left both Germany and Japan in a much better position to pursue their aspirations.[18]

Of course, Szilard's choice of aggressors is now an implausible one, and could certainly be improved upon were the story rewritten today, but the type of situation depicted is entirely plausible. Indeed, as Szilard himself points out in a footnote to his story, it has already occurred in recent history.

The reader may recall that, during the Second World War, a few days after Germany went to war against Russia there was an attack from the air against the Hungarian city of Kassa. The Hungarians examined the bomb fragments and found that the bombs were of Russian manufacture. We know today that the bombs were dropped by the German Air Force to create the impression that Russia was the attacker and to induce Hungary to declare war on Russia. The ruse was in fact successful.[19]

SALT and SSOD

Ideally, the Soviet Union and the United States should have come to the U.S. Special Session on Disarmament (SSOD) with a SALT II Treaty behind them. This would have offered an incentive for strengthening multilateral disarmament programs and mechanisms. Unfortunately, the special session was held in New York City from 23 May to 28 June 1978 without the benefit of a major superpower arms accord.

The SSOD was the first occasion since the 1932 General Disarmament Conference to involve virtually all states on this potentially apocalyptic issue. Although it opened and closed with precious little publicity or general interest, it reflected the deep dissatisfactions of many U.N. members with what they regard as imprudently slow progress in disarmament. Its chief promoters were the nations of the Third

World, who feel threatened both by the burgeoning strategic arsenals of the superpowers and by the prospect of new nuclear powers. Reflecting this view, an oft-expressed theme of the conference was the need for genuine curtailments by the chief actors in the arms race.

But the heads of the two superpowers were conspicuously absent from the proceedings. Ironically, this most probably reflected the understanding on the part of Brezhnev and Carter that any strong endorsement by one of them of the disarmament idea during the highly delicate SALT deliberations could lead to demands for unacceptable concessions by the other. Strangely enough, the objectives of SALT and SSOD are far from congruent: SALT is concerned with the stabilization of mutual nuclear deterrence between the superpowers and excludes disarmament plans which carry the possibility of a radical redistribution of global power.

For the nonaligned initiators of the special session, the principal objectives were greater superpower commitment to steps beyond SALT II, comprehensive test ban negotiations, limitation of nuclear arsenals, and the beginning of real nuclear weapon reductions. For the United States and the Soviet Union, however, these objectives were tempered by a joint, albeit tacit, commitment to the extant distribution of global power—that is, to continuing their present bipolar dominance of the planet. As Professor Hedley Bull has written, Soviet-American cooperation in the arms control area has always been accompanied "by the attempt to legitimize very high ceilings of strategic arms, by political cooperation directed against third parties, and by enunciation of a principle of parity whose effect is to formalize the claims of these two states to a special position in the hierarchy of military power."[20]

"In a curious way," said *New York Times* reporter Richard Burt, Washington and Moscow were "uncomfortable allies" at the special session.[21] Having institutionalized their own competition in strategic arms, the Soviets and Americans were criticized by the "new majority" of nonaligned nations for failing to heed the admonitions of Article VI of the NPT. To a very considerable extent, failure to reach a SALT II agreement placed the superpowers in the role of national hypocrites, ensuring the irrelevance of the special session at the outset. The resultant consequences bode ill not only for the system as a whole, but for a stable Soviet-American relationship in particular. As we have already noted, this is the case because the consequences of proliferation include a heightened probability of nuclear war between the superpowers.

In a world as interdependent as ours, where arms control efforts in one sector invariably have manifestations in other sectors, vertical and horizontal proliferation are a seamless web rather than discrete, isolable conditions. Within this web, the superpowers must learn to set a proper example for a world rid of nuclear weapons. They can do this, as Richard Falk suggests, by striving for a "fuller realization of the juridical promise of sovereign equality" and by creating a "credible program of overall denuclearization." According to Professor Falk:

> Denuclearization means the progressive elimination of nuclear weaponry. The goal is a non-nuclear world in which nuclear weapons are neither legitimate nor possessed. In the context of denuclearization, nonproliferation is obviously integral, but secondary. From the perspective of denuclearization, the wellsprings of danger are not those international actors who *may* acquire nuclear weapons, but rather those who presently possess these weapons, those who have continued to deploy them, and those who improve their nuclear weapons systems—those states, in other words, who actually rely on nuclear weapons as a major policy resource.[22]

The states that are not superpowers in the extant system have come to understand that current forms of Soviet-American cooperation in vertical arms control are conceived with a view to preserving "top-dog" positions in the hierarchy of international power. Unless this perception is changed, the other national members of our global society are bound to resist the high-minded goals stipulated by the NPT and the SSOD. For such a change to take place, arms control and disarmament measures must be undertaken which serve a broader purpose than ratifying the present bipolar dominance of world politics. Distasteful as it may seem to "First Worlders," a more promising approach to global arms control and disarmament requires a shift in power in favor of Third World countries. Such a shift must materialize not through the sanctification of horizontal proliferation, but through substantially more far-reaching modes of curtailing vertical proliferation.

In this connection, it is most important to understand that by agreeing to a shift in global power, the superpowers would contribute significantly to an effective nonproliferation effort, which in turn would increase their own security. By restructuring their arms control efforts along lines that seek to assure the security of international society as a whole, the United States and the Soviet Union could begin to forge a much more durable path to safety from nuclear war. By severing the connection that now obtains between strategies of arms control and attempts to preserve their duopolistic dominance of the international strategic "market," the superpowers would—in effect—acquire an opportunity for a far more genuine form of national security.[23]

A Plan for Meaningful Arms Control
between the Superpowers

In his opening remarks before the Seventeenth Strategy for Peace Conference at Airlie House, Warrenton, Virginia, on 7 October 1976, Conference Chairman C. Maxwell Stanley correctly observed: "Until there is dramatic change, SALT will remain the lowest common denominator of the world community's efforts to halt and reverse the arms race."[24] What, exactly, is this "dramatic change"? Our answer can be framed in a series of four concrete, interrelated, proposals.[25]

Minimum Deterrence

First, the United States and the Soviet Union must return to the relative sanity of strategies based on "minimum deterrence," i.e., strategies based upon the ability to inflict an unacceptable degree of damage upon the aggressor after absorbing a nuclear first strike. It is widely understood by experts in the field that each side has this ability right now, and that each can continue to have such an ability without further deployment of nuclear weapons and with substantial reductions in the existing arsenals. The United States now has 8,500 strategic nuclear warheads, the smallest of which is three times bigger than the Hiroshima bomb. The Russians have at least 4,000 warheads. And both countries have thousands of tactical nuclear weapons.

In short, each side already has far more than is necessary for minimum deterrence. Since the survival of even the smallest fraction of American or Russian ICBMs, bombers, and submarines could assure the destruction of the other, we now have perceptible levels of "overkill." No conceivable breakthrough in military technology can upset either side's minimum deterrence capability. Even if 90 percent of all American nuclear forces were destroyed by a Soviet first strike, the remaining 10 percent could wipe out the 219 major Soviet cities four times over.

These points are corroborated by General Maxwell D. Taylor, former chairman of the Joint Chiefs of Staff:

> In my opinion, the only rational way to measure the adequacy of our strategic forces is by their ability to destroy all Soviet targets and/or systems which they may be ordered to attack, regardless of the circumstances. This measurement, then, is not primarily dependent on the size of the Soviet forces. For the present and foreseeable future, I am convinced that both the United States and the Soviet Union are able to destroy each other utilizing their present or predicted forces and should be able to retain this destructive capability indefinitely.[26]

Within the context of SALT, the return to minimum deterrence would require particular emphasis on the Joint Statement of Principles. This would mean major commitments to further reductions, more comprehensive qualitative constraints on new weapon systems, and provisions to improve verification techniques.

An even more promising strategy, perhaps, would involve the "multilaterization" of SALT and related negotiations.[27] This could be accomplished within the world's principal forum for multilateral arms control negotiations, the Conference of the Committee on Disarmament (CCD), which has met in Geneva each year since 1962. Recently designated more simply as the Committee on Disarmament, its membership was enlarged in 1969 to include thirty-one nations. Its principal credits include the NPT, the Seabed Arms Control Treaty, the Biological Weapons Convention, and the Convention on the Prohibition of Hostile Uses of Environmental Modification Techniques, which were successfully negotiated in the CCD.[28]

In the past several years, the CCD has already held meetings to discuss a comprehensive test ban, a ban on chemical weapons, a proposed ban on new kinds of mass destruction weapons, and the matter of a comprehensive negotiating program of arms control/disarmament measures. Concern for this last matter was institutionalized on 25 August 1977, when the CCD established an ad hoc working group to discuss a draft comprehensive negotiating program. By providing a broad international political context for working out problems of arms control and disarmament, the CCD might profitably subsume SALT on its agenda for vital reform.

In reference to the proposed broader role for the CCD, the U.N. General Assembly's Special Session on Disarmament approved a proposal to enlarge the disarmament commission and eliminate the joint Soviet-American chairmanship. This move was intended to bring France and China into the talks. The proposal increased the thirty-one nation committee to forty members, created a rotating chairmanship among all committee members on an alphabetical basis, and allowed for a permanent secretary to be appointed by U.N. Secretary General Kurt Waldheim.[29]

Comprehensive Test Ban

Second, the time is at hand for a banning of all nuclear weapon testing, i.e., a comprehensive test ban (CTB). Notwithstanding the 1963 Partial Test Ban Treaty, the 1973 Limited Test Ban Treaty, the 1974 Treaty on the Limitation of Underground Nuclear Weapon Tests, the 1974 Threshold Treaty, the 1976 Treaty on Underground Nuclear Explosions for Peaceful Purposes, and the SALT II protocol provisions dealing with flight testing of ICBMs, new types of ballistic missiles, and certain kinds of cruise missiles, only a comprehensive test ban can substantially inhibit further nuclear weapon innovations. Now the subject of a major joint United States-Soviet working group, a comprehensive nuclear test ban would be the culmination of a goal first outlined in the late 1950s. To be genuinely promising, CTB would have to include a moratorium on peaceful nuclear explosion tests (PNEs) as well, since PNE tests are indistinguishable from nuclear weapon tests.[30]

From the point of view of preventing nuclear war between the superpowers, CTB should include all nuclear weapon states and the largest possible number of non-nuclear-weapon states. However, even if France and China initially chose to stay outside such an agreement (neither China nor France has ratified the Partial Test Ban Treaty of 1963), CTB's prospective benefits are apt to be great enough to warrant endorsement. In the words of Jane Sharp, in her introduction to *Opportunities for Disarmament*, disarmament—like charity—should begin at home.[31] Understood in terms of the primary responsibility of the superpowers to make nonproliferation credible in a world of self-assertive states,[32] this means that CTB could offer the critical starting point for wider imitation and reciprocity.

Presently, both superpowers are on record in favor of a comprehensive test ban. President Carter has made such a ban one of the principal objectives of his program for arms control and disarmament. His intentions on this matter were announced before the United Nations on 17 March 1977 and on 4 October 1977, when he told the General Assembly: "The time has come to end all explosions of nuclear devices, no matter what their claimed justification, peaceful or military."[33]

It is, however, the failure of the United States to distinguish between peaceful and military explosions that upsets the Soviets. Although the Soviets have recently backed off from a firm desire not to prevent peaceful nuclear explosions, they are still interested in making some sorts of allowances for PNEs in the future. General Secretary Brezhnev has announced Soviet willingness to accept a moratorium on peaceful nuclear explosions in conjunction with a treaty prohibiting nuclear weapon tests, but he has tied this moratorium to a fixed period of time and to a series of continuing negotiations on the issue.[34] An additional problem in concluding a CTB centers on verification of compliance, but continuing improvements in seismic technology suggest that on-site inspections will become less important and that mutually acceptable procedures are well within the range of feasibility.

No–First-Use Pledge

Third, the United States and the Soviet Union must take the declaratory step of renouncing first use of nuclear weapons.[35] Unfortunately, although a no-first-use pledge would be an important first step in the process of "delegitimizing" nuclear weapons,[36] offering even the fulcrum of more ambitious and universal efforts at denuclearization, the United States continues to oppose such a measure. As we have seen in part 1 of this text, the opposition stems from NATO strategy of deterring Soviet conventional attack with American nuclear weapons.[37] According to Gen. George S. Brown, former chairman of the Joint Chiefs of Staff:

> NATO's defense against growing Soviet strength is based on a strategy of flexible response. Should NATO's primary objective of deterrence fail, its strategy requires that aggression be met with an appropriate response drawn from a range of available options to preserve or restore the territorial integrity of the Alliance. For this strategy to be credible, NATO must deploy conventional forces, theater nuclear forces, and strategic nuclear forces.[38]

Moreover, says Brown, unless "remedial action" is taken to correct deficiencies in NATO's conventional forces, the alliance may be forced to "resort quickly to nuclear warfare or suffer the consequences of intimidation or defeat by superior Warsaw Pact forces."[39]

These views are supported by Secretary of Defense Harold Brown:

> It continues to be U.S. policy that we will resist attacks on the United States and its allies by whatever necessary

means, including nuclear weapons. We have made no secret of our view that conventional forces are an essential component of the collective deterrent, and that any conventional aggression should be met initially by conventional means. We also recognize that nuclear decisions—and especially collective nuclear decisions—would be difficult and could be time-consuming, which makes strong non-nuclear capabilities all the more important. But the United States remains determined to do whatever is required to prevent the defeat of its own and allied forces. Our strategic and theater nuclear forces serve as the ultimate backup to our NATO commitments. Not only do they provide the means to strike NATO-related targets; they also dramatize to a potential attacker that any conventional attack could set off a chain of nuclear escalation, the consequences of which would be incalculable.[40]

It is clear, from existing policy, that a no-first-use pledge would be contrary to the most basic elements of American nuclear deterrence strategy. To permit a renunciation of the first-use option, which originated when the United States had a nuclear monopoly, the United States would have to calculate that the prospective benefits of such renunciation in superpower stability and arms control would outweigh the prospective costs in NATO instability and vulnerability. To allow such a calculation, which would entail final abandonment of the neutron bomb, redeployment of theater nuclear forces away from frontiers, and ultimate removal of these forces altogether, the United States would have to undertake enormous efforts to strengthen conventional forces. These efforts would be necessary in order to preserve a sufficiently high nuclear threshold.

Such efforts would be desirable. Whatever their expense, it must be recognized that current U.S. policy heightens the threat of using nuclear weapons. A no-first-use pledge would counter the buildup of an American counterforce capability, diminish the nuclear arms competition, and lead to genuine reductions in nuclear weapon stockpiles.

Such efforts would be dangerous. But, current alarmist exhortations notwithstanding, they would be less dangerous than continuing with existing policy.[41] To minimize the dangers of a no-first-use pledge, it would be essential to convince the Soviets to reduce their own conventional forces. Such a reduction would be part of an overall plan to achieve an equalization of conventional forces in the European theater.

In terms of the principal arms control effort now underway in Europe—Mutual and Balanced Force Reductions (MBFR)—such equalization would require major policy changes. MBFR negotiations have been in progress in Vienna since November 1973. Their objective has been to increase security through unequal reductions in East-West forces to lower and safer levels. Presently, this objective is being sought through limited NATO ground manpower reductions and through substantial reductions of Warsaw Pact ground manpower and Soviet tanks.

To make MBFR consistent with the requirements of a no-first-use pledge, the ongoing search for joint reductions in conventional and nuclear forces would have to be changed in favor of a plan which allows for the improvement and growth of American conventional forces amidst the progressive elimination of both sides' theater-capable nuclear forces. The objective of such a plan would be a condition in which U.S. and allied conventional forces could deter, and—if necessary—repel any Soviet conventional attack. In exchange for this seemingly one-sided arrangement, one which simultaneously fosters growth of Western conventional forces and reductions of Eastern conventional forces, the United States would agree to a staged redeployment of tactical nuclear weapons away from forward areas with the aim of ultimately withdrawing these weapons.

Such a program would be entirely consistent with what General Brown described as the "overriding objective for NATO," which is "to strengthen its military posture by making the quantitative and qualitative improvements to conventional forces needed to meet the Soviet/Warsaw Pact challenge."[42]

And the Soviets should not find it difficult to permit such improvements in exchange for American concessions on tactical nuclear weapons.[43] However, since the ultimate objective of a transformed MBFR would be a stable military balance in the region based entirely on conventional weapons,[44] American nuclear concessions would have to be paralleled by far-reaching curbs on the growing Russian theater-nuclear-weapons delivery capability. Presently, Warsaw Pact forces are equipped with tactical nuclear delivery systems, and the Soviet Union has deployed even longer range systems with a theater attack capability in the Soviet Union itself. These peripheral attack systems, which are not covered by MBFR or SALT, include light and medium bombers, the large medium range ballistic missile (MRBM) and intermediate range ballistic missile (IRBM) force now being modernized with mobile SS-20 MIRVed missiles, and submarine and surface ships armed with ballistic and cruise missiles.[45]

Nuclear-Weapon–Free Zones

Fourth, the superpowers must supplement their no-first-use pledge with an effective arrangement for nuclear-weapon-free zones. Although the ultimate objective of such an arrangement would be consistent with former prime minister of India Desai's plea to the U.N. General Assembly's Special Session on Disarmament—that the "whole world should be declared a nuclear-free zone"—a more intermediate objective would be limited to particular regions. The incremental effect of such a particularistic strategy might very well be worldwide denuclearization.

The concept of nuclear-weapon-free zones has already received international legal expression in the Treaty for the Prohibition of Nuclear Weapons in Latin America (the Treaty of Tlatelolco), which entered into force on 22 April 1968, and the two additional Protocols to the treaty. Unlike two earlier treaties which seek to limit the spread of nuclear weapons into areas yet to be contaminated—the Antarctic Treaty of 1961 and the Outer Space Treaty of 1967—the Latin American treaty concerns a populated area. The terms of the treaty include measures to prevent the type of deployment of nuclear weapons that led to the Cuban missile crisis, methods of verification by both the parties themselves and by their own regional organization, and IAEA safeguards on all nuclear materials and facilities under the jurisdiction of the parties.[46]

Although it is sometimes argued that nuclear-free zones may have few if any advantages over regional adherence to the existing Non-Proliferation Treaty, such zones do offer certain added opportunities for flexibility. As explained by Professor Robert C. Johansen:

> First of all, they [the nuclear-free zones] may cover regions of the globe, such as the Indian Ocean, where no state exercises sovereignty. Second, in nuclear-weapon free zones states may undertake obligations they refused in the Non-Proliferation Treaty. For example, in the Treaty of Tlatelolco, which prohibits nuclear weapons in the Latin American states that have ratified it, the United States and the United Kingdom both agreed not to use or to threaten to use nuclear weapons against any countries in the zone, a provision they refused to include in the Non-Proliferation Treaty. China and France have also agreed to this provision even though they are not parties to the Non-Proliferation Treaty.[47]

In the coming years, it would surely be helpful if the Treaty of Tlatelolco comes to be regarded as a model for imitation in other sectors of the globe, providing a mobilizing force for the creation of increasingly larger sanctuaries from nuclear weapons. In the absence of far-reaching respect for NPT commitments, nuclear-weapon-free zones offer an especially promising means of reducing the number of potential opportunities for superpower confrontation and conflict. A majority of states already supports the idea of nuclear-weapon free zones, and proposals for regional programs have been advanced for Scandinavia, the Balkans, the Mediterranean, Africa, South Asia, and the South Pacific.

The probable extent of superpower support for this notion is problematic. An indication of this is recognizable in Soviet-American opposition to a 1971 General Assembly declaration which designated the Indian Ocean a "zone of peace." This opposition was based on the declaration's alleged violation of the freedom of the seas.

Although the initiatives for nuclear-weapon-free zones

should come from states within particular regions, the nuclear weapon states—especially the superpowers—must agree to refrain from acts which would violate the zone.[48] In a nuclear-weapon-free zone, not only must the acquisition of nuclear weapons by nonnuclear countries within a region be prohibited, but so must the stationing, transport, and deployment of nuclear weapons by nuclear weapon states in that region. With respect to the Latin Ameircan Nuclear Free Zone Treaty, Protocol II—which commits signatory nuclear powers to respect the denuclearization of Latin America and not to use or threaten to use nuclear weapons in the region—has been ratified by the United States but has not been signed by the Soviet Union. In general, the Soviet Union has favored the creation of nuclear-free zones in other parts of the world, especially Central Europe and the Mediterranean.

All in all, from the standpoint of preventing nuclear war between the superpowers, the idea of nuclear-free zones is a good one. By avoiding certain features of the NPT which are objectionable to certain states, such zones could become a promising security alternative to the NPT for countries that are not parties to that agreement. This does not mean that nuclear-free zones would interfere with the NPT; rather, it means that they could reinforce the treaty's essential objective of promoting an effective nonproliferation regime. Moreover, by obtaining pledges from the superpowers to abstain from nuclear engagement in stipulated regions of the world, nuclear-free zones could limit the number of possible confrontation sites. In the endless minefield of the nuclear age, the nuclear-free zone is an idea whose time has come.

To further acceptance of the idea among the superpowers, Professor William Epstein has proposed four essential steps that warrant careful attention:

1. Undertake to become a party to Protocol I of the Treaty of Tlatelolco (this would apply only to the United States and France);
2. Undertake to become a party to Protocol II of the Treaty of Tlatelolco (this would apply only to the Soviet Union and possibly India);
3. Issue a joint declaration or separate declarations

that they will respect the status of any nuclear free
zone and that they will not use or threaten to use
nuclear weapons against any such zone;
4. Undertake to actively support and promote the establishment of additional nuclear-free zones.[49]

Redefining Superpower Interests

Taken together, the foregoing proposals constitute a coher-
ent strategy for preventing nuclear war between the superpowers. Instead of simply fine tuning overworked scenarios
of nuclear gamesmanship between the U.S. and the USSR,
these proposals point toward a far-reaching disengagement
from existing patterns of strategic competition. Indeed, they
comprise the essential elements of what might reasonably be
called a "nuclear regime"—a system of obligations, force
structures, and doctrinal postures, based upon certain values
and goals, and shaped by certain fearful expectations of the
future.[50] If it were taken seriously as a means of under-
mining the ill-fated vagaries which define the relationship
between the superpowers, this nuclear regime might prove
vital to identifying a new and hopeful sense of direction. By
seeking to remove the corrosive stresses and contradictions
of the present Soviet-American nuclear balance, this alternative system of norms and procedures could foster real mod-
eration and stability between the superpowers.

However, as was indicated at the beginning of this chapter, something else is also needed. This "something else" is
nothing less than a reconceptualization of superpower foreign policies along systemic lines. Responding to what Stanley Hoffman has called "the fragile flickerings of 'universal
consciousness,'"[51] the superpowers must seek conditions
which exploit the foundations of cooperation, commonality,
and pluralism.

The superpowers must jointly attempt to promote a "just
world order," a global society embodying the values of
peace, social justice, economic well-being, and ecological
stability.[52] Without necessarily seeking fundamental changes
in the prevailing state-centric structure of global authority,
the two superpowers must learn to associate their own
security from nuclear war with a more far-reaching search

for worldwide stability and equity.[53] To prevent nuclear war between the superpowers, the prescribed nuclear regime must be augmented by a new awareness of the "connectedness" of states.

Ultimately, the chances for a successful detachment from strategic arms competition will depend upon whether concrete steps are taken to undermine the nuclear threat system, once the superpowers realize that their own security interests are inevitably congruent with those of the world as a whole. The balance of power between the Soviet Union and the United States can never be more stable than the balance of power in the whole of international society. By recognizing this fact, and by subordinating the maintenance of the existing hierarchy of military power to the requirements of more universalized interests, the superpowers can step back from a future that now looms menacingly.

The superpowers will have to take certain risks and hope that arms control and disarmament measures will be offset by the benefits of increased global security. This will require a degree of courage for which there is no meaningful precedent in world affairs. Imagination, the outreaching of national "minds," the casting off of nuclear mooring ropes—these are the qualities that must be displayed by Soviet and American leaders in the years ahead. The will to survive must take precedence over the wish to prevail, and this entails new forms of compromise and interdependence. Although, as Rollo May tells us, "consicousness is the awareness that emerges out of the dialectical tension between possibilities and limitations,"[54] the time has come to place greater emphasis on the former.

In sum, the capacity to prevent nuclear war between the superpowers is inseparable from a new consciousness by our national leaders. Amidst the precarious crosscurrents of global power relations, the United States and the Soviet Union must undertake prodigious efforts to resist the "lure of primacy," focusing instead on the emergence of a new sense of global obligation.[55] And these efforts must be undertaken very soon. The great French Enlightenment philosopher, Jean Jacques Rousseau, once remarked: "The majority of nations, as well as of men, are tractable only in their

youth; they become incorrigible as they grow old." Understood in terms of the superpower imperative to change
direction in the search for peace, this suggests that unless
these nations achieve such a change before losing their
"youth," the chances for later success may be lost forever.

8 Preventing Nuclear War Resulting from Proliferation

The most insidious aspect of nuclear proliferation is the power it bestows on national leaders. History has shown us the destruction that could be wrought by unstable heads of state with far more limited means at their disposal.

How are we to stop the spread? We live in a global society fraught with incentives for governments to acquire nuclear weapons. These incentives include presumed advantages in terms of deterrence and international status as well as bolstered domestic political support, increased strategic autonomy, and leverage over major world powers.[1] Unless would-be members of the nuclear club can be persuaded that these incentives are outweighed by a compelling array of disincentives, these countries are likely to "go nuclear."

To discourage proliferation, states must act together to strengthen and abide by current international treaties and agreements directed at nonproliferation, arms control, and disarmament. They must also join in renouncing the long-discredited principles of realpolitik. These measures closely parallel those recommended for preventing nuclear war between the superpowers. They rest upon the understanding that a successful nonproliferation regime demands not only customary restraints under international law, but also a full-fledged transformation of foreign policy processes. The creative apogee of such antiproliferation thinking can be reached only when all states learn to identify their own best interests with the security of the entire system of world politics. Or, in words from the latest Report to the Club of Rome, we require a "world solidarity revolution" as a pre-condition for survival.[2]

Controlling Nuclear Proliferation

The present nonproliferation regime is founded upon a scaffolding of multilateral agreements, statutes, and safeguards. The important elements of this scaffolding are the Atomic Energy Act of 1954; the Statute of the International Atomic Energy Agency, which came into force in 1957; the Nuclear Test Ban Treaty, which entered into force on 10 October 1963; the Outer Space Treaty, which entered into force on 10 October 1967; the Treaty Prohibiting Nuclear Weapons in Latin America, which entered into force on 22 April 1968; and the Seabeds Arms Control Treaty, which entered into force on 18 May 1972. However, the most important element of the nonproliferation regime is still the Treaty on the Non-Proliferation of Nuclear Weapons, which entered into force on 5 March 1970.

Since, as we have already learned, certain provisions of the NPT—especially Article VI—call for a halt in the nuclear arms race between the superpowers, the SALT treaties and negotiations must also be included as vital parts of the nonproliferation regime. Before the world's nonnuclear powers begin to take nonproliferation seriously, the United States and the Soviet Union will have to sustain a meaningful new SALT agreement. This point was emphasized recently by Paul Warnke, former director of the U.S. Arms Control and Disarmament Agency:

> In the Non-Proliferation Treaty, which came into effect in 1970, the United States and the Soviet Union undertook in Article VI to take prompt steps to bring nuclear armaments under control. We haven't really done enough about that yet. The other countries that signed the treaty in reliance on that promise are reminding us of this fact. At the recently completed United Nations Special Session on Disarmament there was a great deal of complaint about the fact that the two nuclear superpowers had not as yet given meaningful content to that pledge. I think we would be kidding ourselves if we thought that we could wait indefinitely to bring about meaningful measures of nuclear arms control and still expect the rest of the world to continue to forego the acquisition of nuclear weapons capability of their own. They won't indefinitely listen to lectures about nonpro-

liferation without seeing hard evidence that we ourselves and the Soviet Union are prepared to accept
nuclear restraint.[3]

Although it should be clear that proliferation would be
inimical to the security of every state, even if the superpowers fail to live up to the NPT obligation to halt their
own strategic arms competition, the nonweapon states hold
to a different view. As they see it, a "bargain" has been struck
between the superpowers and themselves, and unless the
former begin to take more ambitious steps toward "vertical"
arms control and disarmament they, too, will move in the
direction of strategic capability. Ironically, but understand-
ably, the nonnuclear powers consider this bargain to be the
most prudent path to security.

What this means, from the standpoint of controlling nuclear proliferation, is that the superpowers must restructure
their central strategic relationship. Apropos of the recommendations in the preceding chapter, such restructuring
must be oriented toward a return to strategies of "minimum
deterrence"; a comprehensive nuclear test ban; a joint renunciation of first use of nuclear weapons; and a joint
effort toward creating additional nuclear-weapon-free zones.
Moreover, the declaratory features of these steps must be
backed up by genuine reductions in deployed strategic systems; restraints in qualitative improvements of weapon
systems; improved verification techniques; multilateraliza-
tion of SALT and related negotiations; a moratorium on
peaceful nuclear explosions; major policy changes in the
European theater; and further commitments to the Treaty
of Tlatelolco.

At the moment, the efforts of the superpowers continue
to remind one of Albert Einstein's views on the first disarmament conference of the League of Nations in 1926. As
Einstein passed through Geneva during the conference, re-
porters asked for his assessment of the progress being made.
Said Einstein: "What would you think about a meeting of a
town council which is convened because an increasing number of people are knifed to death each night in drunken
brawls, and which proceeds to discuss just how long and

how sharp shall be the knife that the inhabitants of the city may be permitted to carry?"[4]

The nonnuclear powers are also concerned about the nuclear weapon states that are not superpowers. Strictly speaking, Article VI of the NPT calls upon these states as well as the United States and the Soviet Union to pursue an end to the nuclear arms race and to promote nuclear disarmament. To date, France and China have been particularly intransigent about curbing their own nuclear weapon programs.

By limiting the importance of nuclear weapons through nuclear disarmament, the non-nuclear-weapon states would be offered a significant incentive *not* to proliferate. However, it would surely be unrealistic to believe that curtailments in existing nuclear arsenals, even if they were very substantial, would be sufficient to halt the further spread of nuclear weapons. Additional incentives would also be vital.

Perhaps the most important such incentive is a generalized perception that nuclear weapons would not enhance the security of those states that still do not possess them, and that—in fact—such weapons would even produce insecurity. Although such a view would prove difficult to understand in a world founded upon the classical principles of political "realism," its essential truthfulness suggests some cause for optimism. This cause might be heightened by maintaining the burdensome costs associated with a military nuclear program and by offering superpower security assurances to nonnuclear allies.[5]

The nuclear powers might also contribute to the belief that proliferation would be unattractive by enhancing the security of nonnuclear weapon states in other ways. They might, for example, pledge not to use nuclear weapons against nonweapon states.[6] To the extent that such a pledge would be widely believed, it could contribute to the understanding that nonacquisition of nuclear weapons promotes safety. For example, accession to such a pledge by India and China would provide incentives not to "go nuclear" for Pakistan and Taiwan. And accession by a "near nuclear power" such as Israel might provide similar incentives to the Arab states.

The economic expense involved in going nuclear should also discourage countries from doing so. Coupled with the security disadvantages of going nuclear, these high monetary costs should serve as a disincentive to further proliferation.

However, because of the growth of nuclear power industries, nations that turn to nuclear power for energy purposes would incur a decline in the incremental cost associated with a nuclear weapon program.[7] It follows that in order to control proliferation in a world characterized by the increasing scarcity of fossil fuels, adequate controls and safeguards will have to be applied to civilian nuclear energy programs. With such controls and safeguards, the benefits of the peaceful atom might be obtained without suffering proliferation of nuclear weapons.[8]

To decouple civilian nuclear energy programs from the spread of nuclear weapons, major efforts will have to get underway to strengthen both national and international institutions and procedures concerning the protection of nuclear facilities, materials, and weapons-grade nuclear fuel. The core of these efforts must be a comprehensive non-proliferation regime supported by the Non-Proliferation Treaty. This treaty, which now has more than 100 states as parties, commits signatories to apply IAEA (International Atomic Energy Agency) safeguards to all of their nuclear facilities. To date, the NPT has contributed significantly to fostering the spread of peaceful nuclear power without further nuclear weapon proliferation.

To make the NPT work successfully in the future, a number of changes are called for, particularly in those elements of the treaty which are persistently controversial; namely, (1) the inherently discriminatory features of the NPT, which place an unequal set of obligations on non-nuclear-weapon states, and (2) the inherently weak safeguards system advocated by the treaty. Non-nuclear-weapon states feel that the treaty provides neither effective guarantees for their security nor reliable access to the energy benefits of nuclear power. The nuclear weapon countries fear that the treaty provides too few meaningful constraints to halt proliferation.

To deal with these problematic elements of the NPT, a

number of steps need to be taken. First, non-nuclear-weapon states must be given reasonable assurances that, as NPT signatories, they will be assured an adequate supply of nuclear fuel to meet legitimate energy needs. At the same time, such states must come to understand that this sort of assurance is contingent upon NPT signatory status. It is extremely unfortunate that, until now, the nuclear weapon countries have actually provided more nuclear technology and materials to nonparty states (e.g., Israel, Egypt, Saudi Arabia, India, Pakistan, Brazil, and Argentina) than to party states.[9] This sort of policy, inspired by classical principles of realpolitik, subverts the essential underpinnings of the NPT, especially Article IV. Its net effect, therefore, is to encourage further proliferation rather than to curb it.

For the NPT to work, non-nuclear-weapon signatories must come to believe that there are significant benefits associated with being a party to the agreement. Under the terms of Article IV, which recognizes the "inalienable right" of all parties to full participation in peaceful nuclear activities, nonnuclear parties to the NPT must be provided *preferential* treatment in terms of security assistance, materials, equipment, services, and technical aid. To do otherwise, continuing to favor bilateral collective defense ties over multilateral nonproliferation commitments, would be enormously foolhardy.

Second, the IAEA must be given greater authority with respect to inspection of nuclear facilities, the power to search for clandestine facilities and stockpiles, and the ability to pursue and recover stolen nuclear materials. And, in the not-too-distant future, such authority must be extended to all nuclear facilities of all non-nuclear-weapon states, even if some of these states are not parties to the NPT. In the absence of a truly inclusive application of strengthened IAEA safeguards, a number of non-nuclear-weapon states will inevitably calculate that the benefits of nonproliferation are outweighed by the costs.

This point was explained with great clarity by Ambassador Gerald F. Tape, U.S. representative to the International Atomic Energy Agency, in testimony before the House Subcommittee on International Security and Scientific Affairs:

A world in which all NNWS's (non-nuclear weapons states) have their entire nuclear programs under IAEA Safeguards either by virtue of their being NPT parties or by unilateral submission to Agency Safeguards is a most worthy objective. There are many advantages, most of them arising from the application of a common system: for example, Safeguards are removed from the marketplace—suppliers and customers understand and respect the common standards; all material within a country is under the one system of control, accountability, and inspection; greater uniformity is possible in effecting Agreements and in implementing Agreements, etc.[10]

IAEA safeguards might also be strengthened by the implementation of regional or multinational nuclear-fuel-cycle centers. Under such an arrangement, which was seriously encouraged at the NPT Review Conference in May 1975, nations within a particular region would use a single multinational reprocessing plant. While such centers could not guarantee that certain nations would refrain from clandestine manufacture of nuclear weapons, they could remove the excuse for some states to build their own nuclear fuel reprocessing plants. They could, therefore, constitute an important new approach to solving the problem of plutonium diversion, minimizing the proliferation risks associated with sensitive fuel-cycle activities.[11]

Two potentially promising new approaches to stabilizing nuclear commerce through multinational or regional fuel-cycle centers were offered at the Stanley Foundation's Eighteenth Strategy for Peace Conference in October 1977:

One possibility would locate sensitive fuel-cycle activities, such as reprocessing, in international enclaves under the jurisdiction of an appropriate multinational organization. This international organization would have full custody and control of sensitive materials while in the enclave and during transportation back into the reactor. Technical, managerial, and operational responsibilities would be under national organizations that desire to locate facilities in the enclaves. This approach would separate the sensitive activities, which should be under multinational custody and control from those which need not be, such as the facility's management and operation. This arrangement would perhaps overcome one of the main objections raised in the past to the multinational fuel-center concept. Another possibility would be to establish a multinational facility in a particularly stable country. This facility would provide enriched uranium to countries prepared to forego national reprocessing and enrichment facilities. The spent fuel would be returned to the center in exchange for credit towards additional fuel supplies. Fuel reprocessing using the safest possible technology would be added at a future date, as could breeder or advanced converter reactors (which would use the separated plutonium) thereby minimizing international commerce in weapons-grade materials.[12]

All in all, strengthening and expanding IAEA safeguards and functions is vital to the nonproliferation regime. In addition to the recommendations already offered, steps must be taken to improve the funding and staffing of the agency; to allow the agency complete access to nonnuclear states; to allow the agency to inspect Russian, French, and Chinese nuclear facilities; to allow political sanctions against NPT violators (suspension of U.N. membership might be a particularly effective sanction); to standardize multilateral and bilateral safeguards agreements; to standardize measuring and accounting systems between the IAEA and individual nations; to standardize seals and monitors; to standardize techniques and facilities for the international transport of nuclear fuel, waste storage and disposal, and storage of excess plutonium; to standardize the design, construction, and operation of reactors and other fuel-cycle facilities; to create an international storage regime for fresh and spent fuel; to standardize safety, environmental, and health requirements for multinational fuel-cycle facilities; to standardize designs for physical security systems; to provide technical assistance to civilian nuclear programs in developing countries; and to provide an "international clearing house" for nuclear energy and safeguards data and technology.[13]

An effective nonproliferation regime will also require an

international capability for covert intelligence. At present, IAEA safeguards are more in the nature of a burglar alarm than a lock, simply monitoring facilities to determine if a diversion has already taken place. If these safeguards are to prove genuinely promising in the future, they will have to go beyond confrontation with a *fait accompli* to active prevention measures. In this connection, certain intelligence capabilities that now rest entirely with national governments —e.g., capabilities associated with embassy reporting, monitoring of communications, overflights, and satellites; atmospheric sampling for Krypton-85—will need to be pooled and coordinated.[14]

To strengthen further the nonproliferation regime, additional parts of the world must be declared nuclear-free zones. Such zones are consistent with the letter as well as the spirit of the NPT. According to Article VII: "Nothing in this Treaty affects the right of any group of States to conclude regional treaties in order to assure the total absence of nuclear weapons in their respective territories."

Presently, of course, the only populated area that is off limits to nuclear weapons is Latin America, under the terms of the Treaty of Tlatelolco. To extend the idea of the nuclear-free zone to other populated portions of the world, the states in particular regions will have to perceive the initiative to be in their own best interests. Above all else, this will require efforts that avoid altering existing security arrangements and existing distributions of military power. Moreover, it will require the respect and support of the nuclear weapon states.

To be successful, nuclear-weapon-free zones will also require effective systems of verification and control. Initially, these systems should be provided by the IAEA. The model for such systems is provided by the relationship between the Treaty of Tlatelolco and the IAEA, which obliges the parties to the treaty to conclude a comprehensive safeguards agreement with the IAEA.

As a part of the nonproliferation regime, the existence of nuclear-weapon-free zones can complement collateral measures such as the NPT and SALT. But the problems of implementation are formidable. All regions face internal political obstacles, and none of the nuclear weapon states now favors nuclear-weapon-free zones in all regions.

One way to improve the prospects of the zonal approach would be to redefine the limiting concept of "region" such that states renouncing nuclear weapons need not be territorially contiguous. The idea for such a "swiss cheese" concept of geographical continuity—one that anticipates a truly worldwide nuclear-weapon–free zone—has been incorporated into a Convention for the Renunciation of Nuclear Weapons by the International Council of the Pugwash Movement:[15]

A Convention for the Renunciation of Nucear Weapons

Article I

1. The Contracting Parties undertake not to possess, manufacture, acquire or use nuclear weapons, and therefore to prohibit in their territories:

a. The testing, use, manufacture, production or acquisition by any means whatsoever of any nuclear weapons or other nuclear explosive device by the Parties themselves, directly or indirectly, on behalf of anyone else or in any other way,

b. The receipt, storage, installation, deployment, and any form of possession of any nuclear weapons or other nuclear explosive device, directly or indirectly, by the Parties themselves, by anyone on their behalf or in any other way, and

c. The transit, through the national territories, air space or waterways under the recognized jurisdiction of the Parties, of any nuclear weapon or other nuclear explosive device, except that this provision shall not affect the right of transit through or over straits used for international navigation.

2. The Contracting Parties also undertake to refrain from engaging in encouraging or authorizing, directly or indirectly, or in any way participating in the testing, use, manufacture, production, possession, or control of any nuclear weapon or other nuclear explosive device anywhere.

Article II

For the purposes of this Convention, the territory of a

party State shall include all the land, sea and air space over which it exercises sovereignty according to international law.

Article III

For the purposes of this Convention, a nuclear weapon or other nuclear explosive device is any device capable, as a consequence of a nuclear chain reaction, of producing the release in explosive fashion of the energy stored in atomic nuclei in an amount sufficient to cause significant damage to people and/or structures, and includes such devices whether in an assembled or disassembled state.

Article IV

a. All the Parties to the Convention have the right to participate in the exchange of equipment, materials and scientific and technical information for the peaceful uses of nuclear energy, in accordance with this Convention and under appropriate international supervision and through appropriate international agencies and procedures as provided in the Non-Proliferation Treaty.

b. Peaceful nuclear explosions, if any, shall be performed only with devices provided by states signatory to the Protocol of this Convention, and shall be subject to international supervision and inspection in a manner to be determined by the Parties to the Convention, provided, however, that the Contracting Parties undertake that they will not, in any way, contribute to the development or maintenance of nuclear weapons production by any state not a Party to this Convention or its Protocol, or to abet any such contribution by any third party. Nothing in this treaty shall override any provisions to the contrary in any treaty or agreement limiting the testing of nuclear explosive devices.

Article V

There shall be provision for verifying compliance with the obligations of this Convention in accordance with the following general principles:

1. To the extent suitable, inspection and verification services shall be performed by the International Atomic Energy Agency.

2. Reports of verification activities including inspec-

tion shall be circulated to the Parties to the Convention and its Protocol.

3. At the request of any Party a conference of the Parties shall be convened to consider any such report.

4. In addition to routine verification activities, special inspections shall be conducted.

a. With the consent of the Party concerned, at the request of any Party which suspects that some activity prohibited by this Convention has been carried out or is about to be carried out, or

b. At the request of any Party which is suspected of carrying out some activity prohibited by this Convention.

Article VI

Any dispute concerning the interpretation or application of this Convention which may arise among the Parties to the Convention or its Protocol and which is not otherwise settled shall be referred to a Conciliation Commission.

Each Party to the dispute shall designate one member and the Secretary General of the United Nations shall nominate the President of the Conciliation Commission.

The Conciliation Commission shall attempt to bring the Parties to the dispute to an agreement. If the dispute is not settled, the Commission shall issue a report stating its conclusions and shall transmit its report to the Parties to this Convention and its Protocol.

Article VII

In the case of the threat or use of a nuclear weapon against any Party to this Convention, such Party may call upon the other Parties to provide aid and support to the Party under threat or attack, including non-nuclear military assistance, in accordance with the inherent right of collective self-defense as recognized in Article 51 of the U.N. Charter, and such other Parties may provide such assistance in accordance with their constitutional processes.

Article VIII

Parties to this Convention further pledge that they will strive in good faith for the elimination of nuclear weapons from the arsenals of all states and for the establishment of conditions that will facilitate the adherence of all states to this Convention.

Article IX

Final clauses. Signature, ratification, entry into force, duration, withdrawal, etc.

PROTOCOL

Article 1

States parties to this Protocol agree:

a. To accept and respect the status of the Parties created by the Convention.

b. Not to interfere with any Party in carrying out its obligations under the Convention.

c. Not to use or threaten to use a nuclear weapon against any Party to the Convention.

d. To forbid and prevent the use, or threat of use of nuclear weapons under its control or on its territory against a Party to the Convention.

e. Not to contribute directly or indirectly to the development or maintenance of nuclear weapons production by any state not a party to this Convention or its Protocol, or to abet any such contribution by any third party.

f. To give priority consideration to the Parties to this Convention in their programs of assistance for the peaceful applications of nuclear energy.

Article 2

States parties to this Protocol shall cooperate, when so requested, in the verification procedures provided for by Article V of the Convention.

Article 3

States parties to this Protocol accept and shall have access to the conciliation procedure provided for by Article VI of the Convention.

Article 4

In the case of the threat or use of a nuclear weapon against any Party to the Convention, the Parties to this Protocol, when so requested by the State under threat or attack, shall consider providing such State aid and support in accordance with the right of collective self-defense as recognized in Article 51 of the U.N. Charter.

Article 5
States parties to this Protocol shall have the right to be present as observers and address any Conference of the Parties to the Convention.

Article 6
States parties to this Protocol pledge that they will strive in good faith for the elimination of nuclear weapons from the arsenals of all states and for the establishment of conditions that will facilitate the adherence of all states to the Convention.

Article 7
Final clauses. Signature, ratification, entry into force, withdrawal, etc.

A final arena in which international agreements can contribute to the effectiveness of the nonproliferation regime is nuclear export policy. Since access to a nuclear weapon capability now depends largely on the policies of a small group of supplier states, such policies constitute a vital element in nonproliferation efforts. In the years ahead, those states which carry on international trade in nuclear facilities, technology, and materials will have to improve and coordinate their export policies.

The heart of the problem, of course, is the fact that nuclear exports—while they contribute to the spread of nuclear weapons—are a lucrative market for supplier states. In the United States, for example, the ERDA has estimated that U.S. revenues from the export of reactors and fuel-cycle services could reach $2.3 billion annually by 1980 and $100 billion by the year 2000.[16] Recognizing the conflict in objectives between nonproliferation and a nuclear export market, the IAEA, Euratom, and the NPT impose obligations on nuclear exports concerning the development of nuclear explosives. Article I of the NPT pledges the signatories "not in any way to assist, encourage, or induce any non-nuclear weapon State to manufacture or otherwise acquire nuclear weapons or other nuclear explosive devices." At the same time, Article IV of the NPT ensures that "All parties to the Treaty undertake to facilitate, and have the right to participate in, the fullest possible exchange of equipment, materials, and scientific and technological information for the peaceful uses of nuclear energy."

To avoid the hazards of a worldwide plutonium economy, the United States and other suppliers must press ahead with efforts to halt the diffusion of national plutonium reprocessing and enrichment facilities. If at all possible, prohibitions on the export of sensitive technologies should be carried out on a multilateral basis. While it should be generally understood that it is in every supplier state's best interests to inhibit the spread of technologies with serious proliferation hazards, such an understanding is contingent on the expectation of restraint by every other supplier state.

What this means, in essence, is that all supplier states can be expected to comply with the requirements of a common nuclear export policy only if they all believe that such compliance will be generally reciprocated. From the standpoint of creating an effective consensus on nuclear exports, the problem is one of securing compliance as long as each supplier state is uncertain about the reciprocal compliance of all the other supplier states. Unless each supplier state believes that its own willingness to comply is generally paralleled, it is apt to calculate that the benefits of compliance are exceeded by the costs.

To relieve this problem, two things are needed: (1) an adequate system for verification of compliance with common nuclear export policies; and (2) a system of sanctions for noncompliance in which the costs of departure from such policies are so great as to outweigh the expected benefits of export revenues. In practice, the victory of arms control objectives over commercial goals will depend upon the willingness and capacity of the nuclear supplier states to exert serious political and economic pressures upon recalcitrant "colleagues" to conform with common policies. In the absence of such willingness and capacity, supplier states are apt to pay closer attention to their balance of payments problems than to their long-term security interests, a situation which would have enormously corrosive effects on the nonproliferation regime.

In the management of nuclear exports, sanctions can also play an important role in affecting the decisions of recipient states. In this connection, the threat of such sanctions is already a part of this country's Agreements for Nuclear Cooperation with many countries; the IAEA Statute; and the Foreign Assistance Act as amended by the International Assistance and Arms Export Control Act of 1976. Specific sanctions for noncompliance in these cases include suspension of agreements and the return of transferred materials; curtailment or suspension of assistance provided by the IAEA; suspension from membership in IAEA; and ineligibility for economic, military, or security assistance.[17]

Nonproliferation through Tightened Bipolarity

In the final analysis, the effectiveness of a nonproliferation regime will depend upon a cooperative effort by the superpowers to control[18] limited aspects of their respective alliance systems. Indeed, such an effort will even require extending the reach of these alliance systems to all prospective proliferators who fall within the orbit of superpower influence. Although such a recommendation seems to smack of a new elitism which subordinates the claims of equity and justice to the interests of duopolistic domination, its effect would be to bolster not primacy, but world order. Rather than reassert an earlier form of joint hegemony, a selective tightening of bipolarity in world power processes could provide the framework within which the technological and legal components of the nonproliferation regime would function successfully. This is true because a tightening of superpower control over allies and other states would limit the freedom of these states to "go nuclear." Hence, the "tighter" the dualism of power, the greater the ability of the superpowers to assure broad compliance with nonproliferation objectives.

Of course, taken by itself, the tightening of Soviet and American control over other states is not enough to ensure the success of nonproliferation efforts. It would also require that both superpowers favor the success of the nonproliferation regime and that they are willing to act accordingly. Unless these conditions obtain, there is no reason to believe that the expanded leverage of the superpowers would be conducive to nonproliferation goals.

To what extent are these plausible conditions? At first glance, considering the commonality of interest between the superpowers in halting nuclear spread and the evidence of such interest in major international treaties and agreements, they seem eminently plausible. However, this optimistic view is contingent on the absence of tensions or crises between Russia and the United States, and upon the reaction of each when they do arise. Fear and mistrust make it especially difficult for the superpowers to embark upon a security course based upon cooperative rather than competitive definitions of self-interest.

Similarly, the optimistic view that the superpowers would act in concert to further nonproliferation goals is contingent upon their maintaining an approximate equilibrium of power between them. A dramatically unequal ratio of power between the Soviet Union and the United States might tempt one or the other to value the traditional modalities of realpolitik over collective efforts to assure security. Hence, if the effectiveness of the nonproliferation regime is to depend upon a cooperative tightening of control by the superpowers, it is essential that both the Soviet Union and the United States perceive a condition of rough parity between them.

Summing up, the prospects for nonproliferation success would be improved to the extent that the superpowers could assert limited control over other states in the system, under conditions whereby (1) the superpowers both favor nonproliferation objectives; (2) the superpowers operate within a peaceful and crisis-free environment; and (3) the superpowers perceive a roughly equal ratio of power between them. Where these conditions are satisfied, the tightening of bipolarity improves the prospects for broad compliance on nonproliferation measures. The general point that a reduction in the effective number of decision makers on any issue improves the chances for cooperation has been expressed by the philosopher David Hume in his *Treatise of Human Nature:*

Two neighbors may agree to drain a meadow, which they possess in common; because it is easy for them to know each other's mind; and each must perceive, that the immediate consequences of his failing in his part, is the abandoning of the whole project. But it is very difficult, and indeed impossible, that a thousand persons should agree in any such action; it being difficult for them to concert so complicated a design, and still more difficult for them to execute it; while each seeks a pretext to free himself of the trouble and expense and would lay the whole burden on others.

The states in modern world politics resemble the individuals in Hume's little tale. So long as the number of effectively independent states is low, the prospects for cooperative action are high. However, where this number is increased, the chances for successful cooperation diminish accordingly. Understood in terms of the problem of nonproliferation, this suggests that a tightening of control over individual national decisions must be exerted to prevent additional states from "going nuclear," and that increased superpower control is the best means to this end.

A major part of the nonproliferation problem, then, is not simply the implementation of new procedures, agreements, and treaties, but the control of too large a number of independent national wills. And such control is an instance of the more general problem of decision, which arises when the benefits of common action are dependent upon the expectation that all parties will cooperate. Many years ago, the political philosopher Machiavelli, in his essay *On Fortune*, revealed the essential dynamics of this problem:

> The world is a stupendous machine, composed of innumerable parts, each of which being a free agent, has a volition and action of its own; and on this ground arises the difficulty of assuring success in any enterprise depending on the volition of numerous agents. We may set the machine in motion, and dispose every wheel to one certain end; but when it depends on the volition of any one wheel, and the correspondent action of every wheel, the result is uncertain.

In Machiavelli's metaphor, the "parts" of the machine may be taken to represent the states in world politics, and the "enterprise" for which success is sought may be taken to represent nonproliferation. Understood in such terms, the metaphor suggests that nonproliferation efforts will always be in doubt as long as they depend upon voluntary compliance by states which expect reciprocal compliance by all other states. To remove this dependency, the United States and the Soviet Union must move deliberately and cooperatively to ensure the compliance of other states with all elements of the nonproliferation regime.

Redefining National Interests: Cosmopolitan Steps toward Nonproliferation

The leading role of the superpowers in nonproliferation efforts should not be taken as representing a return to earlier forms of duopolistic domination. Quite the contrary! Unlike earlier forms of joint control, this role would be designed not for national power advantages, but for the assurance of a universal world order. Indeed, in accordance with the requirements for preventing nuclear war between the superpowers discussed in the preceding chapter, this role must be assumed while Russians and Americans move aggressively to curtail their own strategic arms race.

This role must be recognized as both limited in scope and temporary in duration. The exercise of bipolar political pressures must be confined to issues which concern the spread of nuclear weapons and must be terminated as soon as a substantial number of other states in the system begin to follow the nonproliferation norm.

Such pressures, therefore, must never be exerted with a view to preserving top-dog positions in international power. Rather, their rationale must always be a fuller realization of sovereign equality and an improved likelihood of worldwide denuclearization. As long as the leading role of the superpowers is kept limited and temporary, and as long as it is assumed while steps at curtailing vertical proliferation are under way, it is entirely consistent with the goal of a just and secure world order.

To achieve their objective, superpower political pressures must be directed toward creating the conditions wherein all states can begin to redefine their interests along systemic lines. Just as avoidance of nuclear war between the superpowers requires a new consciousness of global community and interdependence, so does the avoidance of nuclear war through proliferation require a generalized renouncement of strategic competition and power politics. Just as the avoidance of nuclear war between the superpowers demands a transformation of American and Soviet foreign policies in ways that recognize the advantages of globalism over nationalism, so does the avoidance of nuclear war through proliferation demand a generalized denunciation of realpolitik.

What is required, then, is a nuclear regime which extends the principles of superpower war avoidance to the rest of international society. The centerpiece of this universal regime must be the cosmopolitan understanding that all states, like all people, form one essential body and one true community. Such an understanding, that a latent oneness lies buried beneath the manifold divisions of our fractionated world, need not be based on the mythical attractions of universal brotherhood and mutual concern. Instead, it must be based on the idea that individual states, however much they may dislike each other, are tied together in the struggle for survival. This point is illustrated colorfully in Stanley Hoffmann's simile:

> In the traditional usage of power, states were like boiled eggs. War, the minute of truth, would reveal whether they (or which ones) were hard or soft. Interdependence breaks eggs into a vast omelet. It does not mean the end of conflict: I may want *my* egg to contribute a larger part of the omelet's size and flavor than *your* egg—or I may want you to break yours into it first, etc. . . . But we all end in the same omelet.[19]

To accomplish the objectives of nonproliferation, it is not enough to provide the customary restraints offered by international treaties and institutions. Although such restraints are essential, they must be surrounded by a new field of consciousness—one that flows from a common concern for an emerging planetary identity. With such a revisioning of national goals and incentives, states can progress from the vapid cliches of "realism" to an awareness of new archetypes for global society. Since all things contain their own contradiction, the world system based upon militaristic nationalism can be transformed into an organic world society.

To succeed in this task will be very difficult. But it need not be as fanciful as some would have us believe. Indeed, we must understand that faith in the new forms of international interaction is a critical step toward their implementation.

Already, there is evidence that such faith is justified. The emergence of nuclear weapons has wrought a significant change in the classic "chessboard" of world political affairs. According to Stanley Hoffmann, this change

> has introduced into the competition of those states that now possess nuclear weapons an element of solidarity that tempers the very logic of separateness that gave rise to the nuclear race in the first place: It is solidarity for survival. The rules that apply are no longer the old rules of interaction.[20]

We are, as philosopher William Irwin Thompson suggests, at the "edge of history."[21] It is time to transcend the clogged conduits of national military power and to reaffirm that the truest forms of realism lie in the imaginings of idealists.

If Nonproliferation Fails: Last Ditch Strategies for Survival

Until this point, we have focused our attention on preventing the spread of nuclear weapons to additional states. It must be conceded, however, that nonproliferation efforts could break down entirely. In this case, steps would have to be taken to limit the hazards of the proliferated global condition. Here, the prevention of nuclear war would rest upon measures designed to manage relations among members of an international nuclear crowd.

In the first place, steps would have to be taken to slow down the rate of proliferation. As long as a significant number of states had not yet attained membership in the nuclear club, efforts geared to inhibiting or halting further proliferation would be called for. Or as Lewis Dunn of the Hudson Institute has argued: "Put simply, the fewer Nth countries the better."[22]

In the second place, steps would have to be taken to ensure the stability of nuclear power relationships and to spread information and technology pertaining to nuclear weapon safeguards. This means that an all-out effort would have to be mustered to prevent intense crises in world affairs and that such an effort would have to be buttressed by technical assistance to Nth country nuclear forces. Since many, if not all, of the new nuclear weapon states would be especially vulnerable to accidental, unauthorized, and first-strike firings, the superpowers would have to take seriously the prospect of helping these states to develop safe weapon systems and reliable command, control, and communications procedures.

The need for such assistance would be dictated by a number of factors. For one, new nuclear powers, in response to the need for quick-reaction forces, would almost certainly turn to automatic or nearly automatic systems of retaliation. For another, new nuclear powers would be unlikely to invest the enormous amount of money needed to equip the nuclear weapons themselves with trustworthy safety design features. It would be essential, therefore, in a proliferated global setting, that the superpowers share many of their safeguard strategies with the newer members of the nuclear club. At a minimum, such sharing would have to include information about (1) making accurate identification of an attacker; (2) rendering nuclear forces survivable for a second strike; (3) ensuring human reliability in the command/control setting; and (4) ensuring weapon-system reliability through such means as coded locking devices and environmental sensing techniques.

In addition to offering technical assistance to Nth countries, the superpowers would also have to influence the strategic doctrines of these new nuclear weapon states. At a minimum, such efforts would have to be directed at underscoring the deterrence function of strategic force, reinforcing the idea that nuclear weapons must not be thought of for war-fighting. In this connection, special emphasis would

have to be placed on the importance of "minimum deterrence" and the disavowal of first-strike capabilities.

Finally, if nonproliferation were to fail, states would be
confronted with the most compelling argument, short of
nuclear war itself, for retreating from principles of realpolitik. They would realize that technology had produced
only radical insecurity. In such circumstances, the resort to
more and more destructive technology would be patently
absurd.

What this suggests is a truly last chance for redefining
national interests and preserving international stability. If
the imperative to prevent proliferation does not prove persuasive enough to cause abandonment of militaristic nationalism, then the hazards of a proliferated world might
provide the necessary incentive. Finding themselves only
"seconds from midnight," states might muster the kind of
consciousness that had previously eluded them. Should this
happen, the actors in world politics might pull back from
unparalleled calamity at the last moment, quickening the
heart of reason with an eleventh-hour awareness of global
oneness.

More than anything else, this kind of awareness would
be crucial to managing in a proliferated world. Moves by
the superpowers toward technical and doctrinal assistance
would be necessary to survive in a nuclear crowd, but they
would not be sufficient. Only a desperate intervention in the
process of global evolution—an intervention born of des-
peration and based on a true world society—would be able
to prevent disaster.

9 Preventing Nuclear Terrorism

Hardening the Target:
Preventing Nuclear Terrorism through
Improved Physical Security

To prevent nuclear terrorism, states must first act to "harden the target,"[1] so to speak. They must develop and implement a wide range of sophisticated physical protection systems to block access to atomic fuel and weapons. A number of ideas are being pursued to this end. They currently include such conventional ideas as improving and increasing guard forces, installing higher and less penetrable fences, employing metal detectors, tags for explosives, and secure communications links[2] as well as more innovative ideas deriving from recent technology such as the use of quick-hardening foam and antipersonnel gas.

Another recent development in this area involves the use of animal sensory systems. Applying the theories of operant psychology, pigeons have been tested in the development of a biological ambush detection system. The nature of these tests, in which motorized convoys are protected by radio link to a team of pigeons, has been described by Robert E. Bailey and Marian Breland Bailey of Animal Behavior Enterprises, Inc.:

> A four-truck convoy is traveling along a highway. Refugees and other non-hostiles are walking along the highway. Coming to a stretch of highway where an ambush is likely, the convoy maintains a speed of about 15 to 25 kilometers per hour (10 to 15 miles per hour) and launches the first pigeon. The pigeon outflight speed is

about 35 to 40 kilometers per hour (20 to 25 miles per hour). The pigeon normally flies out 4 to 8 kilometers (2.5 to 5 miles) and then returns on its own. As soon as the first pigeon is recovered by the moving convoy, a second pigeon is released. The convoy never stops during launch or recovery except during a suspected detection. If, during an outflight, the signal from the pigeon-borne transmitter ceases, this cessation indicates a detection, a malfunction of the equipment, or that the pigeon has exceeded the limits of the radio link. When this occurs, the convoy stops and a second pigeon is released to confirm or deny a detection. If the second pigeon fails to detect a target, recall is sounded, both pigeons are recovered, and the convoy moves on. If target contact is verified, troops are sent ahead to search for hostiles.[3]

Of course, if physical security measures are to be truly helpful in preventing nuclear terrorism, they will have to be implemented internationally. In this connection, special efforts must be made to ensure the success of the nonproliferation regime and to encourage international acceptance of IAEA security standards. Until access to nuclear fuel and assembled nuclear weapons is blocked all over the world, wherever these materials exist, unilateral measures by any one country will be sorely deficient.

Softening the Adversary: Preventing Nuclear Terrorism through Behavioral Measures

Even if high-quality physical security measures are extended throughout the world, they will not be equal to the threat if the terrorist adversary is excluded from strategic calculations. To augment physical safeguards we require a thoughtful behavioral strategy, one that is based upon a sound understanding of the risk calculations of terrorists. Until we understand the special terrorist stance on the balance of risks that can be taken in world politics, we will not be able to identify an appropriate system of threats and punishments.

This is not to suggest, however, that there is any such thing as "the terrorist mind." Rather, there are a great many terrorist minds, a potpourri of ideas, visions, methods, and objectives. What must be established, therefore, are a number of basic strategies of counter nuclear terrorism that are differentiated according to the particular pattern of risk-calculation involved. In this way, governments can begin the development of a suitable behavioral technology, one that correlates deterrent and remedial measures with the terrorist group's particular preference ordering.

Differentiating Strategies of
Counter Nuclear Terrorism:
Four Types of Terrorist Groups

Yasser Arafat has said, "There is nothing greater than to die."[4] Reflecting such thinking, Palestinian commandos often wear explosive belts on missions against Israel, which they are expected to ignite should capture be imminent. Faced with such a form of terrorism, it would be inappropriate to base deterrence on threats of physically punishing acts of retaliation. Instead of orthodox threats of punishment, deterrence in this case would have to be based upon threats which promise to obstruct preferences which the terrorist group values even more highly than physical safety. Such threats, therefore, would have to be directed at convincing terrorists that the resort to nuclear violence would mitigate against their political objectives.

Deterrence, given this type of terrorist group, might also be based upon the promise of rewards. Such a strategy of positive sanctions has been left out of current studies of counterterrorism. Yet, it may prove to be one of the few potentially worthwhile ways of affecting the decisions of certain types of terrorist groups. Of course, in considering whether this sort of strategy is appropriate in particular situations, governments will have to decide whether the expected benefits that accrue from avoiding nuclear terrorism are great enough to outweigh the prospective costs associated with the promised concessions.

Prior to the advent of concern for nuclear terrorism, the idea that governments would engage in substantive bargaining with terrorists was widely criticized. Today, however, we must face up to the fact that the execution of certain terrorist threats could have genuinely system-destructive effects. Recognizing this, the hard-line unwillingness to bargain and make concessions—an unwillingness which is still official U.S. policy—can no longer be a fixed position of responsible governments.[5]

The reasonableness of a strategy of positive sanctions is also enhanced by its probable long-term effects. Just as violence tends to beget more violence, rewards tend to generate more rewards. By the incremental replacement of negative sanctions with positive ones, a growing number of actors in world politics, terrorists as well as states, are apt to become habituated to the ideology of a reward system. The cumulative effect of such habituation is likely to be a more peaceful and harmonious world and national system.

This is not to ignore the problems of strategies based upon positive sanctions, particularly the problem that such sanctions may appear to be bribes. Even if a strategy of positive sanctions is worked out that looks exceptionally promising, the public reaction to it may be exceedingly unfavorable. Matters of honor and courage, therefore, may mitigate against the operation of positive sanctions in counter-nuclear-terrorist strategies.

Another problem associated with the operation of positive sanctions in such strategies centers on the possibility that some terrorists who display the self-sacrificing value system of Fedayeen thrive on violent action for its own sake. They are unconcerned with the political object or matters of personal gain. Here, we are clearly up against a brick wall, the reductio ad absurdum of deterrence logic, since the only incentives that might be extended to deter acts of violence are the opportunities to commit such acts.

And then there is the blackmail problem. The habitual use of rewards to discourage terrorist violence is apt to encourage terrorists to extort an ever-expanding package of "gifts" in exchange for "good behavior." Here, we must confront the prospect of terrorism as a "protection racket" on a global scale.

A second type of terrorist group exhibits a preference ordering very much like that of an ordinary criminal band (e.g., the Italian and South American terrorist groups that have made a business of kidnaping executives for high ransoms, and the American Symbionese Liberation Army, SLA). Here, the group's actions are dictated largely by incentives of material gain, however much these incentives are rationalized in terms of political objectives. If such a terrorist group were to threaten nuclear violence, it would be as inappropriate to base deterrence on threats of political failure or negative public reception as it would be to threaten self-sacrificing ideologues with personal harm. Rather, deterrence in this case should be based largely upon the kinds of threats that are used to counter orthodox criminality. Indeed, in dealing with this particular type of terrorist group, it is not only vital to recognize its particular resemblance to an ordinary criminal band, but to broadcast this resemblance throughout the political system. Once such terrorists have been widely identified as ordinary criminals, the counter-nuclear-terrorist effort could be eased considerably.[6] Ample precedent for such identification already exists in Anglo-American law. Current British and Canadian jurisprudence holds that urban terrorists are clearly common criminals under the law.

A variation of this type of terrorist group is one in which the overarching motives are genuinely political, but where ordinary criminality is engaged in to secure needed capital. Here, the primary activity of the group often centers on "expropriation," the long-established euphemism for robberies designed to supply terrorists with funds. The history of this tactic dates back to the Russian expropriators of the 1860s and 1870s. Later, Lenin was careful about maintaining a firm line between expropriations and ordinary crime, but today's expropriators, such as the Baader-Meinhof group and its successors, the SLA and the Tupamaros, have expressed far less concern about making a distinction. From the standpoint of effective counterterrorism, such diminished sensitivity is clearly desirable, since it makes it much easier for the government to equate the terrorist robberies with orthodox criminality.

This is not to suggest, however, that threats of physically punishing retaliation will always be productive in dealing with this type of terrorist group. Even though this particular type, unlike the self-sacrificing variety considered in the first example, is apt to value personal safety in its ordering of preferences, threats to impair this safety may be misconceived. Indeed, a great deal of sophisticated conceptual analysis and experimental evidence now seems to indicate that —in certain cases—the threat of physical punishment may actually prove counterproductive. Hence, contrary to the widely held conventional wisdom on the matter, taking a "hard line" against terrorists may only reinforce antagonism and intransigence. Recent experience indicates that physical retaliation against terrorists often causes only a shift in the selection of targets and a more protracted pattern of violence and aggression. The threat of physical punishment against terrorists is apt to generate high levels of anger that effectively raise the threshold of acceptable suffering. This is the case because anger can modify usual cost/benefit calculations, overriding the inhibitions ordinarily associated with anticipated punishment.

A third type of terrorist group is primarily oriented toward achieving one form or another of political objective, but the group lacks the self-sacrificing value system of Fedayeen or the Japanese Red Army. If this sort of terrorist group (e.g., the FALN, which supports Puerto Rican independence in the United States; the South Moluccans in Holland; and the Provisional Wing of the IRA) were to threaten nuclear violence, it would be appropriate to base deterrence on a suitable combination of all of the negative and positive sanctions discussed thus far. This means that steps would have to be taken to convince the group that: (1) nuclear violence would mitigate against its political objectives; (2) certain concessions would be granted in exchange for restraint from nuclear violence; and (3) certain physically punishing or otherwise negative acts of retaliation would be meted out if nuclear violence were undertaken.

In this connection, governments would have to avoid the impression that the prospective costs of nuclear violence are so great as to warrant any and all concessions. Rather, prior to the onset of an actual incident, governments should create a hierarchy of concessions, ranging from the most easily satisfied financial demands to the most sweeping transformations of government policy and personnel. With such a hierarchy in hand, responsible officials could at least enter into a protracted bargaining situation with prospective nuclear terrorists, pursuing a concessionary policy that is both incremental and consistent with predetermined calculations of tolerable losses. Such preincident planning might also allow the government to take the offensive position in the bargaining situation.

A fourth and final example that illustrates the need to correlate deterrent and situational measures with the preference orderings of a particular type of terrorist group centers on groups spurred on by the need for spectacular self-assertion. From the standpoint of preventing nuclear violence, this type of terrorist group (e.g., the Weather Underground in the United States and the Red Army Group in West Germany) presents the greatest problems. Moved by the romanticization of violent action exemplified by Sorel and Fanon, such groups confront governments with genuine psychopaths and sociopaths. Clearly, since the preference that would need to be obstructed in this case is neither political success nor personal profit, but rather the violent act itself, and since personal safety is unlikely to figure importantly in the terrorist risk calculus, deterrence of nuclear terrorism must be abandoned altogether as a viable strategy. Instead, all preventive measures must concentrate upon limiting the influence of such terrorists within their particular groups and maintaining a safe distance between such terrorists and the destructive implements of nuclear weapon technologies. Or, if the apparent danger is great enough, governments might feel compelled to resort to preemption.

At the public relations level, all terrorist groups, whether their preeminent motives are altruistic, egoistic, or psychopathic, offer obeisance to Clausewitz's dictum: "The political object . . . will be the standard for determining both the aim of military force and the amount of effort to be made."[7] In fact, however, the particular standard for determining acceptable levels and targets of violence varies from one group of terrorists to another, depending on whether the overarching preference is maximization of political objective, maximization of commercial interest, or escape from one form or another of private anguish. It follows that efforts at counter nuclear terrorism must always be keyed to the preference ordering of the particular group type involved.

In the preceding examples, some of the prospective sanctions available to counter-nuclear-terrorist strategists entail measures that might be injurious to social justice and human rights. Of special interest in this connection are options involving:

1. A total, no-holds-barred military type assault designed to eradicate the terrorist group(s) altogether; and/or
2. A protracted, counterterrorist campaign utilizing "classical" methods of informers, infiltrators, counterterror squads patterned, perhaps, after Israel's *Mivtah Elohim* ("God's wrath"), assassinations,[8] agents provocateurs, and selected raids.

The first option, however effective it might be, is apt to be most destructive of essential citizen rights. Hence, governments contemplating such an option must pay close attention to the necessary tradeoff between efficacy and liberty that is involved. Since this option would almost certainly be repugnant to the most deeply held values of liberal democratic societies, governments—before resorting to this option—would have to be convinced that its prospective benefits were great enough to outweigh its probable costs. In fact, short of its use at the situational level where nuclear acts of terrorist violence have already taken place, it is unlikely that this option would ever be taken seriously in democratic states. Rather, we are likely to see its adoption only by the world's most blatantly authoritarian antidemocratic regimes.

The second option is also apt to score high marks on the efficacy dimension, but its effects on essential citizen rights need not be as injurious. This is not to suggest, however, that a protracted counterterrorist campaign utilizing classical methods of apprehension and punishment would necessarily be any less repulsive to democratic societies. In the final analysis, the problem of conflicting values which emerges from the consideration of harsh deterrent counter-measures can be resolved only by a careful comparison of the costs and benefits involved.

In general, the optimal counter-nuclear-terrorist strategy is one in which effective action leaves the prevailing network of citizen rights and privileges unimpaired. Barring this possibility, however, the requirements of effective strategies should be tempered, to the greatest extent possible, by the assurance of those freedoms which are basic to any democratic order.

To a certain extent, the different ways in which governments balance their commitments to safety and civil liberties are revealed by their different legal conditions. For example, the antiterrorist laws in Germany, France, England, and Sweden reflect different kinds of cost-benefit calculations.

Organizational crimes, or conspiracy, are punishable in the Federal Republic of Germany, France, and England, but not in Sweden.

In reference to grounds for arrest, the West German Criminal Procedure Code stipulates that "urgent suspicion" is sufficient for members of a terrorist association. French law identifies the "endangerment of public safety" as adequate grounds. English law leaves the matter entirely to the court's evaluation of the case made by the prosecuting authorities. And the Swedish solution is very similar to that of the FRG.

The legal situation in the United States is not governed by specific antiterrorist legislation.[9] But important points of comparison do exist. The notion of criminal conspiracy is well defined under American law, but it requires the commission of an overt act—a requirement not present in the West German, English, and French systems. Similarly, the grounds for arrest are generally more stringent than in the other national systems under comparison, even when the arrest is based upon a judgment of "probable cause" rather than a magistrate's warrant. Finally, only minor restrictions are imposed in the United States concerning the prevention of contact between the defense attorney and the defendant, a situation markedly more liberal than that of West Germany and substantially more liberal than those of France and England.[10]

Medical Preparedness as a Measure of Counter Nuclear Terrorism

Although it is rarely taken into account, emergency medical preparedness is an essential part of counter-nuclear-terrorist strategy. Such preparedness is needed not only to limit the number of casualties once an act of nuclear terrorism has actually taken place, but also as an integral part of the strategy of prevention. A visibly sophisticated medical rescue system could figure importantly in the cost-benefit calculations of prospective nuclear terrorists. With a special medical rescue system in place, would-be nuclear terrorists would most likely lower their estimation of potential destructiveness. This would occasion a lowering of their estimation of expected benefits and contribute to the success of deterrence efforts.

This idea flows from recent suggestions by Martin Elliot Silverstein, M.D., who describes medical rescue "as an essential, highly flexible element in the choreography of anti-terrorist efforts."[11] According to Dr. Silverstein, the notion that overwhelming weaponry and large disasters cannot be handled through medical rescue is a myth, one that prevents the creation of a needed medical system of counterterrorism. His conviction is based upon the following three concepts:

1. *The Common Weaponry Model.* Despite the apparent disparate effects of various weaponry upon the human body, the initial injuries follow a common model. The individual effects of specific weaponry are secondary in importance during the initial time period.
2. *The Common Injury Response.* The mammalian body can be considered a system of interacting organ subsystems, brain, heart, lungs, kidney, liver, intestines, and aggregate muscle mass. Barring the complete destruction of any one of those organ subsystems, the body can be kept alive by providing the cells of each organ with sufficient water, oxygen, and certain other blood components, and by maintaining within the

      subsystem's circulation the necessary volume-pressure relationships, whatever the nature of the injury.
3. *The Common Resuscitative Model.* Implicit in the common injury model is the potentiality of sustaining life by supporting the organ subsystems. In general, this is achieved by external oxygen supply, maintenance of adequate filling of the arteriovenous pipeline for oxygen and other transport, and maintenance of the cardiac pump to drive the circulation.[12]

Understanding these concepts, governments that are committed to an effective strategy of counternuclear terrorism must now move toward establishing a uniform emergency medical system. Such a system would involve national management and integration, regional suborganizations, early-warning systems, and reliable communications. To justify the expense involved, it would have to be made clear that a national emergency medical system could be used for other, nonterrorist kinds of emergencies. Even if the etiological agent were a natural disaster rather than a nuclear-terrorist assault, planned emergency medical preparedness would prove valuable.[13]

The International Dimension of Behavioral Measures of Counter Nuclear Terrorism

We have seen that counter-nuclear-terrorist strategies within states require differentiating sanctions according to the particular type of terrorist group involved. However, since nuclear terrorism might take place across national boundaries, the basic principles of these strategies must also be applied internationally. While it is critical for states to harden the target, it is also essential that they learn to soften the adversary. More than anything else, this means learning to understand the variety of terrorist group preferences and the subtlety of ways in which these preferences can be exploited.

Of course, there are special difficulties involved in implementing behavioral measures of counternuclear terrorism internationally. For the most part, these difficulties center on the fact that certain states sponsor and host terrorist groups and that such states extend the privileges of sovereignty to insurgents on their land. While it is true that international law forbids a state to allow its territory to be used as a base for aggressive operations against another state with which it is not at war, a state which seeks to deal with terrorists hosted in another state is still in a very difficult position.

To minimize or remove these difficulties, like-minded governments must create special patterns of international cooperation. These patterns must be based upon the idea that even sovereignty must yield to gross inversions of the norms expressed in the customary laws of war, the Geneva Conventions, the Nuremberg Principles, and the Genocide Convention. They must, therefore, take the form of classical collective defense arrangements between particular states which promise protection and support for responsible acts of counternuclear terrorism.

Such arrangements would have to include plans for cooperative intelligence-gathering on the subject of terrorism and for exchange of the information produced; an expanded and refined tapestry of agreements on extradition of terrorists; multilateral forces to infiltrate terrorist organizations and, if necessary, to take action against them; concerted use of the media to publicize terrorist activities and intentions; and counterterrorism emergency medical networks. Such arrangements might also entail limited and particular acts directed toward effective counter-nuclear terrorism. Examples of such acts include the willingness of Kenya to allow Israeli planes refueling privileges during the Entebbe mission and the assistance of three ambassadors from Moslem states during the Hanafi Moslem siege of Washington, D.C. in March 1977.

Above all else, however, international arrangements for counter-nuclear-terrorist cooperation must include sanctions for states which sponsor or support terrorist groups and activities. As in the case of sanctions applied to terrorists, such sanctions may include carrots as well as sticks, promises of certain kinds of rewards as well as threats of physical or economic punishment. Until every state in the world system calculates that support of counter-nuclear-terrorist measures is in its own interests, individual terrorist groups will have reason and opportunity to escalate their violent excursions.

In principle, such calculations should not be difficult to make. As Secretary General Kurt Waldheim stated in his 1976 Annual Report to the United Nations, international terrorism "is now generally recognized as a threat to the fabric of organized society and a potential danger to all governments and peoples."[14] This statement is eloquently underscored by Professor Robert Friedlander's comment that

> terrorist harm affects all humankind. If the world community cannot conform to the basic human rights concepts that have become a normative part of international law during the past generation, then the United Nations, like the League of Nations, is destined to fail. A determined response to international terrorism is not a matter of choice—it is a question of survival.[15]

Further Counter-Nuclear-Terrorism Measures under International Law

International law has been concerned with transnational terrorism since 1937, when the League of Nations produced two conventions to deal with the problem. These conventions proscribed acts of terror/violence against public officials, criminalized the impairment of property and the infliction of general injuries by citizens of one state against those of another, and sought to create an international criminal court with jurisdiction over terrorist crimes. The advent of the second world war, however, prevented the ratification of either document.[16]

Despite repeated attempts to revive the idea of an international criminal court, it is highly unlikely ever to come into existence. However, there are other measures under international law that could and should be used in the arsenal of international counter-nuclear-terrorism measures.

First, the international legal principle of *aut dedere aut punire* ("extradite or prosecute") needs to be employed against terrorists. And the customary excepting of political offenses as reason for extradition must be abolished for most acts of terrorism. In this connection, the Canadian standard for political crimes, set down by the Canadian Federal Court of Appeals in 1972, would be a suitable model. By this standard, the elements of a political act are so narrowly defined that virtually all acts of terrorism are patently criminal.

To understand the consequences of overemphasizing political motives for refusing extradition in matters concerning terrorism, one need only consider the case of several American black militants who hijacked a Delta DC-8 jet from Miami to Algiers in 1972. In 1975, a French court refused a U.S. request for their extradition because their admitted crime had been inspired by "political motives." In November 1978, the group received very light sentences, ranging from two-and-a-half to three years, in a trial hailed by the defense as a "slap at American racism" and a "trial on American history."[17]

In another case that took place in the same month as the French hijacking trial, Yugoslavia refused to extradite four West Germans wanted by Bonn on charges including the abduction and murder of Hans-Martin Schleyer, an important industrialist. Moreover, instead of prosecuting the alleged terrorists themselves, Yugoslavia declared the four *persona non grata* and allowed them to leave "to a country of their own choice." Speculation suggests that this country was one of the following: Libya, Iraq, or Southern Yemen.[18] Under international law, the Yugoslavian action is improper for at least two reasons: (1) the political-offense exception for refusing extradition must be waived in matters involving homicide; and (2) pursuant to long-standing customary norms and a number of recent conventions, the extradite-or-prosecute formula applies.

Second, states must encourage compliance with such important documents of international law as the Universal Declaration of Human Rights; the International Covenant on Civil and Political Rights; the International Covenant on Economic, Social and Cultural Rights; the Convention on the Prevention and Punishment of the Crime of Genocide; and the United Nations Declaration on Principles of International Law Concerning Friendly Relations and Co-operation among States in Accordance with the Charter of the United Nations. Taken together, these documents and their incorporated principles provide a corpus of law that might be used to counter nuclear terrorism.

Third, states must broaden the Definition of Aggression approved by the General Assembly in 1974. This definition condemns the use of "armed bands, groups, irregulars or mercenaries, which carry out acts of armed force against another State," but supports wars of national liberation against "colonial and racist regimes or other forms of alien domination."[19] Clearly, such a distinction leaves international law with inadequate leverage in counter-nuclear-terrorist strategies.

Fourth, invoking the long-established principle of *hostes humani generis* ("common enemies of mankind") terrorists must come to be viewed as outlaws subject to universal jurisdiction. The basic objective of such a policy, which would be based upon an implicit identification of modern terrorists with pirates, must be the disruption of collaboration between different terrorist groups. As we have already noted, extraordinary instances of such collaboration have already taken place between widely scattered and ideologically divergent groups.

For example, a Revolutionary Coordinating Council (*Junta de Coordinación Revolucionaria*) was established for Latin America in 1974 "to facilitate the expansion of joint operations and an acceleration of personnel exchanges and mutual support activities."[20] Latin American terrorists have worked cooperatively outside the region with various Japanese, Palestinian, and European organizations. But the most widely observed transnational connections between terrorists have been between the Japanese Red Army faction and the Popular Front for the Liberation of Palestine. These connections have been institutionalized through the creation of a permanent liason office in Tokyo and through offices in Paris and other European cities.[21]

Redefining National Interests: Planetization and Freedom from Nuclear Terrorism

In the final analysis, the effectiveness of international patterns of counter-nuclear-terrorist cooperation will depend upon the reactions of proterrorist states. Just as the avoidance of nuclear war between countries requires a new consciousness of global community and interdependence, so does the avoidance of nuclear terrorism require a real commitment by these states to unity and relatedness. To realize this commitment, the states which now sponsor and host terrorist groups will have to build upon the cosmopolitan understanding that is vital to nuclear war avoidance, working toward the replacement of our fragile system of realpolitik with a new world politics of globalism.

What this suggests is nothing less than the total intersection of the three principal paths to nuclear catastrophe in world politics. Each of these paths—nuclear war between the superpowers, nuclear war through proliferation, and nuclear terrorism—is occasioned by competitive definitions of national interest. And each of these paths can be obstructed only when these competitive definitions are replaced by cooperative ones. Should we fail to make the necessary transformations, all three paths will remain wide open. But if we move toward a new ecumenical spirit of oneness, all three paths will face powerful barriers.

Preventing nuclear terrorism, therefore, must be one part of an even larger strategy, one that is geared to the prevention of all forms of nuclear violence. It would be futile to try to tinker with the prospect of nuclear terrorism without affecting the basic structure of modern world politics. This structure is integral to all possibilities of an atomic apocalypse, and its revisioning and reformation is central to all possibilities for survival.

Notes

Introduction

1. Public concern over nuclear catastrophe in world politics seems to have increased considerably after the Soviet invasion of Afghanistan late in 1979. Indeed, during the weekend preceding the president's State of the Union Message in January 1980, at least five major political commentators warned of a nuclear war between the United States and the Soviet Union. These five, as documented in the "Talk of the Town" column of the February 4, 1980, issue of *The New Yorker*, were Jack Nelson of the Los Angeles *Times;* Hugh Sidey of *Time;* and the syndicated columnists George Will, Carl Rowan, and James Kilpatrick.

2. For more than thirty years, a prophesying clock in the editorial offices of the *Bulletin of the Atomic Scientists* has symbolized the threat of nuclear doomsday. Recently, in January 1980, the minute hand of this clock has been advanced from nine to seven minutes before midnight.

3. The explosive equivalent of the Hiroshima bomb was roughly 14,000 tons of TNT, or 14 kilotons, while the Nagasaki bomb yielded approximately 20,000 tons of TNT, or 20 kilotons. The yield of a nuclear weapon is described in terms of the quantity of chemical explosive needed to release an equivalent amount of energy.

4. The term "nuclear" covers both fission and fusion weapons.

5. See "Nuclear War by 1999?," *Harvard Magazine*, November 1975, p. 25.

6. According to Frank M. Chilton, a California nuclear physicist who specializes in explosion engineering, the student's scheme would be "pretty much guaranteed to work." (See John D. Fox, "Reinventing the PU-239 Bomb," *Princeton Alumni Weekly*, 25 October 1976, p. 6.)

7. Ibid.

8. See Mason Willrich and Theodore B. Taylor, *Nuclear Theft: Risks and Safeguards* (Cambridge: Ballinger, 1974), p. 22.

9. Ibid., pp. 20–21.

10. See John S. Foster, "Nuclear Weapons," *Encyclopedia Americana*, 1973.

11. Willrich and Taylor, pp. 24–25.

12. See Robert R. Jones, "Nuclear Reactor Risks—Some Frightening Scenarios," *Chicago Sun-Times*, 30 April 1976.

13. Ibid.

Chapter One

1. The total world military expenditure each year is now about equal to the entire national income of the poorer half of mankind. Moreover, resources granted to medical research are less than one-fourth the amount devoted to military research and development. Together, the United States and the Soviet Union account for a little less than two-thirds of annual world military expenditure. For reliable and up-to-date figures on world military expenditure, see the most recent editions of *World Armaments and Disarmament*, the Yearbook of the Stockholm International Peace Research Institute (SIPRI); Frank Barnaby and Ronald Huisken, *Arms Uncontrolled* (Cambridge, Mass.: Harvard University Press, 1975); and Ruth Legar Sivard, *World Military and Social Expenditures*, prepared annually under the sponsorship of the Arms Control Association, the Institute for World Order, and the Members of Congress for Peace through Law Education Fund, and published by WMSE Publications, Leesburg, Va.

2. Megadeath signifies death in the millions; gigadeath signifies death in the billions.

3. Paul H. Nitze, "Assuring Strategic Stability in an Era of Detente," *Foreign Affairs*, 54, no. 2 (January 1976): 211. This does not imply, however, that the Soviet civil defense effort could effectively prevent an American nuclear retaliation from producing consequences that satisfy all meaningful definitions of "assured destruction." The destabilizing implications of the inequality between Soviet and American civil defense capabilities lie in the prospect that the Soviets might underestimate the damage surviving U.S. strategic forces could inflict on the USSR, and overestimate the damage the USSR could inflict on U.S. strategic forces with a surprise "counterforce" attack on U.S. long-range missile and bomber forces.

4. See James R. Schlesinger, "The Theater Nuclear Force Posture in Europe," Report to the United States Congress in com-

pliance with Public Law 93-365 (Washington, D.C.: Government Printing Office, 1975), p. 22. This position is reaffirmed by the latest statements of the Department of Defense. See, for example, Secretary of Defense Harold Brown, 2 February 1978, in *U.S. Department of Defense Annual Report FY 1979* (Washington, D.C.: Government Printing Office), p. 68; and Gen. George S. Brown, 20 January 1977, in *United States Military Posture of FY 1978* (Washington, D.C.: Government Printing Office), p. 35.

5. This position is supported by the scenario offered by Gen. Sir John Hackett and other top-ranking NATO generals and advisors in *The Third World War: August 1985* (New York: Macmillan, 1978).

6. See Arthur S. Collins, Jr., "The Enhanced Radiation Warhead: A Military Perspective," *Arms Control Today*, 8, no. 6 (June 1978): 5.

7. This concept involves making a threat credible by demonstrating a commitment to its fulfillment. The stationing of American troops in Europe, for example, is believed to constitute a "trip wire" on the assumption that any injury to them could not possibly go unpunished.

8. Present American NATO policy includes both theater (tactical) nuclear forces and strategic nuclear forces as prospective deterrents against Warsaw Pact aggression. In his report to the Congress on "The Theater Nuclear Force Posture in Europe," former Secretary of Defense Schlesinger describes the respective roles of these two nuclear components: "Theater nuclear forces deter and defend against theater nuclear attacks; help deter and, if necessary, defend against conventional attack; and help deter conflict escalation. The final leg of the Triad, strategic forces, deter and defend in general nuclear war, deter conflict escalation and reinforce theater nuclear forces if needed" (p. 1).

9. See Richard Shearer, "Nuclear Weapons and the Defense of Europe," *NATO Review*, no. 6 (December 1975), pp. 12–14.

10. See John F. Kennedy, *The Strategy of Peace* (New York: Harper & Row, 1960), p. 185.

11. See *The Defense Monitor*, 4, no. 2 (February 1975): 3.

12. See Schlesinger, "Theater Nuclear Force Posture," p. 2.

13. See *The Defense Monitor*, p. 3.

14. A similar argument is made by Herbert F. York, the distinguished physicist who served as director of Defense Research and engineering under Presidents Eisenhower and Kennedy, in "The Nuclear 'Balance of Terror' in Europe," *Bulletin of the Atomic Scientists*, 32, 5, (May 1976) pp. 8–17.

15. See *The Defense Monitor*, p. 3.

16. It is worth noting here that the superpower with the vulnerable retaliatory forces might also decide preemption is worthwhile. This could occur if the vulnerable superpower perceived that its condition was known to the other superpower, that the other superpower was seriously entertaining the thought of a first strike, and that it would stand to lose less by striking first itself.

17. Fred C. Iklé in remarks to the Milwaukee Institute of World Affairs, 24 November 1975 (summary available from ACDA).

18. U.S. Department of Defense, *Annual Defense Department Report*, 27 January 1976, p. iv.

19. See Harold Brown, in *DOD Annual Report FY 1979*, p. 62.

20. See Gen. George S. Brown, *U.S. Military Posture for FY 1978*, p. 5.

21. Of course, the continued American reaffirmation of a "first use" policy of nuclear weapons coupled with its search for a "counterforce" or damage-limiting capability gives the Soviets ample cause for concern about an American first strike.

22. See "Nuclear War by 1999?" *Harvard Magazine*, November 1975, p. 22.

23. See *Public Papers of the Presidents of the United States: John F. Kennedy, 1961* (Washington, D.C.: Government Printing Office, 1962), p. 230.

24. James R. Schlesinger, at press conference before the Godfrey Sperling Group, Washington, D.C., 1 July 1975.

25. 6 July 1975.

26. Rooted in President Truman's decision to drop atomic bombs over Hiroshima and Nagasaki, this policy has been adopted by every succeeding administration. Consider the following statements, taken from *Congressional Quarterly: Weekly Report*, 33, no. 32 (9 August 1975): 1748.

Question: "In your opinion, can the United States be defeated in an all-out first-blow nuclear war, and is it your position that we must take the first blow?" Answer: "I don't see any reason, therefore, for saying we necessarily have to take the first blow. But I do say this: always we must be alert. And I think it is silly to say that we can be defeated in a first-blow attack, for the simple reason that we have so much strength, retaliatory strength, that any nation foolish enough to resort to that kind of an effort—that is, the exchange of nuclear attacks—would itself be destroyed. There is no question in my mind." (President Dwight D. Eisenhower at press conference, 27 August 1958)

I have stated on several different occasions . . . that we will use whatever weapons are necessary to protect our interests, including nuclear weapons. (Secretary of Defense Robert S. McNamara before Senate Armed Services Committee, 22 February 1963)

If a state which has accepted this treaty does not have nuclear weapons and is a victim of aggression, or is subject to a threat of aggression, involving nuclear weapons, the United States shall be prepared to ask immediate Security Council action to provide assistance in accordance with the Charter [of the United Nations]. (President Lyndon B. Johnson at signing of the NPT, 1 July 1968)

Potential enemies must know that we will respond to whatever degree is required to protect our interests. They must also know that they will only worsen their situation by escalating the level of violence. (President Richard Nixon, in foreign policy report to Congress, 25 February 1971)

First use could conceivably, let me underscore conceivably, involve what we define as strategic forces and possibly, possibly, underscore possibly, involve selective strike at the Soviet Union. We do not necessarily exclude that but it is indeed a very, very low probability. (Secretary of Defense James R. Schlesinger before the Godfrey Sperling group, 1 July 1975)

27. The refusal of the United States and the Soviet Union to adopt a no-first-use posture creates still another problem for *both* superpowers, namely the incentive for *other* nuclear powers to adopt hair-trigger strategics for protection against anticipated preemptive strikes.

28. From Barton J. Bernstein, "The Week We Almost Went to War," *Bulletin of the Atomic Scientists*, 32 no. 2 (February 1976): 13.

29. See Herman Kahn, *On Escalation: Metaphors and Scenarios* (New York: Praeger, 1965), p. 10. The "chicken" analogy was first introduced into the strategic literature, however, not by Kahn, but by Bertrand Russell in his *Common Sense and Nuclear Warfare* (New York: Simon & Schuster, 1959), p. 30.

30. Kahn, *On Escalation*, p. 12.

31. See U.S. Arms Control and Disarmament Agency, *Arms Control: Moving Toward World Security* (Washington, D.C.: Government Printing Office, 1975), p. 10.

32. From U.S. Department of Defense undated press release sent to the author by W. Y. Smith (Lieutenant General, USAF, and assistant to the chairman of the JCS), on 16 June 1976.

33. See *The Defense Monitor*, p. 9.

34. Ibid.

35. According to William B. Maxson [Brigadier General USAF, and deputy assistant to the secretary of defense (atomic energy)], "We have no information concerning Soviet safeguards against the accidental or unauthorized use of nuclear weapons." (From letter to the author of 17 November 1976).

36. See U.S. Department of Defense (DOD) Directive No. 5030.15, *Safety Studies and Reviews of Nuclear Weapons Systems*, 8 August 1974, pp. 3–4.

37. Ibid., p. 2.

38. However, no matter how reliable American safety systems are presumed to be, security from accidental nuclear war is still contingent upon the reliability of Soviet safety systems. Since we know very little about the character of Soviet safety systems, considerable uncertainty necessarily surrounds the issue of security from accidental nuclear war between the superpowers.

39. I received special briefings on this program from the USAF Directorate of Nuclear Surety at Kirtland AFB, New Mexico, on 11 May 1976, and from SAC officers at Headquarters, Offut AFB, on 13 May 1976. They revealed that each armed service is charged with enforcing such a program pursuant to DOD directives 5210-41 and 5210-42. The Air Force's Human Reliability Program stipulates a scrupulous and continuing review of every pertinent individual's medical and personnel records, although it is not necessary that each individual under review be examined by a psychological professional. The basic judgment of reliability rests with the commanding officer. At SAC, a total of approximately 1,500–2,000 individuals screened under its Human Reliability Program are disqualified annually for nuclear weapon assignments. Of these, about one-third are disqualified at the initial screening and two-thirds during the first two years of service. There is very little disqualification after two years of service have been completed.

40. See U.S. Department of Defense, *Nuclear Weapons Safeguards* [a publication issued by the deputy assistant to the secretary of defense (atomic energy)], (Washington, D.C.: Government Printing Office, n.d.).

41. This information is based on the author's 11 May 1976 briefings by the USAF Directorate of Nuclear Surety.

42. Although this point is generally accepted in the declassified literature on the subject (see especially Phil Stanford, "The Deadly 'Move to Sea,'" *The New York Times Magazine*, 21 September 1975, pp. 16–17, 44–69; and "The Talk of the Town," *The New Yorker*, 3 May 1976, p. 29), the Department of Defense

has refused to corroborate it for me. It is a highly classified piece of information.

43. With respect to the ICBM force, however, there once did appear to be some difference between the Minuteman and Titan forces. At the special Command Control Briefing conducted for me at SAC's Underground Command Post on 13 May 1976, I was told that while coded switches were already operative in Titan forces, their installation in Minuteman forces would not take place until 1977. Both elements of the strategic bomber force—B-52s and FB-111s—are allegedly governed by coded switch systems that transmit firing capability as well as firing authority. Of course, all elements of the triad are safeguarded by the requirement that at least two (and usually more than two) individuals who are certifiably "reliable" must act in concert within very close time tolerances.

44. Stanford, "The Deadly 'Move to Sea,' " pp. 16–17.

45. See the unofficial publication of the House Select Committee on Intelligence Report (the Pike Papers after Committee Chairman Otis Pike) presented in a 24-page supplement of *The Village Voice*, 21, no. 7 (16 February 1976): 88. In reply (12 March 1976) to my inquiry to the Department of Defense about the accuracy of the House Intelligence Committee's final report, Brig. Gen. William B. Maxson states: "We do not possess any information on collisions involving U.S. nuclear submarines."

46. See *The Indianapolis Star*, 16 February 1976.

47. See Lloyd J. Dumas, "National Insecurity in the Nuclear Age," *Bulletin of the Atomic Scientists*, 32, no. 5 (May 1976): 28.

48. For an interesting discussion of some of these problems, see the statement by Herbert F. York prepared for the Committee on International Relations, House of Representatives, 94th Cong., 2d sess., 18 March 1976.

49. See *Strategic Air Command Information*, current as of 1 July 1975, p. 16.

50. Ibid., p. 17.

51. In this connection, it is important to point out that although the overall strategy of peace through nuclear deterrence is monumentally misconceived, the elements of the military that are charged with the maintenance of the weapon systems themselves seem to be performing their ill-fated task with a remarkable degree of skill and intelligence.

52. These incidents are discussed in Dumas, "National Insecurity in the Nuclear Age." I am especially indebted to Professor Dumas for his far-reaching and penetrating examination of this problem.

53. Ibid., p. 27.

54. Nor are these missiles equipped with in-flight destruction mechanisms, since an adversary might learn the secret signal and render the attacking missiles impotent.

55. *SAC Information*, p. 30.

56. Based on my briefings by USAF Directorate of Nuclear Surety and SAC officers, the prospect of an accidental launch by launch crew members would be minimal for a number of reasons: ICBMs cannot be launched out of a single silo; several launch crew members must "vote" within very close time tolerances (in the case of Minuteman missiles, at least four individuals operating out of two launch control centers must be involved); launch crew members are under continual screening by the Air Force's Human Reliability Program; each launch crew member has an "inhibit capability" whereby an improper launch vote by any other crew member can be nullified; and since 1977, no ICBM has been capable of firing without a coded release by authorities outside the launch control facility itself.

57. See Dumas, "National Insecurity in the Nuclear Age," pp. 28–29.

58. Cited in Herman Kahn, *On Thermonuclear War* (Princeton: Princeton University Press, 1960), p. 525.

59. It should be noted that this discussion of tactical nuclear accidents has been conservative, since it has assumed the reliability of permissive action links, environmental sensing devices, human reliability programs, and the two-man concept. Moreover, there is also considerable danger from the possibility of accidents involving Soviet tactical nuclear weapons (although Soviet deployment is almost certainly less extensive). Presently, we know very little about Soviet safety measures in this area.

60. See *First Use of Nuclear Weapons: Preserving Responsible Control*, Hearings before the Subcommittee on International Security and Scientific Affairs of the Committee on International Relations, House of Representatives, 94th Cong., 2d sess., 18 March 1976, pp. 46–57.

61. Ibid., p. 72.

62. See "The Tripwire Scenario," *Saturday Review*, 17 April 1976, p. 21.

63. See *The Defense Monitor*, p. 9.

64. See David R. Inglis, *Nuclear Energy: Its Physics and its Social Challenge* (Reading, Mass.: Addison-Wesley, 1973), p. 206.

65. See Sid Moody, "Missile Subs—Cops on Ultimate Beat," *The Chicago Tribune*, 10 October 1976.

66. See *The Defense Monitor*, p. 8.

67. For more detailed information, the following Department

of Defense directives and instructions are related directly to the safety and safeguards program:

DOD Directive 5210.41, 30 July 1974, Security Criteria and Standards for Protecting Nuclear Weapons.

DOD Directive 5210.42, 24 April 1975, Nuclear Weapon Personnel Reliability Program.

DOD Directive 4540.3, 19 December 1972, Logistic Movement of Nuclear Weapons.

DOD Instruction 4540.4, 20 December 1972, Safety Standards and Procedures for the Logistic Movement of Nuclear Weapons.

DOD Directive 5030.15, 8 August 1974, Safety Studies and Reviews of Nuclear Weapons Systems.

DOD Directive 5100.1, 31 December 1958, revised 1969, Functions of the Department of Defense and its Major Components.

68. See *The Defense Monitor*, p. 9.

69. See Statement by former Sen. Stuart Symington in the U.S. Senate concerning "Controlling the Cancer of Nuclear Proliferation," 13 March 1975. Printed in the First Annual Report to the U.S. Congress by the Joint Committee on Atomic Energy, 30 June 1975, app. II, pp. 54–59.

70. See *The Defense Monitor*, p. 8.

71. See "First Annual Report," 1975, app. F, pp 47–51.

72. Ibid., p. 50. Recent testimony by representatives of the Department of Defense before the Military Installations and Facilities Subcommittee of the House Committee on Armed Services revealed the following information: (1) the incentive to upgrade criteria for nuclear storage sites came in 1972, after the Munich Olympics terrorist incident; (2) the official U.S. upgraded criteria were published in July 1975; (3) the Department of Defense is currently seeking $6.8 million to continue to upgrade overseas nuclear storage sites; and (4) the intended improvements center on arming guard force facilities, establishing a complete set of intrusion detection devices, and improving the lighting and communications facilities. (See the following Hearings: *To Authorize Certain Construction at Military Installations: H.R. 5692*, 95th Cong., 1st sess., 24 and 25 February 1977; and *For Other Purposes and Full Committee Consideration of H.R. 6690*, 95th Cong., 1st sess., 19, 20, 21, 25, and 27 April 1977.)

73. The United States continues to rely on the early-warning satellite system and the ballistic missile early-warning system

(BMEWS) radars for warning of ICBM attacks. For warning of SLBM attacks, the United States relies upon satellites and 474N SLBM detection and warning system radars. It is expected that the 474N radars will eventually be replaced with newer SLBM phased-array radars.

74. "First Use of Nuclear Weapons," p. 73.

75. Ibid., p. 61.

76. See Theodore H. White, *Breach of Faith: The Fall of Richard Nixon* (New York: Dell, 1975), p. 35.

77. From a letter to author of 14 March 1976.

78. Jerome D. Frank, *Sanity and Survival: Psychological Aspects of War and Peace* (New York: Random House, 1967), p. 57.

79. Ibid., p. 59.

80. Ibid., p. 61.

81. Ibid., p. 62.

82. Ibid., pp. 60–61.

83. See Theodore Sorensen, *Kennedy* (New York: Harper and Row, 1965), p. 705.

Chapter Two

1. As it is used herein, proliferation refers not only to the spread of nuclear weapons themselves to states not yet members of the nuclear club, but also to the spread of the capability to make nuclear weapons. And while nuclear-weapon-grade materials can be produced either by the enrichment of uranium or by the recovery of plutonium from spent reactor fuel, it is the second possibility that generates the greatest current hazard to world peace, because of the very close relationship that exists between the acquisition of civilian nuclear energy facilities and the capability to develop nuclear explosives.

2. See *Nuclear Proliferation: Future U.S. Foreign Policy Implications*, Hearings before the Subcommittee on International Security and Scientific Affairs, Committee on International Relations, House of Representatives, 94th Cong., 1st sess., October-November 1975.

3. See *Nuclear Reduction, Testing, and Non-Proliferation*, Hearing before the Subcommittee on Arms Control, International Organizations, and Security Agreements, Committee on Foreign Relations, Senate, 94th Cong., 2d sess., 18 March 1976.

4. See Hearings on "Nuclear Proliferation."

5. Cited by Daniel Yergin, "The Terrifying Prospect: Atomic Bombs Everywhere," *The Atlantic Monthly*, April 1977, p. 49.

6. See William Epstein, *The Last Chance: Nuclear Proliferation and Arms Control* (New York: The Free Press, 1976), p. 40.

7. See Harold A. Feiveson and Theodore B. Taylor, "Security Implications of Alternative Fission Futures," *Bulletin of the Atomic Scientists*, 32, no. 10 (December 1976): 16.

8. A country might also seek entry into the nuclear club by using a "research reactor" to make weapon-grade plutonium, or by enriching U-235 to weapon-grade levels. The first of these routes, and the one taken by India in its successful bid for membership, involves producing plutonium from a natural uranium reseach reactor and then separating it from the remaining uranium and other accumulated radioactive fission products. The result of such separation by a small chemical reprocessing plant can be weapon-grade plutonium. In comparison to the plutonium that is made from power reactors, the plutonium from research reactors is cheaper, faster, and of higher weapon-making quality. The second route, uranium enrichment, was used to make the Hiroshima bomb, and is a costly, complex process requiring a special plant to separate isotopes which are chemically identical. At the moment, only five countries have the capability to enrich uranium (particularly by gaseous diffusion): the United States, the Soviet Union, the United Kingdom, France, and China. In the not too distant future, however, substantial enrichment facilities are apt to exist in West Germany, Japan, the Netherlands, and South Africa. Centrifuge enrichment is presently being adapted to commercial use, and it appears that more efficient and less expensive new technologies—especially laser isotopic separation—might soon become commercially feasible.

9. See Frank C. Barnaby, "How States Can 'Go Nuclear,'" *Annals of the American Academy of Political and Social Science*, 430 (March 1977): 30.

10. The main provisions of U.S. nuclear export policy, as articulated by President Carter in April 1977, are described as follows in "U.S. Nonproliferation Policy," Bureau of Public Affairs, Department of State, August 1977:

> To reduce inventories abroad of weapons-grade fuel, the U.S. will avoid new commitments to export large amounts of highly enriched uranium (HEU), except when the project is of exceptional merit and the use of low enriched fuel or some other less weapons-usable material is clearly shown to be technically infeasible.
>
> Export of small quantities of separated plutonium will be permitted for research and analytical uses.
>
> Supply of HEU greater than 15 kilograms (the approximate

amount needed for a bomb) will require direct Presidential approval.

Efforts will be made to identify projects and facilities that might be converted to the use of low enriched uranium instead of HEU.

The U.S. does not export uranium enrichment facilities or reprocessing plants, as they are not presently safeguardable.

11. This expression is used by Epstein in *The Last Chance.*

12. See "Nuclear War By 1999?" *Harvard Magazine,* November 1975.

13. See R. Robert Sandoval, "Consider the Porcupine: Another View of Nuclear Proliferation," *Bulletin of the Atomic Scientists,* 32, no. 5 (May 1976): 19.

14. Cited in John Herz, *International Politics in the Atomic Age* (New York: Columbia University Press, 1959), p. 212.

15. See Pierre M. Gallois, "Nuclear Strategy: A French View," in David Brook, ed., *Search for Peace* (New York: Dodd, Mead, 1970), p. 165. The article is reprinted from Eleanor Lansing Dulles and Robert Dickson Crane, eds., *Detente: Cold War Strategies in Transition* (New York: Praeger, 1965), pp. 215–20; 223–40.

16. This scenario, of course, could just as reasonably have been written in reverse, with the Egyptians striking first, or it could also have been written around other conflictual states in the arena of world politics.

17. This expression is borrowed from Daniel Yergin in "The Terrifying Prospect."

18. At the time of this writing, South Korea has two research reactors in operation, and two power reactors under construction.

19. See Sean MacBride, "A New Morality for a New World," *Bulletin of the Atomic Scientists,* 33, no. 7 (September 1977): 23.

20. The non-nuclear-weapon nations that have accepted the NPT must maintain their own systems of accounting for and control of all their nuclear material. The IAEA then applies its own safeguards:

    1) *Design Review.* The nation must supply the IAEA with information on relevant design characteristics of its existing nuclear plants and of new plants in the planning stage.

    2) *Records.* The nuclear plant operator must keep a precise account of all nuclear materials he has, receives, sends out, etc., based on exact measurements of the material.

    3) *Reports.* On the basis of information given by the plant

operator, the national authority sends the IAEA regular reports on the amount of nuclear material in each plant and of all changes in these amounts so that the IAEA can keep its own state of accounts for verification and comparison purposes.

4) *Inspections.* IAEA inspectors perform independent measurements and observations for verifying the information submitted by the country concerned. All inspectors have to be approved by the IAEA's Board of Governors (34 Member States) and designated with the consent of the country involved.

(The above is taken directly from *International Nuclear Safeguards* (Vienna: IAEA, March 1976), p. 1.

21. See Epstein, *The Last Chance.*

22. Remarks entitled, "The Nonproliferation Treaty and our Worldwide Security Structure," Public Information Release, ACDA, p. 3.

23. See "On the Manner of Settling Disputes in a State of Natural Liberty," *The Law of Nature and of Nations* (New York: Occana, 1964), p. 562.

24. The world's leading nuclear supplier nations are the United States, the Soviet Union, Japan, Canada, France, the United Kingdom, and West Germany.

25. See William Epstein, "Retrospective on the NPT Review Conference: Proposals for the Future," Occasional Paper No. 9, The Stanley Foundation, Muscatine, Iowa, 1975.

Chapter Three

1. Among some of the better known are Japan's United Red Army; West Germany's Baader-Meinhof group; Italy's Red Brigades; the United States' New World Liberation Front; and the various groups for which the PLO acts as an umbrella organization: Al Fatah, Al Saiqa, Arab Liberation Front (ALF), Popular Front for the Liberation of Palestine (PFLP), Popular Front for the Liberation of Palestine—General Command (PFLP-GC), and the Popular Democratic Front for the Liberation of Palestine (PDFLP).

2. See *The Defense Monitor,* no. 2 (February 1975), p. 8.

3. See especially "Security Review at Certain NATO Installations," *Congressional Record* 121 S 7184–S 7189 no. 68 (30 April 1975); *First Annual Report to the United States Congress by the Joint Committee on Atomic Energy* (30 June 1975), app. II, pp. 54–59; and app. F, pp. 47–51; and "Nuclear Theft and Terrorism,"

a discussion group report of the Sixteenth Strategy for Peace Conference, The Stanley Foundation, Muscatine, Iowa, October 1975. In the past several years, the Department of Defense, in response to these fears, has increased security around its nuclear arsenals, employing such means as ground sensors, infrared cameras, metal detectors, sophisticated identification systems, and customized vans for secure transport. In this connection, see Hearings before the Military Installations and Facilities Subcommittee of the House Committee on Armed Services, 95th Cong., 1st sess., February and April, 1977.

4. See especially Mason Willrich and Theodore Taylor, *Nuclear Theft: Risks and Safeguards* (Cambridge, Mass.: Ballinger, 1974); William Epstein, *The Last Chance: Nuclear Proliferation and Arms Control* (New York: The Fress Press, 1976); David Krieger, "Terrorists and Nuclear Technology," *Bulletin of the Atomic Scientists* 31, no. 6 (June 1975); and Ralph Lapp, "The Ultimate Blackmail," *New York Times Magazine*, 4 February 1973, p. 31.

5. See Robert M. Press, "Atom Bomb Developers Warn of Nuclear Dangers," *Christian Science Monitor*, 23 December 1975, p. 13.

6. See "Nuclear Theft and Terrorism."

7. See Gilinsky, *NRC Safeguards and Related Issues*, remarks of the commissioner, U.S. Nuclear Regulatory Commission, before the Institute of Nuclear Materials Management, New Orleans, La., 18 June 1975.

8. See Frank, "Nuclear Terrorism and the Escalation of International Conflict" (Paper presented to the Annual Meeting of the Midwest Political Science Association, Chicago, Ill., 1 May 1976).

9. See *Final Report of the Joint ERDA-NRC Task Force on Safeguards* (Washington, D.C., 12 July 1976), pp. 55–56.

10. A similar problem of "inventory differences" and "materials unaccounted for" was reported in 1974. (See David Burnham, "Thousands of Pounds of Materials Usable in Nuclear Bombs Unaccounted For," *New York Times*, 29 December 1974. Accounting for nuclear materials is, of course, a very difficult process. Since each measurement involves an unavoidable uncertainty, the cumulative effect of several thousand measurements can involve a very large loss.

11. See Office of Management Program and Analysis, U.S. Nuclear Regulatory Commission, "Domestic Safeguards," *Annual Report to Congress FY 1978* (Washington, D.C.: Government Printing Office, January 1979), p. 9.

12. See David Rosenbaum, "Nuclear Terror," *International Security* 1, no. 2 (Winter 1977): 143.

13. See Willrich and Taylor, *Nuclear Theft*, p. 1.

14. See Rosenbaum, "Nuclear Terror," pp. 142–43.

15. See Frank, "Nuclear Terrorism," pp. 3–4.

16. In this connection, see, for example, U.S. Army Mobility Equipment Research and Development Command, *Capability for Intrusion Detection at Nuclear Fuel Sites*, prepared for the U.S. Nuclear Regulatory Commission, March 1978.

17. See David Burnham, "Nuclear Facilities Told to Strengthen Antiterrorist Guard," *New York Times*, 20 February 1977. The obvious inference that can be drawn from this statement is that terrorist inclinations to nuclear materials theft exceed their interest in reactor sabotage and/or that the task of reactor sabotage is intrinsically more difficult. Comparatively speaking, it would be more difficult for terrorists to "pulse" a nuclear reactor core to destruction than to make a radiological weapon or crude fission bomb.

18. See B. L. Welch, statement before the Joint Committee on Atomic Energy, p. 32.

19. See Robert R. Jones, "Nuclear Reactor Risks—Some Frightening Scenarios," *Chicago Sun-Times*, 30 April 1976. For the improved security regulations, see Comptroller General of the United States, General Accounting Office, *Improvements Needed in the Program for the Protection of Special Nuclear Material*, June 1974.

20. See Jones, "Nuclear Reactor Risks," p. 12.

21. Ibid.

22. This information was disclosed by ERDA's Division of Safeguards and Security to Mr. James M. Cubie of Congress Watch, an organization associated with Ralph Nader, in a letter dated 26 January 1976. The author has received and reviewed a copy of this letter and the attached listing of threats or acts of violence with regard to ERDA unlicensed nuclear facilities.

23. See Rosenbaum, "Nuclear Terror," p. 154. The citation for the French newspaper article mentioned by Rosenbaum is *Le Gaeule Ouverte*, 9 June 1975, M. Goulet.

24. See U.S. Nuclear Regulatory Commission, WASH-1400, *Reactor Safety Study* 1975; and *Risk Assessment Review Group Report to the U.S. Nuclear Regulatory Commission*, H. W. Lewis, Chairman (Washington, D.C., September 1978).

25. See "Nuclear Theft and Terrorism," p. 35.

26. See *Joint ERDA-NRC Task Force on Safeguards, Final Report*.

27. Political scientist Michael Waltzer cites three historical examples of an earlier form of terrorism which operated according to a code distinguishing between individuals who can

and cannot be killed. These examples are drawn from Russian revolutionary activity in the 1870s; the IRA bombing campaign in Britain during the years 1938–1939; and the activities of the Stern Gang in Palestine in 1944. See "The New Terrorists," *The New Republic*, 30 August 1975, pp. 12–14.

28. See Eric Hobsbawm, *Bandits* (New York: Dell, 1969), pp. 54–55.

29. The German original reads: "Die Lust zur Zerstörung ist zugleich eine schaffende Lust." This much quoted statement goes back to Bakunin's "Dresden days." It is found at the end of a fairly long essay entitled "The Reaction in Germany (Fragment from a Frenchman)," written sometime in 1842 in Dresden. It was published under the pseudonym Jules Elizar and marks the transition of Bakunin's intellectual evolution from a philosopher to a man of "practical action." The essay was originally published as "Die Reaktion in Deutschland," in *Deutsche Jahrbücher für Wissenschaft und Kunst*, ed. Arnold Ruge, Leipzig, V. nos. 247–51 (17–21 October 1842), pp. 985–1002. An English translation is found in James M. Edie, James P. Scanlon, and Mary-Barbara Zeldin, eds., *Russian Philosophy* (Chicago: Quadrangle Books, 1965), 1: 385–406. Citation on p. 406.

30. *The Wretched of the Earth*, trans. Constance Farrington (New York: Grove Press, 1963), p. 73.

31. Preface to Fanon, *The Wretched of the Earth*, p. 73.

32. See R. W. Apple, Jr., "A Loose Alliance of Terrorists Does Seem to Exist," *New York Times*, 23 October 1977; Robert Fisk, "The World's Terrorists Sometimes Are United," *New York Times*, 17 August 1975; Yonah Alexander, "Some Perspectives on International Terrorism," *International Problems* 14, nos. 3–4 (Fall 1975): 27; and John B. Wolf, "Black September: Militant Palestinianism," *Current History*, January 1973, p. 37.

33. See the *Report of the Ad Hoc Committee on International Terrorism*, General Assembly, 1973, Official Records, Twenty-Eighth Session, Supplement No. 28, A/9028; and U.N. General Assembly, *Definition of Aggression*, 1974, in Benjamin B. Ferencz, *Defining International Aggression: The Search for World Peace*, vol. 2, (New York: Oceana, 1975).

34. See Ferencz, *Defining International Aggression*, p. 18.

Chapter Four

1. Hiroshima's current mayor, Takeshi Araki, says that at least 140,000 persons were killed by the blast.

2. See Robert Jay Lifton, *Death in Life: Survivors of Hiroshima* (New York: Vintage, 1967), pp. 20–21.

3. See M. Hachiya, *Hiroshima Diary*, ed. and trans. Warner Wells (Chapel Hill: University of North Carolina Press, 1955), p. 54. Also cited in Lifton, *Death in Life*, p. 25.

4. See Terrence Des Pres, *The Survivor: An Anatomy of Life in the Death Camps* (New York: Oxford University Press, 1976).

5. Cited in Lifton, *Death in Life*, p. 48.

6. After the blast, it was widely feared that plant life would be blighted for decades. When first buds appeared unexpectedly the next spring, there were wet eyes everywhere in Japan.

7. See Henry Kamm, "A 'Hiroshima Maiden' Conquers Bitterness," *New York Times*, 22 May 1977.

8. See Lifton, *Death in Life*, p. 7.

9. Recent evidence also seems to indicate that some Americans may have suffered the effects of the Hiroshima bomb in a much more immediate and dramatic way, i.e., as actual victims of the blast. Although the U.S. government has never confirmed the suspicion, it is now widely believed that a number of American prisoners of war were being held in Hiroshima on 6 August 1945. That is the date placed on a tombstone at Jefferson Barracks near St. Louis for crew members of the B-24 "Lonesome Lady," which was hit by enemy fire in the vicinity of Hiroshima on 28 July 1945. Ten crewmen bailed out, and most were reportedly taken prisoner.

10. See Robert Jay Lifton, *The Life of the Self: Toward a New Psychology* (New York: Simon & Schuster, 1976), pp. 132–33.

11. See *Protection in the Nuclear Age*, Defense Civil Preparedness Agency, Department of Defense, H-20, February 1977, p. iii.

12. Ibid., p. 2.

13. Ibid., p. 49.

14. Ibid., pp. 50–51.

15. Ibid., p. 54.

16. See *Ready to Serve the President: 5000 Executives*, Federal Preparedness Agency, General Services Administration, February 1977, p. 9.

17. See "Civil Defense Seen as a Fading Program," *New York Times*, 20 February 1977.

18. Ibid.

19. Ibid.

20. See Kevin N. Lewis, "The Prompt and Delayed Effects of Nuclear War," *Scientific American* 241, no. 1 (July 1979), pp. 35–47; and *Economic and Social Consequences of Nuclear Attacks on the United States*, a study prepared for the Joint Committee on Defense Production, Congress of the United States, published by the Committee on Banking, Housing, and Urban Affairs, U.S.

Senate (March 1979), 150 pp. According to *Consequences of Nuclear Attacks*, "to provide a retaliatory force capable of highly destructive attacks on sources of national strength, only 10 percent of current U.S. strategic force loadings, or 30 percent of equivalent Soviet forces, must survive an initial exchange" (p. v).

21. *Consequences of Nuclear Attacks*, p. v.

22. See Richard Pipes, "Why the Soviet Union Thinks It Could Fight and Win a Nuclear War," *Commentary* 64, no. 1 (July 1977): 30.

23. Ibid., p. 34.

24. See Bernard T. Feld, "The Consequences of Nuclear War," *Bulletin of the Atomic Scientists* 32, no. 6 (June 1976): 12.

25. Ibid.

26. See Tom Stonier, *Nuclear Disaster* (New York: Meridian, 1964), p. 24.

27. Ibid.

28. See Dr. Handler's letter of transmittal, which is contained at the beginning of the report, *Long-Term Worldwide Effects of Multiple Nuclear-Weapons Detonations*, National Academy of Sciences, Washington, D.C., 1975.

29. This point, made by NAS President Philip Handler in his letter of 12 August 1975, transmitting the report to ACDA, is by no means uncontroversial. In fact, in the belief that it is an "overstated conclusion," the Federation of American Scientists issued a public declaration which effectively accused NAS of inadvertently encouraging nuclear war. The federation, whose membership includes half of America's living Noble laureates, charged that the academy had reached a "false conclusion" in suggesting mankind's probable survival. The federation's statement was prepared by Jeremy Stone, the organization's director, and was approved by a majority of the organization's executive committee. The FAS position is also supported by Bernard Feld, editor-in-chief of the *Bulletin of the Atomic Scientists*, who believes that the NAS conclusion concerning the survival of the human race is "too sanguine." (See Feld's, "Consequences of Nuclear War," p. 13.)

30. Taken from Nevil Shute's work of fiction on the aftermath of system-wide nuclear war, *On the Beach* (New York: William Morrow, 1957).

31. A rad is a unit of radiation dose which measures the amount of ionization produced per unit volume by the particles from radioactive decay.

32. See Feld, "Consequences of Nuclear War," p. 13.

33. See *Worldwide Effects of Nuclear War . . . Some Perspectives*, A Report of the U.S. Arms Control and Disarmament Agency, not dated, but produced after the 1975 NAS report, pp. 23–24.

34. For a comprehensive treatment of such formulations, see *Analysis of Effects of Limited Nuclear Warfare*, prepared for Subcommittee on Arms Control, International Organizations and Security Agreements of the Committee on Foreign Relations, Senate, 94th Cong., 1st sess., September 1975, pp. 26–28.

35. This view was based on the assumptions of (1) a Soviet attack on all American Minuteman and Titan ICBMs with one one-megaton warhead targeted on each silo and (2) extensive civil defense protection.

36. Known officially as the Ad Hoc Panel on Nuclear Effects, it comprised the following members:

Jerome Wiesner (chairman), president of MIT

Harold Brown, president of California Institute of Technology

Sidney Drell, deputy director of SLAC (former member of PSAC)

Richard Garwin, IBM (former member of PSAC and the Defense Science Board)

Spurgeon Keeny, MITRE Corp. (formerly assistant director of ACDA)

Gordon MacDonald, Dartmouth College (former member of Council on Environmental Quality)

Gerald Miller (former deputy director of Joint Strategic Targeting and Planning Staff)

James Neel, Department of Human Genetics, University of Michigan (formerly acting director of Field Studies Atomic Bomb casualty Commission)

Archie Wood, Brookings Institution (formerly deputy assistant secretary of defense)

The Panel's single meeting was held on 1, February 1975. The Technology Assessment Board's vice chairman, Sen. Clifford Case of New Jersey, attended part of the session. Also in attendance were OTA Deputy Director Daniel DeSimone, William Mills, Tom McGurn, Buford Macklin, and Henry Kelly, all of the OTA staff.

37. See *Effects of Limited Nuclear Warfare*, pp. 4–5.

38. See Senator Sparkman's letter to Dr. Schlesinger of 17 March 1975, in *Effects of Limited Nuclear Warfare*, pp. 9–10.

39. See opening statement by Senator Case to Hearing before the Subcommittee on Arms Control, International Organizations

and Security Agreements of the Committee on Foreign Relations, U.S. Senate, on "Possible Effects on U.S. Society of Nuclear Attacks Against U.S. Military Installations," 94th Cong., 1st sess., 18 September 1975, p. 3.

40. Testimony in Hearing of 18 September 1975, p. 10.

41. Testimony in Hearing of 18 September 1975, p. 19. For more by Dr. Drell on this subject, see Sidney D. Drell and Frank Von Hippel, "Limited Nuclear War," *Scientific American* 235, no. 5 (November 1976), pp. 27–37.

42. See Drell's testimony in Hearing of 18 September 1975, p. 21.

43. Cited by Dr. Richard L. Garwin (IBM Fellow at the Thomas J. Watson Research Center, adjunct professor of physics at Columbia University, and member of the Ad Hoc Panel on Nuclear Effects for the OTA) at Hearing of 18 September 1975, p. 53.

44. See Kissinger's *Problems of National Strategy* (New York: Praeger, 1965), cited by Dr. Drell in his testimony at Hearing of 18 September 1975, p. 18.

45. Cited by Dr. Drell at Hearing of 18 September 1975, p. 19.

46. See, for example, the Drell testimony.

47. See Secretary of Defense Donald H. Rumsfeld in *Annual Defense Department Report for FY 1978*, p. 73.

48. Ibid.

49. Scenario taken from *Time*, 25 July 1977, p. 29.

50. From *Der Spiegel*, cited by Ellen Lentz, "West Germany Aroused Over Neutron Bomb Prospect," *New York Times*, 24 July 1977.

51. The above information on radiation casualty criteria is from Jorma K. Miettinen, "Enhanced Radiation Warfare," *Bulletin of the Atomic Scientists* 33, no. 7 (September 1977): p. 35.

52. Editor-in-chief's editorial in *Bulletin of the Atomic Scientists* 33, no. 7, (September 1977): 11.

53. Smoking, drinking, and drug-taking are perhaps the most easily understood examples today. Although individuals who engage in these activities often admit being self-destructive, such admissions are not typically deeply felt. Rather, they reflect the absurd narcissism that death is something that occurs only to others. Similarly, individuals functioning as residents of particular countries exhibit blithe unconcern over the prospects of nuclear annihilation because—in the deepest recesses of their minds—they cannot really believe in the "mortality" of their most established and expansive institutional creation.

54. See Ernest Becker, *The Denial of Death* (New York: The Free Press, 1973), p. 17.

Chapter Five
1. See Bernard T. Feld, "The Consequences of Nuclear War," *Bulletin of the Atomic Scientists* 32, no. 6 (June 1976): 13.
2. These effects, of course, are the ones used by the Committee to Study the Long-Term Worldwide Effects of Multiple Nuclear-Weapons Detonations.
3. See the NAS Report, *Long-Term Worldwide Effects of Multiple Nuclear-Weapons Detonations*, (Washington, D.C.: Government Printing Office 1975), p. 60.
4. Ibid, p. 9.
5. Ibid., p. 66.
6. Ibid., p. 85.
7. Ibid.
8. Ibid., pp. 12–13.
9. See Robert Jay Lifton and Eric Olson, *Living and Dying* (New York: Praeger, 1974), chap. 6.
10. See Tom Stonier, *Nuclear Disaster* (New York: Meridian, 1964), p. 54.
11. Ibid., p. 112.
12. Ibid., p. 135.
13. See *Worldwide Effects of Nuclear War . . . Some Perspectives*, A Report of the U.S. Arms Control and Disarmament Agency, not dated, but produced after the 1975 NAS report, p. 7.
14. See Ruth Leger Sivard, *World Military and Social Expenditures 1977* (Leesburg, Va.: WMSE Publications, 1977), p. 5. This publication, now in its third updating, contains a foreword by Robert S. McNamara, and is sponsored by the Arms Control Association, Institute for World Order, Members of Congress for Peace Through Law Education Fund, The Rockefeller Foundation, and the Canadian Peace Research Institute—Dundas.
15. See Roy L. Prosterman, *Surviving to 3000: An Introduction to the Study of Lethal Conflict* (Belmont, Calif.: Duxbury Press, 1972), p. 285.
16. See *Worldwide Effects of Nuclear War*, pp. 7–8.
17. Ibid., p. 14.
18. Ibid., pp. 14–15.
19. Ibid., p. 16.
20. See Samuel Glasstone, ed., *The Effects of Nuclear Weapons*, prepared by the U.S. Department of Defense, U.S. Atomic Energy Commission (Washington, D.C.: Government Printing Office, 1964).
21. See, for example, statements by de Gaulle cited in Herman Kahn, *On Thermonuclear War* (Princeton: Princeton University Press, 1960), pp. 30–31.

22. Ibid.

23. Even where these new weapons are not adopted by new nuclear powers, they may still affect the consequences of nuclear war through proliferation. This is the case because their deployment by the superpowers may increase the chances for nuclear war involving new nuclear powers.

24. A somewhat more technical definition is provided by Kosta Tsipis, a physicist at MIT who writes on questions of defense policy and arms control: "A cruise missile can be defined as a dispensable, pilotless, self-guided, continuously powered, air-breathing warhead-delivery vehicle that flies just like an airplane, supported by aerodynamic surfaces." See Kosta Tsipis, "Cruise Missiles," *Scientific American* 236, no. 2 (February 1977): 20.

25. See Kosta Tsipis, "The Long-Range Cruise Missile," *Bulletin of the Atomic Scientists* 31, no. 4 (April 1975), pp. 22–23.

26. See "Strategic Balance: Trends and Perceptions," *Washington Report* (Washington, D.C.: American Security Council, April 1977), pp. 13–15.

Chapter Six

1. A significant nuclear yield is defined as a yield *much greater* than the yield of an equal mass of high explosive.

2. See U.S. Congress, Office of Technology Assessment, *Nuclear Proliferation and Safeguards* (New York: Praeger, 1977), pp. 140–41.

3. Ibid., p. 142.

4. See *Nuclear Power: Issues and Choices* (Cambridge, Mass.: Ballinger, 1977), p. 306. This report by the Nuclear Energy Policy Study Group was sponsored by the Ford Foundation, and administered by the Mitre Corporation.

5. See Mason Willrich and Theodore B. Taylor, *Nuclear Theft: Risks and Safeguards* (Cambridge, Mass.: Ballinger, 1974), pp. 21–22.

6. Ibid., p. 22.

7. The nuclear weapon dropped on Hiroshima was exploded 1,850 feet above the ground.

8. See Frank Barnaby, "The Continuing Body Count at Hiroshima and Nagasaki," *Bulletin of the Atomic Scientists* 33, no. 10 (December 1977), pp. 50–51.

9. Ibid., p. 51.

10. Ibid., p. 53.

11. Kataoka Osamu, "A Survivor's Story: 'Friends, Please Forgive us,'" *Bulletin of the Atomic Scentists* 33, no. 10 (December 1977): 52.

12. See Barnaby, "The Continuing Body Count," p. 53. For more detailed information on the effects of the Hiroshima and Nagasaki bombs, see the report of the Natural Science Group, organized by the Geneva-based International Peace Bureau, to appraise Japanese studies of the aftereffects of the Hiroshima/Nagasaki bombings: "The Physical and Medical Effects of the Hiroshima and Nagasaki Bombs," *Bulletin of the Atomic Scientists* 33, no. 10 (December 1977), pp. 54–56.

13. See Barnaby, "The Continuing Body Count," p. 53.

14. The *FRPPNE* (April 1977) comprises three parts: a basic report and two annexes: Annex I—*Guidelines For Federal-State Relationships* and Annex II—*An Analysis of Legal Authorities in Support of the Federal Response Plan for Peacetime Nuclear Emergencies.*

15. Ibid., pp. 4–5.

16. See OTA, *Nuclear Proliferation and Safeguards*, p. 146.

17. Ibid.

18. See Willrich and Taylor, *Nuclear Theft*, pp. 24–25.

19. Ibid., pp. 25–26.

20. Such scenarios may be abstracted from fictive conjectures, as in the film *The China Syndrome*, or from actual events, as in the case of the Three Mile Island nuclear power plant accident in Pennsylvania in March 1979. While such scenarios deal with malfunctions rather than sabotage, the effective consequences would be very similar. Indeed, the U.S. Nuclear Regulatory Commission, *Reactor Safety Study*, WASH-1400, October 1975, known generally as the Rasmussen Report, indicates that the worst consequences from nuclear reactor sabotage would not exceed the worst cases from accidents.

21. See OTA, *Nuclear Proliferation and Safeguards*, p. 116; Brian Michael Jenkins, *The Potential for Nuclear Terrorism*, The Rand Paper Series, The Rand Corporation, p-5876, May 1977, p. 6.

22. See U.S. Senate Subcommittee on Internal Security of the Senate Judiciary Committee, "Terroristic Activity: International Terrorism," 14 May 1975, p. 197.

23. See MITRE Corporation, Technical Report MTR-7022, *The Threat to Licensed Nuclear Facilities*, September 1975, p. 55.

24. See Peter Kihss, "Suit to Bar Nuclear Reactor Cites Terrorist Risk," *New York Times*, 12 March 1978.

25. See OTA, *Nuclear Proliferation and Safeguards*, p. 117.

26. See Willrich and Taylor, *Nuclear Theft*, p. 27.

27. See *Answers to your questions about nuclear dangers . . . and solar potential*, a brochure published by the Union of Concerned Scientists, undated.

28. See Kurt H. Hohenemser, "The Fail-Safe Risk," *Environment* 17, no. 1 (January/February 1975): 7.

29. See U.S. Atomic Energy Commission, *The Safety of Nuclear Power Reactors and Related Facilities*, Washington, D.C., June 1973, 1250.

30. See *Nuclear Power: Issues and Choices*, p. 214.

31. See WASH-1400.

32. According to the Report of the Nuclear Energy Policy Study Group, which disagrees with the Rasmussen Report (WASH-1400), the consequences of sabotage are apt to be *more* severe. See *Nuclear Power: Issues and Choices*, p. 308.

33. Ibid., p. 224. For an interesting assessment of the Rasmussen Report, see H. A. Bethe, "The Necessity of Fission Power," *Scientific American* 234, no. 1 (January 1976), pp. 21–31.

34. See H. W. Lewis, et al., *Risk Assessment Review Group Report to the U.S. Nuclear Regulatory Commission*, NUREG/CR-0400, 1978. Among this report's specific findings, which concern the adequacy and accuracy of the earlier *Reactor Safety Study* (WASH-1400) are the following: (1) the statistical analysis performed in the *Reactor Safety Study* is deeply flawed; (2) the *Reactor Safety Study* model of reactor accident consequences is deficient; the *Reactor Safety Study* "greatly understated" the uncertainty of its estimates regarding the probability of severe reactor accidents.

35. See *Nuclear Power: Issues and Choices*, p. 307.

36. Ibid., p. 22.

37. A comprehensive assessment of these effects can be found in WASH-1400.

38. Ibid.

39. See *Nuclear Power: Issues and Choices*, p. 224.

40. Ibid., p. 178.

41. See *Threat to Licensed Nuclear Facilities*, p. 81.

42. Ibid., p. 82.

43. See *Nuclear Power: Issues and Choices*, p. 313.

44. Similarly, goaded by the kidnapping of former Premier Aldo Moro in March 1978, Italian authorities declared a "situation of emergency" and ordered broadened police powers to cope with the threat. These powers included greater discretion in wiretapping and authorization to question suspects immediately without a lawyer being present.

45. See Walter Sullivan, "Nuclear Safeguards Assessed at Meeting," *New York Times*, 22 May 1977.

Chapter Seven

1. For a contrary view—one' that displays confidence in the extant system of superpower nuclear competition and argues for its continuation—see Michael Mandelbaum, "International Stability and Nuclear Order: The First Nuclear Regime," in David C. Gompert, et al., *Nuclear Weapons and World Politics: Alternatives for the Future*, 1980s Project/Council on Foreign Relations (New York: McGraw-Hill, 1977), pp. 15–80.

2. See Jimmy Carter, letter of transmittal to the Congress of the United States, 22 March 1978, *Seventeenth Annual Report of the U.S. Arms Control and Disarmament Agency* (Washington, D.C.: Government Printing Office, released May 1978).

3. Bilateral Arms Control Agreements between the United States and the Soviet Union as of February 1978

	Signed	Entered Into Force
"Hot Line" Agreement	6/20/63	6/20/63
Improved "Hot Line" Agreement	9/30/71	9/30/71
Nuclear Accidents Agreement	9/30/71	9/30/71
ABM Treaty	5/26/72	10/ 3/72
Interim Agreement on Offensive Strategic Arms	5/26/72	10/ 3/72
Standing Consultative Commission for SALT	12/21/72	12/21/72
Basic Principles of Negotiations on the Further Limitation of Strategic Offensive Arms	6/21/73	6/21/73
Threshold Test Ban Treaty with Protocol	7/ 3/74	
Protocol to the ABM Treaty	7/ 3/74	5/24/76
Treaty on the Limitation of Underground Explosions for Peaceful Purposes	5/28/76	
Convention on the Prohibition of Military or Any Other Hostile Use of Environmental Modification Techniques	5/18/77	

(Taken from app. 1, *Seventeenth Annual Report*, p. 48.)

4. Ibid., p. 6.

5. Ibid., p. 7.

6. Cruise missiles, it will be recalled, are unmanned, self-propelled, guided missiles that can be launched from aircraft, submarines, surface ships, and ground platforms.

7. For more on these differences, see Richard Burt, "The Scope and Limits of SALT," *Foreign Affairs* 56, no. 4 (July 1978): 751–70.

8. Ibid., p. 755.

9. See *Seventeenth Annual Report*, p. 9.

10. For the complete text of the SALT II Agreement, see *Selected Documents No. 12A*, United States Department of State, Bureau of Public Affairs, Washington, D.C., 1979.

11. This is the case because the Soviets perceive MX as an American first-strike weapon which might jeopardize their ICBM forces.

12. See Richard Burt, "New Killer Satellites Make 'Sky-War' Possible," *New York Times*, 11 June 1978.

13. See David K. Shipler, "Soviet Warns that Policy of U.S. is 'Fraught with Dangers' to Peace," *New York Times*, 18 June 1978.

14. A corollary to this argument suggests that the superpowers must also begin to distinguish between their overarching interest in avoiding nuclear war and their associated interest in maintaining joint dominance of the system. For an explanation of its importance, see Hedley Bull, "Arms Control and World Order," *International Security* 1, no. 1 (Summer 1976): 12.

15. See Paul Warnke, "Arms Control: A Global Imperative," *Bulletin of the Atomic Scientists* 34, no. 6 (June 1978): 33–34.

16. See Wayland Young, "Disarmament: Thirty Years of Failure," *International Security* 2, no. 3 (Winter 1978): 49.

17. Regrettably, it does not appear that the new test ban treaties between the United States and the Soviet Union will do much to convince nonnuclear countries that the superpowers are fulfilling their strategic arms control obligations under the NPT. For a fine explanation of this argument concerning the Threshold Test Ban Treaty (TTBT) signed 3 July 1974 and the Treaty on the Limitation of Underground Explosions for Peaceful Purposes (PNET) signed 28 May 1976, see Robert W. Helm and Donald R. Westervelt, "The New Test Ban Treaties: What Do They Mean? Where Do They Lead?," *International Security* 1, no. 3 (Winter 1977): 162–78. The main line of the authors' argument is that the TTBT and the PNET "are not likely to help promote the objective of nonproliferation since they neither reduce present superpower military capabilities nor remove the PNE asymmetry contained in the NPT" (p. 168).

18. See Leo Szilard, *The Voice of the Dolphins and Other Stories* (New York: Simon & Schuster, 1961), p. 49.

19. Ibid.

20. See Bull, "Arms Control," p. 5.

21. See Richard Burt, "Is the Bang Worth 400 Billion Bucks?," *New York Times*, 28 May 1978.

22. See Richard A. Falk, "Nuclear Weapons Proliferation as a World Order Problem," *International Security* 1, no. 3 (Winter 1977): 85.

23. For more on this point, see Bull, "Arms Control."

24. See *Seventeenth Strategy for Peace Conference Report*, The Stanley Foundation, Muscatine, Iowa, 1977, p. 9.

25. These proposals are offered by the author.

26. See Maxwell D. Taylor, "The United States—A Military Power Second to None," *International Security* 1, no. 1 (Summer 1976): 51. See, also, Mandelbaum, "International Stability and Nuclear Order," p. 39.

27. This is one of the recommendations offered by Alva Myrdal in her book, *The Game of Disarmament* (New York: Pantheon, 1976).

28. See *Seventeenth Annual Report*, p. 24.

29. It had often been suggested that the Conference undergo some essential restructuring to permit the participation of France and China. According to a recent publication by the Carnegie Endowment for International Peace concerned with the 1978 U.N. Special Session on Disarmament, one promising proposal for bringing all the nuclear weapon states into CCD negotiations would have involved implementation of Article 26 of the U.N. Charter, which gives the Security Council responsibility for regulating armaments. Since France and China are permanent members of the Security Council, this would automatically have brought them into the deliberations. See Jane Sharp, ed., *Opportunities for Disarmament: A Preview of the 1978 United Nations Special Session on Disarmament* (New York: Carnegie Endowment for International Peace, 1978), p. 7.

30. Ibid., p. 2.

31. Ibid., p. 6.

32. See Falk, "Nuclear Weapons Proliferation," p. 87.

33. See *Seventeenth Annual Report*, p. 14.

34. Ibid.

35. A frequently recommended corollary to this proposal is one suggesting that all nuclear weapon states accept a pledge never to use nuclear weapons against non-nuclear-weapon states. While this sort of pledge would allegedly be an antiproliferation

measure, it is extremely doubtful that it would be genuinely re-assuring to the non-nuclear-weapon states.

36. See Robert C. Johansen, *The Disarmament Process: Where To Begin* (New York: The Institute for World Order, 1977), p. 13.

37. Although U.S. policy excludes the use of nuclear weapons as the first offensive (first-strike) move of war, it does not ex-clude their retaliatory use to stave off defeat in a major conven-tional conflict.

38. Gen. George S. Brown, 20 January 1977, in *United States Military Posture for FY 1978* (Washington, D.C.: Government Printing Office), p. 35.

39. Ibid., p. 41.

40. Secretary of Defense Harold Brown, 2 February 1978, in *Department of Defense: Annual Report for FY 1979* (Washington, D.C.: Government Printing Office), p. 68.

41. One reason that the dangers of a no-first-use pledge have been exaggerated is simply that tactical nuclear weapons are less credible deterrent forces than is often believed. In view of the enormously high probability of Soviet nuclear counterretaliation and the terrible destruction that would be visisted upon the European theater "in order to save it," it is altogether likely that Soviet strategists entertain serious doubts about American will-ingness to use theater nuclear forces. Indeed, in the aftermath of an overwhelming Russian conventional assault involving West Germany and France, it would probably be more rational for American decision makers to bypass the tactical nuclear weap-ons altogether, urging instead that the president resort imme-diately to a strategic first strike.

42. See General Brown in *U.S. Miliary Posture for FY 1978*, p. 41.

43. Some cogent points concerning the difficulties in negotiat-ing MBFR are raised in Jane Sharp, "MBFR As Arms Control," *Arms Control Today* 6, no. 4 (April 1976).

44. Currently, the MBFR reduction process is geared to a pro-gressive, asymmetric scaling down of all forces, conventional and nuclear, with a goal of approximate parity. Parity, however, would be based on a mix of both kinds of forces, and it is not geared to the ultimate elimination of nuclear components.

45. See Harold Brown in *DOD Annual Report FY 1979*, p. 69.

46. See U.S. Arms Control and Disarmament Agency, *Arms Control and Disarmament Agreements: Texts and History of Ne-gotiations*, June 1977, p. 59.

47. See Johansen, *The Disarmament Process*, p. 9.

48. See *Multilateral Disarmament and the Special Session,*

Twelfth Conference on the United Nations of the Next Decade, San Juan del Rio, Mexico, 19–25 June 1977, published by The Stanley Foundation, Muscatine, Iowa, 1977, p. 23.

49. See William Epstein, *The Last Chance: Nuclear Proliferation and Arms Control* (New York: The Free Press, 1976), p. 220.

50. This definition is based upon the very fine development of the "nuclear regime" idea in Gompert, et al., *Nuclear Weapons and World Politics*.

51. See Stanley Hoffmann, "The Uses of American Power," *Foreign Affairs* 56, no. 1 (October 1977): 29.

52. These are the guiding values of the Institute for World Order's World Order Models Project.

53. See Falk, "Nuclear Weapons Proliferation," p. 82.

54. See Rollo May, *The Courage to Create* (New York: Norton, 1975), p. 117.

55. See Hoffmann, "Uses of American Power," p. 30.

Chapter Eight
1. A complete list of incentives may be found in the study by the Office of Technology Assessment, *Nuclear Proliferation and Safeguards* (New York: Praeger, 1977), pp. 25–26.

2. See Ervin Laszlo, et al., *Goals for Mankind: A Report to the Club of Rome on the New Horizons of Global Community* (New York: Signet, 1977).

3. See Paul Warnke, "SALT: Its Contribution to U.S. Security and World Peace" (Speech to the Conference on U.S. Security and the Soviet Challenge, Hartford, 25 July 1978), *Current Policy*, no. 27 (August 1978): 7.

4. Cited by Leo Szilard in *The Voice of the Dolphins and Other Stories* (New York: Simon & Schuster, 1961), p. 54.

5. Such assurances would be particularly important in the case of sheltered states from which tactical nuclear weapons and other forward-based systems had been removed in order to fulfill superpower arms control commitments, e.g., West Germany, Japan, Taiwan, Turkey, and South Korea.

6. On this point, see Ted Greenwood, et al., *Nuclear Proliferation: Motivations, Capabilities, and Strategies for Control* (New York: McGraw-Hill, 1977), p. 13.

7. On this point, see OTA, *Nuclear Proliferation and Safeguards*, p. 96.

8. Ibid., p. 61.

9. Ibid., p. 79.

10. See Ambassador Tape's testimony in "Nuclear Proliferation: Future U.S. Foreign Policy Implications," Hearings Before

the Subcommittee on International Security and Scientific Affairs of the House Committee on International Relations, 94th Cong., 1st sess., 30 October 1975, p. 138.

11. See "Non-Proliferation Strategy for the Late '70s," a Discussion Group Report to the Eighteenth Strategy for Peace Conference, The Stanley Foundation, Muscatine, Iowa, 13–16 October 1977, p. 8.

12. Ibid., pp. 8–9.

13. See OTA, *Nuclear Proliferation and Safeguards*, pp. 80–81.

14. Ibid., p. 81.

15. See *Bulletin of the Atomic Scientists* 34, no. 5 (May 1978), pp. 43–44. This Convention, submitted to the Preparatory Committee of the U.N. Special Session on Disarmament, was drafted by the following: E. Bauer (France); A. Chayes (U.S.); C. Dominice (Switzerland); B. T. Feld (U.S.); E. E. Galal (Egypt); A. Parthasarathi (India); J. Prawitz (Sweden); and V. G. Trukhanovsky (USSR).

16. See Report of the Nuclear Energy Policy Study Group, The Ford Foundation, *Nuclear Power: Issues and Choices* (Cambridge, Mass.: Ballinger, 1977), p. 377.

17. See Lewis A. Dunn, "The Role of Sanctions in Non-Proliferation Strategy," Final Report of the Hudson Institute, prepared for the Office of Technology Assessment, U.S. Congress, 2 February 1977, pp. 1–2.

18. The intended meaning of the word "control" is expressed better by its French equivalent, *contrôle* or "general supervision."

19. See Stanley Hoffman, *Primacy or World Order: American Foreign Policy Since the Cold War* (New York: McGraw-Hill, 1978), p. 117.

20. Ibid., p. 119.

21. See William Irwin Thompson, *Passages About Earth: An Exploration of the New Planetary Culture* (New York: Harper & Row, 1974), pp. 131–32.

22. See Lewis A. Dunn, "Changing Dimensions of Proliferation Policy, 1975–1995," Report to the U.S. Arms Control and Disarmament Agency, Hudson Institute, New York, 15 February 1977, p. 83.

Chapter Nine

1. For this term, I am indebted to Dr. Robert H. Kupperman, *Facing Tomorrow's Terrorist Incident Today*, U.S. Government, Law Enforcement Assistance Administration, October 1977, p. 7.

2. Ibid., p. 5.

3. See Robert E. Bailey and Marian Breland Bailey, "Uses of Animal Sensory Systems and Response Capabilities in Security Systems," in Joel Kramer, ed., *The Role of Behavioral Science in Physical Security*, Proceedings of the Second Annual Symposium, U.S. Department of Commerce, National Bureau of Standards, June 1978, p. 52.

4. See "Palestinians: Return to Terror," *Time*, 27 March 1978, p. 36.

5. According to a recent publication of the Department of State, "The U.S. will make no concessions to terrorist blackmail." See *"Terrorism,"* GIST, a publication of the Bureau of Public Affairs, Department of State, August 1978, p. 2.

6. In the United States, the example of the Black Panther Party best illustrates the progressive take-over of a militant, political organization by criminal elements. For information on this take-over, see especially *Gun-Barrel Politics: The Black Panther Party, 1966–1971*, Report by the Committee on Internal Security, House of Representatives (Washington, D.C.: Government Printing Office, 18 August 1971).

7. See Clausewitz, *On War*, chap. 1, "What Is War?"

8. Despite the revulsion that is typically generated by the suggestion of assassination in liberal, democratic societies, there is a well-established tradition in political philosophy that regards it as permissible under certain circumstances, e.g., the writings of Cicero, St. Thomas Aquinas, and Sir Thomas More. However, these writers were concerned with the question of tyrannicide rather than the elimination of insurgents.

9. It should be noted, however, that at the time of this writing, an antiterrorist bill sponsored by Senators Ribicoff and Javits and Congressman Anderson has been introduced into the Congress.

10. These points are taken from a comparative survey of the main antiterrorist laws in Germany, France, England, and Sweden published in *Der Spiegel*, 5 December 1977, and a translation of this survey by Ronald F. Storette and Axel Heck, prepared for the German Information Center, Federal Republic of Germany.

11. See Silverstein, "Emergency Medical Preparedness," *Terrorism: An International Journal* 1, no. 1, (1977): 51.

12. Ibid., p. 55.

13. Ibid., p. 61.

14. See 13 *UN Chronicle* 58 (1976) pp. 58–59.

15. See Friedlander, "Terrorism and International Law; What is Being Done," *Rutgers Camden Law Journal* 8, no. 3 (Spring 1977): 392.

16. Ibid., p. 386.

17. See "Hijackers Receive Light Sentence," *Lafayette Journal and Courier*, Lafayette, Ind. 25 November 1978.

18. See "Serbian Court Refuses to Extradite Four Sought by Bonn in Terrorism," *New York Times* 19 November 1978.

19. See Friedlander, "Terrorism and International Law," p. 389.

20. See Charles A. Russell, "Transnational Terrorism," *Air University Review*, January/February 1976, pp. 2–3.

21. Ibid., pp. 5–6.

Index